BRITISH SHIPPING LAWS

ARNOULD'S LAW OF MARINE INSURANCE AND GENERAL AVERAGE

BRITISH SHIPPING LAWS

ARNOULD'S LAW OF MARINE INSURANCE AND GENERAL AVERAGE

FIRST SUPPLEMENT TO THE SEVENTEENTH EDITION

By

JONATHAN GILMAN, QC, MA

and

ROBERT MERKIN

Professor of Commercial Law, University of Southampton

SWEET & MAXWELL

THOMSON REUTERS

Published in 2010 by Thomson Reuters (Legal) Limited
(Registered in England and Wales, Company No. 1679046.
Registered Office and address: 100 Avenue Road, London, NW3 3PF)
trading as Sweet and Maxwell

For further information on our products and services, visit
www.sweetandmaxwell.co.uk

No natural forests were destroyed to make this product; only farmed
timber was used and replanted.

Computer set by LBJ Typesetting Ltd
Printed and bound in Great Britain by CPI Anthony Rowe,
Chippenham and Eastbourne

A CIP catalogue record for this book is available from the British Library

ISBN 9780414044524

PREFACE

In the short time since the seventeenth edition of Arnould was published, there has been a number of significant developments in the law of marine insurance. The Cargo Clauses have been revised and replaced with new wordings which make limited but important changes to the standard coverage provided. The Third Parties (Rights against Insurers) Act 1930 has been repealed and replaced by the 2010 Act from a date to be determined. The choice of law rules in the Rome Convention ceased to operate with effect from December 2009, and a new regime was introduced by the Rome I Regulation. Market and legislative matters aside, the courts have maintained the level of activity in insurance matters established over the last decade and have handed down a series of important rulings affecting most parts of the work and too numerous to be listed here. As will be seen from the content of this Supplement, almost all of the chapters have been affected to a greater or lesser extent.

Publishing deadlines have meant that the Supplement was required to go to press at a time when two major decisions remain outstanding. The first is the appeal to the Supreme Court in *The Cendor Mopu*, and the ruling is likely to have substantial impact upon the law relating to perils of the seas, inherent vice and causation. Arguments were heard in July 2010, but at the date of the writing of this preface the judgment had not been handed down. The second is the appeal to the Court of Appeal in *Masefield v Amlin*, the arguments being heard early in October 2010. This decision, when it appears, will have important implications for the definitions of actual and constructive total loss in the context of piracy as well as for public policy. Given the significance of these decisions, it is intended that a special Supplement will be published in 2011 to accompany the present volume. In the meantime, the editors have stated the law as it stands and have indicated at appropriate points the matters that remain unresolved pending the decisions.

The text for the Supplement went to press in November 2010, and it has been possible to add at proof stage references to relevant cases decided after that date. The cut-off date was 12 November 2010, and we have attempted to incorporate into the Supplement all material available to us up to and including that date.

(For further information on the Special Supplement post the judgements, please email sweetandmaxwell.customerservices@thomson.com.)

Jonathan Gilman
Rob Merkin

ACKNOWLEDGMENTS

The following documents which appear in the appendices are reproduced with the kind permission of Lloyd's Market Association and the International Underwriting Association:

Institute Cargo Clauses (A) 1/1/09

Institute Cargo Clauses (B) 1/1/09

Institute Cargo Clauses (C) 1/1/09

Institute Strike Clauses (Cargo) 1/1/09

Institute War Clauses (Cargo) 1/1/09

HOW TO USE THIS SUPPLEMENT

This is the First Supplement to the 17th Edition of *Arnould on the Law of Marine Insurance and General Average* and has been compiled according to the structure of the main work volume.

Within each chapter, updating information is referenced according to the relevant paragraph in the main volume. Where it has been necessary to insert additional paragraphs, their place in the main work has been indicated. It has been necessary to replace only one chapter in its entirety, Chapter 5 (Jurisdiction and Applicable Law).

CONTENTS

CONTENTS

Table of Statutes

CONTENTS

CONTENTS

Table of Cases

TABLE OF CASES

Table of Statutory Instruments

CHAPTER 2

FORM AND CONTENTS OF MARINE POLICIES

What insurances must be made by a policy

The English and Scottish Law Commissions, by their Issues Paper No.9 **2–02**
published in October 2010, have recommended the repeal of s.22 of the Marine
Insurance Act 1906.

Statutory requisites of a policy

The English and Scottish Law Commissions, by their Issues Paper No.9 **2–03**
published in October 2010, have recommended the repeal of ss.23 and 24 of the
Marine Insurance Act 1906.

Scratching a slip

The proposition that there may be a binding contract between the parties before **2–10**
the slip has been scratched has been applied in a number of cases. In *Allianz
Insurance Company-Egypt v Aigaion Insurance Co SA (No 2)*[1] reinsurers were
sent a slip for a marine reinsurance policy. The slip contained a "Deferred
Premium Clause" which, although its terms were not set out in the slip itself,
provided that the premium was payable in quarterly instalments and that notice
of cancellation was required if the reinsurers wished to cancel the cover for
non-payment. The reinsurers did not scratch the slip but replied "Cover is bound
with effect from 31.03.05 as we had quoted ... Our documents to follow."
Subsequently the reinsurers supplied policy documents which stated that the
premium was due within 60 days from inception. The Court of Appeal held that
a binding contract had been made once the reinsurers had signified their acceptance, and that there was no need for the slip to be scratched and the terms could
not be altered thereafter. It followed that the reinsurers could not argue that there
was no contract at all[2] or, if there was, that it contained their premium payment
obligation. In other proceedings arising out of the same agreement, *Allianz
Insurance v Aigaion*,[3] it was held that the reinsurers' acceptance of the slip on the
terms presented to them meant that they were bound by the terms of the slip and
were unable to assert that the parties had agreed to a class warranty which had

---

[1] [2009] Lloyd's Rep. IR 69. See also *Markel Capital Ltd v Gothaer Allgemeine Versicherung AG*
[2009] Lloyd's Rep. IR 433, where the court refused, in an application for summary judgment, to
come to a decision on the limited evidence before it.
[2] The assertion that the phrase "Deferred Premium Clause" was too uncertain to be enforced and that
the entire policy was void, was rejected by the Court of Appeal.
[3] [2008] 2 Lloyd's Rep. 595.

by error been omitted from the slip. In *Crane v Hannover Ruckversicherungs-Aktiengesellschaft*[4] reinsurers issued a standing offer of cover to reinsureds who accepted direct risks and notified the insurers of such acceptance. Following notification, slips were scratched. It was held that a contract of reinsurance came into existence as soon as the reinsurers had been notified of any acceptance of a direct risk, and that the slips merely confirmed what had already been agreed. In *Dunlop Haywards (DHL) Ltd v Barbon Insurance Group Ltd*,[5] brokers prepared a Firm Order Notification (FON) sheet, which was stated to be subject to slips, and this was scratched by underwriters. Thereafter slips were scratched and policies were issued. The parties accepted that the FON was a contract in its own right[6] although the effect of the slips on the FON did not arise for decision.

Relationship between slip and policy

2–14 The leading authority on rectification is now *Chartbrook Ltd v Persimmon Homes Ltd*.[7] The House of Lords confirmed that rectification is possible if four conditions are met: (i) there was a previous common intention as to what was intended to be in the policy, together with some outward expression of the accord; (ii) the common intention continued up to the date that the parties entered into a binding contract; (iii) there was clear evidence that the instrument as executed did not accurately represent the true agreement of the parties at the time of its execution; and (iv) the instrument would, if rectified, accurately represent the true agreement of the parties at that time.

Note 84: See also *Dunlop Heywards (DHL) Ltd v Erinaceous Insurance Services Ltd* [2009] Lloyd's Rep. IR 464.

Rectification of policy by reference to slip

2–15 *Note 93*: The decision in *Dunlop Heywards (DHL) Ltd v Erinaceous Insurance Services Ltd* referred to in this footnote was upheld on appeal [2009] Lloyd's Rep. IR 464.

The Lloyd's S.G. policy

2–22 The English and Scottish Law Commissions, by their Issues Paper No.9 published in October 2010, have suggested that there is no longer a need for the Lloyd's S.G. policy to be retained in the schedule to the Marine Insurance Act 1906 and that it should be repealed.

---

[4] [2010] Lloyd's Rep. IR 93.
[5] [2010] Lloyd's Rep. IR 149.
[6] See the earlier proceedings, *Dunlop Haywards (DHL) Ltd v Erinaceous Insurance Services Ltd* [2009] Lloyd's Rep. IR 464.
[7] [2009] UKHL 38.

Major changes in cargo insurance

The approach which was adopted by the draftsmen of the 1982 Cargo Clauses has **2–35** been continued under the revised Clauses introduced in 2009, which are reproduced in the Appendix below.

The description of "the modern system for insuring cargoes" in this paragraph of **2–36** the main work (which referred to the then current Institute Cargo Clauses 1/1/82) remains valid with regard to the new 2009 Clauses. The basic structure of the (A)(B) and (C) Clauses has been retained, and the Risks Clauses in each of those sets of Clauses are substantially unaltered in the 2009 Clauses. There have been several important changes affecting other provisions in the (A), (B) and (C) Clauses which are discussed at appropriate points in this Supplement. Major changes have been made in relation to the Transit Clause,[8] the Change of Voyage Clause,[9] and the wording of the exclusions relating to insufficiency of packing,[10] insolvency or financial default of the owners of the vessel,[11] unseaworthiness and unfitness of vessel or craft and unfitness of containers,[12] and terrorism.[13] The 1982 Clauses may continue for some time to be used alongside the new Clauses, but it appears that the 2009 Clauses have already gained wide acceptance even in insurance markets (such as Japan) where the 1963 Cargo Clauses mentioned at para.2–34 in the main work were still frequently used in preference to the 1982 Clauses.[14]

---

[8] See paras 13–39, 13–40 below.
[9] The new wording in cl.10.2 is designed to mitigate the effect of *The Prestrioka* decision [2003] 2 Lloyd's Rep. 327. See paras 13–17 *et seq*, below.
[10] See para.22–28 below.
[11] Para.23–74 below.
[12] Analysed at para.20–41 below.
[13] See para.24–30 below. It is questionable whether the introduction of a definition of "act of terrorism" is a change of any real substance.
[14] See J. Dunt and W. Melbourne "Insuring Cargoes in the new millennium" in R Thomas (ed), *The Modern Law of Marine Insurance*, Vol. 3 (2009), Ch.6 at para.6.128.

CHAPTER 3

THE CONSTRUCTION OF MARINE POLICIES

The intentions of the parties: factual matrix

The principles set out in *Investors Compensation Scheme v West Bromwich* **3–03**
Building Society[1] were confirmed by the House of Lords in *Chartbrook v
Persimmon*.[2] Lord Hoffmann, giving the leading judgment, emphasised that the
previous negotiations of the parties (point (3) of the guidelines in *Investors
Compensation Scheme*) are to be excluded from the factual matrix.

The comments of Lord Steyn in *Sirius International Insurance Co (Publ) v FAI
General Insurance Ltd*[3] were echoed in *Re Sigma Finance Corporation*.[4] Lord
Collins, speaking for the majority, commented at para.35 that:

"An over-literal interpretation of one provision without regard to the whole may
distort or frustrate the commercial purpose. This is one of those too frequent
cases where a document has been subjected to the type of textual analysis more
appropriate to the interpretation of tax legislation which has been the subject
of detailed scrutiny at all committee stages than to an instrument securing
commercial obligations . . ."

See also *Pratt v Aigaion*[5] for similar sentiments.

Note 19: In *Chartbrook v Persimmon* [2009] UKHL 38 the House of
Lords confirmed the exclusionary rule and similarly doubted the validity of the
exceptions to it.

Certainty and uniformity

Note 61: See also *Durham v BAI (Run-Off)* [2009] Lloyd's Rep. IR 295 reversed **3–13**
on appeal, [2010] EWHC Civ 1096.

Incorporation of policy terms

Note 171: The reference should be to Chapter 33.   **3–37**

---

[1] [1998] 1 All E.R. 98.
[2] [2009] UKHL 38.
[3] [2005] 1 Lloyd's Rep. 461.
[4] [2009] UKSC 2.
[5] [2009] Lloyd's Rep. IR 149.

Ambiguity: *contra proferentem*

3–38 In *Pratt v Aigaion*[6] the Court of Appeal applied the *contra proferentem* principle to hold that the phrase "Warranted Owner and/or Owner's skipper on board and in charge at all times" was to be construed in favour of the assured, and meant that the crewing warranty applied only when the vessel was sailing or preparing to sail: any other construction would have made compliance impractical, and warranties—being draconian in effect—were generally to be construed *contra proferentem*.

---

[6] [2009] Lloyd's Rep. IR 149. For a full discussion of this case, see Ch.19 below in this Supplement.

Chapter 4

DIFFERENT CLASSES OF INSURERS ON MARINE POLICIES

Insurance companies and the Financial Services and Markets Act 2000

Note 8: These Directives will be repealed and replaced in 2012 by the Solvency **4–03**
II Directive, European Parliament and Council Directive 2009/138/EC.

A distinction is to be drawn between an insurance company which does not **4–04**
have any authorisation to carry on a regulated activity but nevertheless does so,
and an insurance company which does have authorisation to carry on a regulated
activity but issues policies which fall outside the scope if its authorisation. The
latter situation is straightforward: the insurer does not commit a criminal offence
and the validity of the policy is unaffected.[1] By contrast, if the former situation
applies and the insurance company has no authorisation to carry on a regulated
activity, any issue of marine policies constitutes a criminal offence.[2] The policy
itself is unenforceable by the insurer,[3] but the assured has the option either to
disaffirm the contract and recover sums paid (in particular by way of premium)
plus compensation,[4] or to enforce the contract.[5] However, the court has the power
to permit enforcement of the policy by the insurer where it is just and equitable
in the circumstances to do so, having regard to whether the insurer reasonably
believed that it was acting lawfully.[6] In practice an assured who has been paid
claims is unlikely to want to disaffirm the contract, as that requires the repayment
by him of those claims, and the same applies where there are unpaid outstanding
claims which will be lost if the policy is disaffirmed, assuming of course that the
amount of the premium does not exceed those claims.[7]

Regulation of Lloyd's

The internal regulation of Lloyd's as established by the Lloyd's Act 1982 **4–06**
was modified by the Legislative Reform (Lloyd's) Order 2008.[8] The Council,
consisting of 16 elected members of Lloyd's, eight of whom are external, remains

---

[1] 2000 Act, s.20.

[2] 2000 Act, s.23.

[3] 2000 Act, s.26(1).

[4] In *Re Whiteley Insurance Consultants* [2009] Lloyd's Rep. IR 212 it was noted that compensation is
likely to be a relatively small figure, perhaps confined to interest on the premium paid by the assured.

[5] 2000 Act, s.26(2).

[6] 2000 Act, s.28. See *Re Whiteley Insurance Consultants* [2009] Lloyd's Rep. IR 212, where the
insurer was aware of its contravention.

[7] If the insurer is in liquidation, it will be necessary to value the amount of the outstanding claims
possessed by the assured in accordance with the Insurance Companies (Winding Up) Rules 2001, SI
2001/3635.

[8] SI 2008/3001.

the governing body.[9] The Council in turn is to elect a Chairman and Deputy Chairmen, The Chairman is to be elected annually by all members. The Committee of Lloyd's, responsible for issuing Codes of Practice, was abolished in 2008. Discipline is administered by the Disciplinary Committee[10] and Appeal Tribunal.

Lloyd's and its members

4–07   *Note 53*: The residual liabilities of Equitas have been transferred under a scheme of arrangement to an associated company, Equitas Insurance Ltd: *Re Equitas Ltd* [2010] Lloyd's Rep. IR 69.

Risks and liabilities insured by clubs

4–11   The Third Parties (Rights against Insurers) Act 1930 is to be replaced, from a date to be announced, by the Third Parties (Rights against Insurers) Act 2010. The point made in the text is unaffected by the new Act.

Article 81 of the EC Treaty has been replaced, without amendment, by Article 101 of the Lisbon Treaty 2007, which came into force on December 1, 2009.

Rules of mutual insurance associations

4–14   The Third Parties (Rights against Insurers) Act 1930 is to be replaced, from a date to be announced, by the Third Parties (Rights against Insurers) Act 2010. The 2010 Act modifies the statements in the text that conditions precedent in Club policies can be relied upon as a defence to proceedings and that "pay to be paid" clauses are permissible.

Under the 2010 Act the general rule remains that policy conditions have to be complied with (s.9(1)), but this is modified in three respects: the third party is himself entitled to satisfy the condition, if he can (s.9(2)); any condition which requires the assured to provide information or assistance to the insurers is to be disregarded where the assured cannot comply because it is a dissolved corporation or a deceased individual (s.9(3)); and any condition requiring the assured to provide information or assistance to the insurers remains in force insofar as the assured has not died or been dissolved, but that condition is ineffective insofar as it requires the assured to notify a claim to the insurer (s.9(4)).

As regards "pay to be paid" clauses, the rule under the 1930 Act that such clauses are valid and enforceable has been retained by the 2010 Act, s.9(5). However, in the specific case of a claim for death or personal injury, s.9(5) of the 2010 Act has reversed the earlier rule and negatives the effect of a pay to be paid clause. Accordingly there will be a direct claim against the Club despite the presence of a pay to be paid clause.

---

[9] The 2008 Regulations removed the need for approval of members by the Bank of England.
[10] The 2008 Regulations repealed the requirement for a majority of the Disciplinary Committee to be members of Lloyd's.

Contributions: claims by members and non-members

Note 133: The Third Parties (Rights against Insurers) Act 2010, s.17, has the **4–15** same effect as s.1(3) of the Third Parties (Rights against Insurers) Act 1930, and outlaws any policy term which seeks to alter the rights of the assured in the event of his insolvency.

Underwriting pools

Note 163: The Court of Appeal has unanimously dismissed an appeal in the **4–18** *Temple* case, *Temple Legal Protection v QBE Insurance* [2009] Lloyd's Rep. IR 544, although Rix L.J. was of the view that the agreement did confer the necessary authority on the underwriting agent to conduct run-off but that the underwriting agent had repudiated the agreement and thus lost the right.

CHAPTER 5

JURISDICTION AND APPLICABLE LAW[1]

Jurisdiction: legal structure

The principles which determine the jurisdiction of the English courts over a **5–01** dispute relating to a marine policy depend upon the domicile of the defendant in the proceedings. If the defendant is domiciled in a European Union country, jurisdiction depends upon the provisions of the Brussels Regulation 2001[2]; if the defendant is domiciled in the EFTA countries of Switzerland or Iceland,[3] jurisdiction depends upon the provisions of the Lugano Convention 1989, which for all purposes relevant to the present discussion is identical to the Brussels Regulation[4]; if the defendant is domiciled in Norway, jurisdiction depends upon the Lugano Convention 2007, a revised version of the 1989 Convention which has been brought further into line with the Brussels Regulation; and in all other cases the jurisdiction of the English courts is determined by domestic procedural law as enshrined in Pt 6 and the relevant Practice Directions in the Civil Procedure Rules.

Jurisdiction: domestic law

If the defendant is not domiciled in a Brussels Regulation/Lugano Convention **5–02** country the English courts have jurisdiction over the dispute if the defendant can be served with a claim form. This is possible where the defendant is physically present in England: a company may be served if its registered office is in England[5] or if it is an overseas company but has a place of business in England.[6] A defendant may also be served if he has agreed to accept service in England[7] or if he has accepted service other than purely to contest jurisdiction.[8] In the absence of physical presence or submission by the defendant, the claimant may seek

---

[1] As a result of substantial changes to the law effected by the replacement of the Rome Convention with the Rome I Regulation, and also of the renumbering of the provisions of the Civil Procedure Rules relating to jurisdiction, Ch.5 has been entirely recast and is reproduced here in its new form.

[2] European Council Regulation 44/2001/EC, replacing with some amendments the Brussels Convention 1968. Until December 2006 the Brussels Convention remained in force only in respect of Denmark, but in that month Denmark became subject to the Brussels Regulation.

[3] Liechtenstein, the remaining EFTA country, has refused to participate.

[4] References in this chapter are to the numberings in the Brussels Regulation only.

[5] Companies Act 2006, s.1139.

[6] Companies Act 2006, s.1139.

[7] Such agreement may be subject to the right of the defendant to contest jurisdiction: *Sphere Drake Insurance plc v Sigorta Anonim Sirketi* [1988] 1 Lloyd's Rep.139; *Burrows v Jamaica Private Power Co Ltd* [2002] 1 Lloyd's Rep. 472.

[8] *Finnish Marine Insurance Co Ltd v Protective National Insurance Co* [1989] 2 All E.R. 929.

permission from the English courts to serve the defendant outside the jurisdiction. The court may give permission if three conditions are satisfied. First, the claimant must show that on the merits there is a serious question to be tried[9] in that the claim has a reasonable prospect of success.[10] Secondly, the claimant must show that he has a good arguable case—in the sense that he has a much better argument on the material available[11]—that the claim falls within one of the specific grounds of jurisdiction listed in CPR PD 6B. The most important heads of jurisdiction for present purposes are that the claim is made in respect of a contract[12] which is: made within the jurisdiction[13]; made outside England but through an agent of the defendant[14] trading within the jurisdiction[15]; governed by English law[16]; or broken within the jurisdiction.[17] Thirdly, the claimant must show that England is the forum in which the case should properly be tried.[18] Permission will in these cases almost always be sought without notice to the defendant, and if permission is granted the defendant may contest the grant of permission at a subsequent hearing at which he is represented.[19]

---

[9] *Seaconsar Far East Ltd v Bank Marzaki Jomhouri Islami Iran* [1993] 4 All E.R. 456; *De Molestina v Ponton* [2002] 1 Lloyd's Rep. 271; *Swiss Reinsurance Company Ltd v United India Insurance Company* [2005] Lloyd's Rep. IR 341.

[10] See CPR r.6.37.

[11] *Canada Trust v Stolzenberg (No 2)* [1998] 1 W.L.R. 547; *Carvill America Incorporated v Camperdown UK Ltd* [2005] 2 Lloyd's Rep. 457; *Konkola Copper Mines plc v Coromin Ltd* [2006] 1 Lloyd's Rep. 410; *Cherney v Deripaska* [2008] EWHC 1530 (Comm); *Sharab v Al Saud* [2009] 2 Lloyd's Rep. 160; *AstraZeneca UK Ltd v Albemarle International Corporation* [2010] EWCH 1028 (Comm).

[12] This phrase appears to encompass all disputes affecting a marine policy, including its validity and the right of the insurers to terminate for breach or avoid for non-disclosure or misrepresentation: *DR Insurance Co v Central National Insurance Co of Omaha* [1996] 1 Lloyd's Rep. 74; *HIB Ltd v Guardian Insurance Co Ltd* [1997] 1 Lloyd's Rep. 412.

[13] CPR PD 6, para.3.1(6)(a).

[14] A broker is the agent of the assured, so that if the assured wishes to bring proceedings in England against insurers not present within the jurisdiction it is not enough for him to show that his own broker was trading in England—it will be necessary for him to point to an agent of the insurers, e.g., an underwriting agent. See *Union International Insurance Co Ltd v Jubilee Insurance Co Ltd* [1991] 1 All E.R. 740.

[15] CPR PD 6, para.3.1(6)(b). See *Lincoln National Life Insurance Co v Employers Reinsurance Corporation* [2002] Lloyd's Rep. IR 853.

[16] CPR PD 6, para.3.1(6)(c). See below.

[17] CPR PD 6, para.3.1(7). Breach may consist of the sending of notification of an intention to break (anticipatory breach) or actual breach. It is uncertain whether notice of anticipatory breach takes effect where the notice was given or where it was received although modern authority favours the latter: *Atlantic Underwriting Agencies v Compania di Assicurazioni di Milano SpA* [1979] 2 Lloyd's Rep. 240. Actual breach in the form of non-payment of sums due takes effect where the sums were payable to the claimant or his: *Citadel Insurance Co v Atlantic Union Insurance Co SA* [1982] 2 Lloyd's Rep. 543. A failure by the assured to disclose material facts is probably not a breach of contract for this purpose.

[18] CPR r.6.37(3). See: *Spiliada Maritime Corp v Cansulex Ltd* [1987] A.C. 460; *Cherney v Deripaska* [2009] EWCA Civ 849; *AstraZeneca UK Ltd v Albemarle International Corporation* [2010] EWCH 1028 (Comm).

[19] Not just on jurisdictional and discretionary grounds, but also on the basis that the claimant failed in the without notice application to disclose all material facts to the court, including the defendant's possible defences. See *Albon v Naza Motor Trading SDN BHD* [2007] EWHC 9 (Ch).

Discretion

Assuming that jurisdiction has been made out in any of the above cases or under **5–03** CPR PD 6, the English court may stay or strike out the proceedings if England is not the most appropriate forum for the resolution of the dispute.[20] England will almost inevitably be the most appropriate forum if the parties have agreed to submit their disputes to English jurisdiction, and in the same way other than in exceptional circumstances England will not be the most appropriate jurisdiction if the parties have agreed on some other forum.[21] In the absence of any arbitration or jurisdiction provision, the court will weigh up the circumstances of the case to decide whether England is the most appropriate forum. The most important consideration is the applicable law. If English law is the applicable law, either because it has been chosen as such[22] or because the policy has the closest connection with England,[23] then it is normally appropriate for the English court to hear the dispute, although this is not necessarily the case if the issues are purely factual or the foreign court has the competence to apply English law[24] and under its conflict of laws rules would do so.[25] Equally, if the policy is governed by a foreign law then, unless there is good reason for hearing the action, the English court will stay its proceedings.[26] Other relevant considerations include the location of the witnesses and the evidence,[27] and whether there are in existence other proceedings which have reached an advanced stage.[28] All of this means in practice that if the risk has been placed in London and there is a non-disclosure, misrepresentation, interpretation or other issue of law, England is almost certain to be the most appropriate forum,[29] although a different result may be appropriate

---

[20] *Spiliada Maritime Corporation v Cansulex* [1986] 3 All E.R. 843.

[21] See below.

[22] *Stonebridge Underwriting Ltd v Ontario Municipal Insurance Exchange* [2010] EWHC 2279 *(Comm)*. This is the case whether or not, independently of that choice, the contract would have any connection with England: *Britannia Steamship Insurance Association Ltd v Ausonia Assicurazioni SA* [1984] 2 Lloyd's Rep. 98; *Standard Steamship v Gann* [1992] 2 Lloyd's Rep. 528.

[23] *Islamic Arab Insurance Co v Saudi Egyptian American Reinsurance Co* [1987] 1 Lloyd's Rep. 315; *Stonebridge Underwriting Ltd v Ontario Municipal Insurance Exchange* [2010] EWHC 2279 (Comm).

[24] *Amin Rasheed Shipping Corporation v Kuwait Insurance Co* [1983] 2 All E.R. 884.

[25] If there is a risk that the court will not apply English law to a policy which the English court regards as governed by English law, a stay may be refused: *Brotherton v Aseguradora Colseguros* [2002] Lloyd's Rep. IR 848; *Dornoch Ltd v Mauritius Union Assurance Co Ltd* [2006] Lloyd's Rep. IR 786. See also the situation in which the foreign court is likely to apply local public policy rules to strike down an English law contract: *Seashell Shipping Corporation of Panama v Mutualidad de Seguros del Instituto Nacional de Industria* [1989] 1 Lloyd's Rep. 47; *Overseas Union Insurance Ltd v Incorporated General Insurance* [1992] 1 Lloyd's Rep. 439.

[26] *Atlantic Underwriting Agencies Ltd v Compagnia di Assicurazioni SpA* [2979] 2 Lloyd's Rep. 240; *BP plc v Aon Ltd* [2006] 1 Lloyd's Rep. 549.

[27] *Tiernan v Magen Insurance* [2000] I.L. Pr. 517 (Comm); *Limit (No 3) Ltd v PDV Insurance Co Ltd* [2005] 1 Lloyd's Rep. 552; *Travelers Casualty & Surety Co of Europe Ltd v Sun Life Assurance Co of Canada (UK) Ltd* [2004] Lloyd's Rep. IR 846.

[28] On the *lis alibis pendens* principle: *The Abidin Daver* [1984] A.C. 398.

[29] *El Du Pont de Nemours & Co v Agnew* [1987] 2 Lloyd's Rep. 585; *Seashell Shipping Corporation of Panama v Mutualidad de Seguros del Instituto Nacional de Industria* [1989] 1 Lloyd's Rep. 47; *Meadows Insurance Co Ltd v Insurance Corporation of Ireland* [1989] 2 Lloyd's Rep. 298; *Berisford v New Hampshire Insurance Co* [1990] 1 Lloyd's Rep. 454; *Gan Insurance Co v Tai Ping Insurance*

if the issue is purely factual and relates to the knowledge or conduct of an assured whose enterprise is situated in some other jurisdiction.[30] It is irrelevant that the English proceedings have taken the form of an application by the insurers for negative declaratory relief as long as the intervention of the English court serves a useful purpose,[31] although negative declaratory relief will be refused if the court is asked to resolve an issue which is purely hypothetical[32] or which has no connection with England.[33] The fact that, if the assured loses his action against the insurers it will be necessary for him to commence a fresh action against the brokers in some other jurisdiction is not of itself enough to require the proceedings to be consolidated within a single jurisdiction.[34] The power to stay on the ground of *forum non conveniens* is in any event removed where the defendant is domiciled in England and the English court is seised of the proceedings earlier than any another court[35] whether inside or outside the EU.[36]

Co [1999] Lloyd's Rep. IR 472; *Agnew v Lansforsakrings* [2001] 1 A.C. 223; *Commercial Union Assurance Co plc v Simat Helleisen & Eichner Inc* [2001] Lloyd's Rep. IR 172; *Assicurazioni Generali v Ege Sigorta* [2002] Lloyd's Rep. IR 480; *General Star International Indemnity Ltd v Stirling Cooke Brown Reinsurance Brokers Ltd* [2003] Lloyd's Rep. IR 719; *Markel International Insurance Co Ltd v La Republica Compania Argentina de Seguros Generales SA* [2005] Lloyd's Rep. IR 90; *Tryg Baltica International (UK) Ltd v Boston Compania de Seguros SA* [2005] Lloyd's Rep. IR 32; *Tonicstar Ltd v American Home Assurance Co* [2005] Lloyd's Rep. IR 40; *Dornoch Ltd v Mauritius Union Assurance Co Ltd* [2006] Lloyd's Rep. IR 786.

[30] *Insurance Co of Ireland v Strombus International Insurance Co* [1985] 2 Lloyd's Rep. 138; *Trade Indemnity v Forsakrings Njord* [1995] LRLR 367; *Chase v Ram Technical Services Ltd* [2000] 2 Lloyd's Rep. 418; *Navigators Insurance Co Ltd v Atlantic Methanol Production Co LLC* [2004] Lloyd's Rep. IR 418.

[31] *Meadows Insurance Co Ltd v Insurance Corporation of Ireland* [1989] 2 Lloyd's Rep. 298; *New Hampshire Insurance Co v Philips Electronics North America Corporation (No 1)* [1999] Lloyd's Rep. IR 58; *Gan Insurance Co Ltd v Tai Ping Insurance Co Ltd* [1999] Lloyd's Rep. IR 472; *CGU International Insurance plc v Szabo* [2002] Lloyd's Rep. IR 196; *Lincoln National Life Insurance Co v Employers Reinsurance Corporation* [2002] Lloyd's Rep. IR 853; *Travelers Casualty & Surety Co of Europe Ltd v Sun Life Assurance Co of Canada (UK) Ltd* [2004] Lloyd's Rep. IR 846; *Munchener Ruckversicherungs Gesellschaft v Commonwealth Insurance Co* [2005] Lloyd's Rep. IR 99; *Sun Alliance & London Insurance plc v PT Assuransri Dayin Mitra TBK* [2006] Lloyd's Rep. IR 860.

[32] *Tryg Baltica International (UK) Ltd v Boston Compania de Seguros SA* [2005] Lloyd's Rep. IR 40; *Royal & Sun Alliance Insurance plc v Retail Brand Alliance Inc* [2005] Lloyd's Rep. IR 510.

[33] *Chase v Ram Technical Services* [2000] 2 Lloyd's Rep. 418; *Burrows v Jamaica Private Power Co Ltd* [2002] Lloyd's Rep. IR 466; *American Motorists Insurance Co v Cellstar Corporation* [2003] Lloyd's Rep. IR 295. In the context of a claim for negative declaratory relief by reinsurers, it is not appropriate for the English court to determine the liability of the reinsured to the direct assured under a policy which has no connection with England: *Meadows Insurance Co Ltd v Insurance Corporation of Ireland* [1989] 2 Lloyd's Rep. 298; *Royal & Sun Alliance Insurance plc v Retail Brand Alliance Inc* [2005] Lloyd's Rep. IR 510; *Limit (No 3) Ltd v PDV Insurance Co Ltd* [2005] Lloyd's Rep. IR 553.

[34] *Munchener Ruckversicherungs Gesellschaft v Commonwealth Insurance Co* [2005] Lloyd's Rep. IR 99.

[35] Under art.30 of the Brussels Regulation, as applied to England, the court is first seised when the claim form issued, as long as it has been served within the period of its validity: *WPP Holdings Italy SRL v Benatti* [2006] EWHC 1641 (Comm).

[36] Case C-281/02 *Owusu v Jackson* [2005] 1 Lloyd's Rep. 452. There are doubts as to whether *Owusu* applies if there are parallel proceedings in a court of competent jurisdiction outside the EU: *Royal & Sun Alliance Insurance Plc v Rolls-Royce Plc* [2010] EWHC 1869 (Comm). *Owusu* is also potentially subject to an exception where the English court is satisfied that the parties have agreed to submit their dispute to the exclusive jurisdiction of the courts of some other place: *Konkola Copper Mines plc v Coromin* [2006] Lloyd's Rep. IR 71 (Colman J).

In the case of a claim against a number of insurers who are domiciled in different countries, the existence of a leading underwriter clause under which an English-based insurer may act on behalf of the market empowers the court to treat the leading insurer as the representative of the insurers as a whole and to order under CPR r.19.6(1) that the claim be continued against all of the subscribing insurers without any need for the assured to seek permission to serve them outside the jurisdiction.[37] The power to order a representative action may be exercised even in the absence of a leading underwriter clause, as there is otherwise a risk that the English insurer facing the claim may face liability for the entire costs of the action[38] even though he cannot be liable on the policy for any sum in excess of his own participation.

Exclusive jurisdiction clauses: domestic law

English domestic law does not impose any restrictions on the right of the parties **5–04** to enter into exclusive jurisdiction agreements specifying the country in which disputes between them are to be resolved. The English courts regard an exclusive jurisdiction clause as severable from the contract to which it relates, so that an allegation that a marine policy containing an exclusive jurisdiction clause is void will not prevent the court from asserting jurisdiction in accordance with that clause over that very question.[39]

Where the parties have an agreed to submit their dispute to the exclusive jurisdiction of the English courts, permission for service abroad can be given[40] and the English court will proceed to hear the matter[41]: it will only in exceptional circumstances be appropriate for the English court to stay its proceedings so that the matter can be resolved in some other court, as where there is a risk of the fragmentation of proceedings.[42] Indeed, if proceedings are brought in another jurisdiction in breach of an exclusive jurisdiction clause nominating the English courts,[43] the usual outcome will be an anti-suit injunction restraining the claimant in the foreign proceedings from maintaining the action.[44] Such an injunction will

---

[37] *Irish Shipping Ltd v Commercial Union Assurance Co plc, The Irish Rowan* [1989] 2 Lloyd's Rep. 144.

[38] *Bank of America National Trust and Savings Association v Taylor* [1992] 1 Lloyd's Rep. 484; *National Bank of Greece SA v Outhwaite* [2001] Lloyd's Rep. IR 652.

[39] *IFR Ltd v Federal Trade SpA* 2001 [2001] EWHC 519 (Comm). The law which would have governed the clause, assuming its validity, will be applied to determine such validity: *AstraZeneca UK Ltd v Albemarle International Corporation* [2010] EWCH 1028 (Comm).

[40] CPR PD 6, para.3.1(6)(d).

[41] *Akai Pty v People's Insurance Co* [1998] 1 Lloyd's Rep. 90; *Youell v Kara Mara Shipping Co* [2000] 2 Lloyd's Rep. 102.

[42] *Donohue v Armco Inc* [2002] 1 Lloyd's Rep. 425.

[43] It is not appropriate for the English court to intervene and to act as a referee between two foreign courts: *Airbus Industrie v Patel* [1998] 1 Lloyd's Rep. 631.

[44] *Akai Pty v People's Insurance Co* [1998] 1 Lloyd's Rep. 90; *Youell v Kara Mara Shipping Co* [2000] 2 Lloyd's Rep. 102. An anti-suit injunction may be granted even if there is no exclusive jurisdiction or arbitration clause, although it is necessary for the applicant to show that the foreign proceedings are vexatious or oppressive. See: *Commercial Union Assurance Co plc v Simat Helliesen Eichner Inc* [2000] Lloyd's Rep. IR 172. Such relief is rare: *El Du Pont de Nemours & Co v Agnew* [1987] 2 Lloyd's Rep. 585; *SCOR v ERAS International Ltd (No 2)* [1987] 3 All E.R. 510.

normally[45] be refused only if the applicant has delayed in making the application,[46] if he has submitted to the jurisdiction of the foreign court or, perhaps most importantly, if the action has been brought in a court of a country which is party to the Brussels Regulation or Lugano Convention: in the latter case, the first seised rule in the Regulation and the Convention means that only the court in which the action has been brought may determine its own jurisdiction.[47]

A clause under which the parties agree to submit any dispute to the exclusive jurisdiction of a foreign court will be honoured and English proceedings in breach of the clause will be stayed[48] other than in highly exceptional circumstances.[49]

Non-exclusive jurisdiction clauses: domestic law

5–05 A jurisdiction clause, rather than requiring the parties to submit their dispute to the courts of a particular jurisdiction, may entitle one or both of them to commence proceedings in a named jurisdiction, in which case the other agrees to submit to the jurisdiction of the court in question. Whether a clause is exclusive or non-exclusive is a matter of its proper construction: there is a presumption in favour of exclusivity,[50] although it has been held in a marine case that the words "This insurance is subject to English jurisdiction" merely created a permissive clause which entitled, but did not require, the assured to sue in England.[51]

The mere existence of a non-exclusive jurisdiction clause is not of itself of particular in any decision of the English courts on whether or not to stay proceedings if the clause has not been invoked.[52] However, if the clause permits a party to sue in England and he has asserted his right to do so, the parties will be held to their agreement and the exercise of the option will be treated as akin to an exclusive jurisdiction provision. Equally, the nomination of some other court as having non-exclusive jurisdiction will, once the option to sue in that jurisdiction has been exercised, generally cause the English court to stay its proceedings in much the same way as it would if faced with an exclusive jurisdiction clause.[53] A clause which requires the assured to sue in England while giving the insurers the

---

[45] See *Donohue v Armco Inc* [2002] 2 Lloyd's Rep. 425.

[46] *Aggeliki Charis Compania Maritima SA v Pagnan SA, The Angelic Grace* [1995] 1 Lloyd's Rep. 87.

[47] So held by the European Court of Justice in its controversial decision *Erich Gasser GmbH v MISAT Srl* (C-116/02), [2004] 1 Lloyd's Rep. 222. See also *Turner v Grovit* (C-159/02) [2004] 1 Lloyd's Rep. 216, applying the same principle where the applicant's allegation was that the action against him was oppressive and an abuse of process. Contrast the position where an anti-suit injunction is sought to restrain judicial proceedings in breach of an arbitration clause: see para.5–09, below.

[48] *ACE Insurance SA-NV v Zurich Insurance Co* [2001] Lloyd's Rep. IR 504; *Burrows v Jamaica Private Power Co Ltd* [2002] Lloyd's Rep. IR 466.

[49] Enumerated in *The Eleftheria* [1970] P.90.

[50] *Sohio v Gatoil* [1989] 1 Lloyd's Rep. 588; *IP Metal Ltd v Ruote OZ SpA* [1993] 2 Lloyd's Rep. 60. See, for illustrations of the distinction in the insurance context: *Beazley v Horizon Offshore Contractors Inc* [2005] Lloyd's Rep. IR 231; *Konkola Copper Mines plc v Coromin* [2007] Lloyd's Rep. IR 307.

[51] *Berisford v New Hampshire Insurance Co* [1990] 1 Lloyd's Rep. 454. Cf *Standard Steamship Owners Protection and Indemnity Association (Bermuda) Ltd v Gann* [1992] 2 Lloyd's Rep. 528.

[52] *BP plc v Aon Ltd* [2006] 1 Lloyd's Rep. 549.

[53] *Munchener Ruckversicherungs Gesellschaft v Commonwealth Insurance Co* [2005] Lloyd's Rep. IR 99; *Travelers Casualty & Surety Co of Europe Ltd v Sun Life Assurance Co of Canada Ltd* [2004] Lloyd's Rep. IR 846.

right to sue in any court of competent jurisdiction is not to be treated as an exclusive jurisdiction clause where the insurers choose to sue in England, but in such circumstances the clause is of great weight and it will be difficult for the assured to persuade the court that English proceedings should be stayed.[54] A "service of suit" clause under which a party agrees to accept service in a given jurisdiction is not a jurisdiction clause as such, but if service has been effected in some other jurisdiction under the terms of such a clause then the English courts are most unlikely to assert jurisdiction themselves.[55]

Jurisdiction: Regulation/Convention rules

The jurisdiction rules under the Brussels Regulation have generated a mass of **5–06** complex litigation. In outline, an action must be brought against a defendant in the place of his domicile within an EU or Lugano Convention country,[56] although there are various alternative countries in which an action may be brought depending upon the nature of the proceedings.[57] There is no need for the claimant to seek the permission of the English court to serve a claim form upon a person who is domiciled within an EU or Lugano Convention country providing that there are no other proceedings between the parties concerning the same claim pending in any EU or Lugano Convention country.[58] Where two or more courts have jurisdiction over a dispute under the rules in Regulation, the court "first seised"[59] has exclusive jurisdiction, and all other courts are required to stay or strike out their proceedings.[60] Further, if the English court is first seised of a dispute in which the defendant is domiciled in England, there is no discretion to stay the proceedings in any circumstances.[61] Fortunately it is unnecessary for the generality of the Brussels Regulation to be considered in any detail in the present work, because there are special jurisdictional rules for insurance contracts set out in arts 8 to 13 of the Regulation, which are designed to protect the assured as the perceived weaker party to an insurance transaction. The articles apply to "matters relating to insurance",[62] a term which is not defined but which has been held to cover all forms of insurance, whether domestic or commercial,[63] other than reinsurance[64] and actions between insurers, e.g., contribution claims[65] or claims

---

[54] *Groupama Insurance Co Ltd v Channel Islands Securities Ltd* [2002] Lloyd's Rep. IR 843.
[55] *Excess Insurance v Allendale Mutual Insurance Co* [2001] Lloyd's Rep. IR 524; *Ace Insurance SA-NV v Zurich Insurance Co* [2001] Lloyd's Rep. IR 504; *Catlin Syndicate Ltd v Adams Land & Cattle Co* [2007] Lloyd's Rep. IR 96.
[56] Brussels Regulation, art.2.
[57] In particular in art.5, which applies to contract actions and to tort actions. See also art.6, which allows joinder, e.g., where there are co-insurers: *Dornoch Ltd v Westminster International BV* [2009] Lloyd's Rep. IR 540; *Glacier Reinsurance AG v Gard Marine & Energy Ltd* [2010] EWCA Civ 1052.
[58] CPR r.6.33.
[59] See fn.46, above.
[60] Brussels Regulation, art.21.
[61] See fn.46, above.
[62] Brussels Regulation, art.8.
[63] *New Hampshire Insurance Co v Strabag Bau AG* [1992] 1 Lloyd's Rep. 361.
[64] *Group Josi Reinsurance Co SA v Universal General Insurance Co* (C-412/98), [2001] 1 Lloyd's Rep. 483, a decision of the European Court of Justice which confirmed the view to this effect of the House of Lords in *Agnew v Lansforsakringsbolagens AB* [2000] Lloyd's Rep. IR 483.
[65] *GIE v Zurich Espana & Softrans* (C-77/04), [2006] Lloyd's Rep. IR 215.

against co-insurers which have been assigned to the insurers by the assured.[66] Other claims arising out of the insurance relationship, e.g. the right to avoid the policy or to recover damages for fraud or misrepresentation, are also matters relating to insurance,[67] although a claim for costs against a third party under s.51 of the Senior Courts Act 1981 is not such a matter.[68]

The jurisdictional rules vary depending upon whether the proceedings are brought by or against the assured. A claim by the insurer against a policyholder, assured or policy beneficiary domiciled in an EU or Lugano Convention country may be brought only in the place of that person's domicile,[69] and this is the case irrespective of the place of the insurer's own domicile.[70] The only situations in which the insurer can bring an action in some other place are:

(a) if the policyholder, assured or beneficiary has himself initiated the proceedings and the insurers have counterclaimed,[71] although even here the insurers cannot join co-assureds domiciled elsewhere who were not parties to the original claim[72];

(b) if the claim arises out of the operations of the assured's agent, in which case the insurers may action sue Member State where the agent carries on its operations[73]; and

(c) if there is a direct action against liability insurers by a third party victim, where the law of the forum allows joinder of the assured.[74]

A claim against an insurer who is domiciled in an EU or Lugano Convention country may be brought by the policyholder, the assured or the beneficiary of the policy in that country,[75] or in the country of that person's own domicile if he has an EU or Lugano Convention country domicile.[76] If the claim is brought under a liability policy, it may be brought by the policyholder, assured or beneficiary in the EU or Lugano Convention country where the "harmful event" occurred,[77] and the insurer may—if the law of the forum so permits—be joined to proceedings by

---

[66] *Youell v La Reunion Aerienne* [2009] Lloyd's Rep. IR 405. It is doubtful whether a subrogation claim brought by the insurers in the name of the assured would be treated in the same way.
[67] *Jordan Grand Prix Ltd v Baltic Insurance Group* [1999] Lloyd's Rep. IR 93.
[68] *National Justice Compania Naviera SA v Prudential Assurance Co Ltd, The Ikarian Reefer (No.2)* [2000] 1 Lloyd's Rep. 129.
[69] Brussels Regulation, art.12.1.
[70] *Jordan Grand Prix Ltd v Baltic Insurance Group* [1999] Lloyd's Rep. IR 93.
[71] Brussels Regulation, art.12.2.
[72] *Jordan Grand Prix Ltd v Baltic Insurance Group* [1999] Lloyd's Rep. IR 93.
[73] Brussels Regulation, art.5.5.
[74] Brussels Regulation, art.11.3.
[75] Brussels Regulation, art.9.1(a).
[76] Brussels Regulation, art.9.1(b). An assured who is not domiciled within an EU or Lugano Convention country may bring an action based on these rules if he so chooses: *Berisford v New Hampshire Insurance Co* [1990] 1 Lloyd's Rep. 454.
[77] Brussels Regulation, art.11.1. The harmful event, a concept derived from the tort jurisdiction rules in art.5.3 of the Brussels Regulation, is either the act which gives rise to the claim or the loss suffered by the victim, so in many cases there will be a choice of jurisdictions under this provision. See generally *Bier v Mines de Potasse d'Alsace* Case 21/76, [1976] E.C.R. 1735.

the third party victim against the assured.[78] The law is particularly complex where a direct action is brought against liability insurers by the third party victim. Under art.11.2 of the Brussels Regulation, the insurance rules are stated to "apply to actions brought by the injured party directly against the insurer, where such direct actions are permitted." It has been held by the European Court of Justice in *FBTO Schadeverzekeringen NV v Odenbreit*[79] that the injured party is to be treated as if he were the policyholder, assured or beneficiary and thus can sue the insurers in his own domicile, and the English courts have ruled that whether or not a direct action is permitted is to be determined by the law applicable to the insurance policy and not the law of the place in which the proceedings are brought.[80] There is no general right of direct action under English law, so in the absence of the assured's insolvency[81] the English courts will not have jurisdiction to hear a direct claim against insurers not domiciled in England if the policy is governed by English law. There are no additional jurisdictional options in respect of a marine policy.

A claim against an insurer who is not domiciled in an EU or Lugano Convention country is subject to ordinary English jurisdictional rules, discussed above, with two modifications. First, if the policy is subscribed to by a number of insurers, and the leading underwriter is domiciled in an EU or Lugano Convention country, then all co-insurers may be sued in that country.[82] Secondly, an insurer who has a branch, agency or other establishment in an EU or Lugano Convention country is, in disputes arising out of its operations,[83] deemed to be domiciled in that country.[84] A broker is not an agent of the insurer for this purpose.[85]

Jurisdiction clauses: Regulation/Convention rules

The special European jurisdiction rules for matters relating to insurance are, as noted above, designed as consumer protection measures. Accordingly, there are strict rules regulating the extent to which the parties can contract out of those rules. It is possible to depart from the insurance rules only in the following situations.[86]   **5–07**

First, by means of an agreement which has been entered into after the dispute has arisen.[87]

---

[78] Article 11.1.
[79] Case C-463/06, [2008] Lloyd's Rep. IR 354.
[80] *Thwaites v Aviva Assurances* Unreported December 16, 2009, Mayors and City of London Court.
[81] In which case a direct action is permitted by the Third Parties (Rights against Insurers) Act 2010.
[82] Art 9.1(c).
[83] This means the making of the contract, and it is irrelevant that the contract was not made in the EU or a Lugano Convention country as long as the contract was made by an agent so domiciled: *Lloyd's Register of Shipping v Societe Campenon Bernard* [1995] All E.R. (EC) 531.
[84] Article 9.2.
[85] *New Hampshire Insurance Co v Strabag Bau AG* [1992] 1 Lloyd's Rep. 361. The position may be different where the broker is a coverholder operating under a binding authority with the power to accept risks on behalf of the insurer.
[86] Article 13.4 provides another possibility, but this is confined to compulsory insurance and to insurance of immovable property and thus is not relevant to marine insurance.
[87] Article 13.1.

Secondly, the agreement must be one which allows the assured to bring proceedings in courts other than those specified in the Brussels Regulation.[88] In a marine case, the clause may, therefore, permit the assured to sue in the place of his own domicile, the domicile of the insurer (or that of any relevant agent) or in any other agreed country. The clause cannot restrict the right of the assured to sue in his own domicile or the domicile of the insurer, and it is not permissible under this ground for the insurer to seek to add to the number of jurisdictions in which proceedings can be brought against the assured.

Thirdly, if at the time of the conclusion of the policy the assured and the insurer are domiciled or habitually resident in the same Convention or Regulation state, the parties may agree to confer jurisdiction on the courts of that state as long as its domestic law so allows: there is nothing in English law to preclude such an agreement.[89]

Fourthly, the parties are free to enter into an exclusive or non-exclusive jurisdiction agreement in so far as it covers one or more of a number of risks, set out in art. 14.[90] Those risks relevant to marine insurance, are:

1. any loss of or damage to:

   (a) seagoing ships [or] installations situated offshore or on the high seas ... arising from perils which relate to their use for commercial purposes;
   (b) goods in transit other than passengers' baggage where the transit consists of or includes carriage by such ships . . .;

2. any liability, other than for bodily injury to passengers or loss of or damage to their baggage:

   (a) arising out of the use or operation of ships [or] installations
   (b) for loss or damage caused by goods in transit as described in point 1(b);

3. any financial loss connected with the use or operation of ships, installations or aircraft as referred to in point 1(a), in particular loss of freight or charter-hire;

4. any risk or interest connected with any of those referred to in points 1 to 3;

5. notwithstanding points 1 to 4, all large risks.

Employers' liability cover issued to a shipowner falls within art.14.3 and also within art.14.4.[91]

Finally, if the assured voluntarily submits to the jurisdiction of a court which would not otherwise possess jurisdiction over the claim against him, such submission operates to confer jurisdiction upon the court.[92]

---

[88] Article 13.2.
[89] Article 13.3.
[90] Article 14.5.
[91] *Standard Steamship Owners' Protection and Indemnity Association (Bermuda) Ltd v GIE Vision Bail* [2005] Lloyd's Rep. IR 407.
[92] *Vienna Insurance Group v Bilas* (C-111/09), [2010] EUECJ, applying the general provisions of art.24 of the Brussels Regulation.

In *Charman v WOC Offshore BV*[93] the Court of Appeal decided that the inclu- **5–08**
sion of risks in a marine policy but falling outside paras 14.1 to 14.3 does not
remove the freedom of contract conferred by art.14 as long as the policy remains
primarily one of marine insurance. Here, the assured engineering contractors
agreed to supply equipment and personnel for construction works to be carried
out in Algeria, and a policy was taken out against the risk that the refusal of an
export licence by the Algerian authorities would prevent the removal of the equipment from Algeria. The question was whether a jurisdiction clause in the policy
was binding on the parties. It was common ground that the detention of a vessel
fell within art.14, but a dispute arose as to whether heavy machinery not capable
of floating fell within art.14.4. The Court of Appeal held that it did. The word
"risk" in art.14.4 referred back to the losses referred to in the earlier paragraphs
and that the word "interest" was not used in a technical sense but referred back to
ships and goods. Accordingly, art.14.4 applied to risks not mentioned in paras
14.1 to 14.3 as long as there was a connection with the risks or property
mentioned in those paragraphs. As far as the required connection was concerned,
a broad approach was to be taken, and other risks were covered providing that
they were not disproportionately large compared with those falling within arts
14.1 to 14.3, as would be the case where the policy covered land-based risks and
incidentally covered a marine risk. In the present case the value of property
falling outside arts 14.1 to 14.3 was about 20 per cent of the total insured value,
so that the policy remained primarily marine. It was also decided in this case that
if a policy covers risks falling outside art.14 then the jurisdiction clause is void.

The definition of "large risk" in art.14.5 is taken from EU law,[94] and in the
context of marine insurance means:

(i) all damage to or loss of river and canal vessels, lake vessels and sea
vessels[95];

(ii) all damage to or loss of goods in transit or baggage[96]; and

(iii) all liability arising out of the use of ships vessels or boats on the sea, lakes,
rivers or canals (including carriers' liability).[97]

It will be seen from these definitions that the vast majority of marine policies,
whether on ships, goods or freight, fall within art.14.

Where art.14 applies, the parties are free to enter into any form of exclusive or
non-exclusive jurisdiction clause as long as the clause is[98]:

---

[93] [1993] 2 Lloyd's Rep. 551.
[94] Council Directive 73/239/EEC (First Non-Life Directive), art.5(d), inserted by the Second Non-Life
Directive, art.5 (as amended).
[95] First Non-Life Directive, Annex, point 6.
[96] First Non-Life Directive, Annex, point 7.
[97] First Non-Life Directive, Annex, point 12.
[98] The tests laid down for the validity of jurisdiction clauses in art.23 of the Brussels Regulation.

"(a) in writing or evidenced in writing[99]; or

(b) in a form which accords with practices which the parties have established between themselves[100]; or

(c) in international trade or commerce, in a form which accords with a usage of which the parties are or ought to have been aware and which in such trade or commerce is widely known to, and regularly observed by, parties to contracts of the type involved in the particular trade or commerce concerned."[101]

It has been held it is well known that insurance issued in London on the MAR form contains a standard form exclusive jurisdiction clause in favour of England, so that possibility (c) applies to give the clause binding effect,[102] and a similar conclusion has been reached with respect to jurisdiction clauses in P&I Club rules.[103] A clause does not satisfy any of these requirements if it is contained in some other contract the terms of which have been incorporated by general words into the policy without express reference in the policy to the jurisdiction clause,[104] although a clause agreed by the authorised agents of the parties is binding on them.[105]

Arbitration

5-09 An arbitration clause in a marine policy precludes judicial proceedings in breach of that clause. The English courts can give effect to an arbitration clause in one of two ways. First, if the action is brought in the English courts, then once the court is satisfied that there is a valid arbitration clause which extends to the dispute between the parties,[106] the court is required under s.9(1) of the Arbitration Act 1996 to stay its proceedings unless satisfied that the arbitration clause is void,

---

[99] An exchange of correspondence between the parties which refers to a jurisdiction clause suffices here: *Standard Steamship Owners' Protection and Indemnity Association (Bermuda) Ltd v GIE Vision Bail* [2005] Lloyd's Rep. IR 407.

[100] A course of dealing between the parties, in which they have adopted a jurisdiction clause, satisfies this requirement: *Standard Steamship Owners' Protection and Indemnity Association (Bermuda) Ltd v GIE Vision Bail* [2005] Lloyd's Rep. IR 407.

[101] Brussels Regulation, art.23.

[102] *Denby v Hellenic Mediterranean Liners Co Ltd* [1994] 1 Lloyd's Rep. 320.

[103] *Standard Steamship Owners' Protection and Indemnity Association (Bermuda) Ltd v GIE Vision Bail* [2005] Lloyd's Rep. IR 407.

[104] *AIG Group (UK) Ltd v The Ethniki* [1999] Lloyd's Rep. IR 221; *AIG Europe SA v International QBE Insurance* [2002] Lloyd's Rep. IR 22. There is a long line of authority for the same proposition as regards arbitration clauses.

[105] *Denby v Hellenic Mediterranean Lines Co Ltd* [1994] 1 Lloyd's Rep. 320; *Standard Steamship Owners' Protection and Indemnity Association (Bermuda) Ltd v GIE Vision Bail* [2005] Lloyd's Rep. IR 407.

[106] In principle the court could refer either of these matters to the arbitrators for the determination of their own jurisdiction under the "kompetenz-kompetenz" principle established by s.30 of the Arbitration Act 1996. However, other than in exceptional circumstances, the court will not exercise its inherent jurisdiction to stay the proceedings where the validity or scope of arbitration clause is at stake. Any challenge to the existence of the marine policy itself, and indirectly to the arbitration clause, will, however, be stayed so that the validity of the policy can be determined by the arbitrators under s.30. For these principles, see: *Fiona Trust & Holding Co v Privalov* [2007] EWCA Civ 20; *Albon v Naza Motor Trading (No 3) SDN BHD* [2007] EWHC 665 (Ch).

inoperative or incapable of being enforced[107]: the arbitrators themselves are to resolve these issues and also any question as to whether there is an existing dispute between the parties.[108] It is immaterial for the purposes of s.9 whether the seat of the arbitration is England or elsewhere, so that a stay may be granted to support a foreign arbitration.

Secondly, if the judicial proceedings are brought in some other jurisdiction, then the English court may in principle grant an anti-suit injunction preventing the claimant in the foreign proceedings from continuing the action in breach of the arbitration clause[109] if the court is satisfied that the clause is valid and extends to the dispute.[110] If the proceedings are brought in a court outside the EU or EFTA, the English court can grant injunctive relief if it possesses jurisdiction over the claimant in the foreign proceedings,[111] so that, unless he is domiciled in England, the arbitration clause must be made in England or governed by English law or the arbitration must have its seat in England so that there can be said to have been a breach of contract in England. Further the claimant in the foreign proceedings must be in breach of the arbitration clause or otherwise acting in a vexatious fashion. There is no breach of the arbitration clause where the claimant is not a party to the insurance contract containing the arbitration clause but rather is seeking to enforce a right under a foreign law to bring a direct action against the insurers. In this type of case, which will typically arise where the third party has a claim against the assured under a liability policy which may be enforced under some foreign law by a direct claim against the assured's liability insurers, the English court need go no further than grant a declaration that the third party is bound by the arbitration clause: such a declaration may be regarded as conclusive by the foreign court, or if not then it will at the very least prevent enforcement in England of a foreign judgment against the insurers and in favour of the third party.[112] The power to issue an anti-suit injunction does exist, it will only be exercised if the remedy is sought without delay.[113]

By contrast if the claim is one which has been, or which is capable of being, brought in an EU or EFTA court, the English court cannot grant an anti-suit

---

[107] These grounds assume the validity of the arbitration clause, and that something has otherwise occurred which prevents its enforcement: *A v B* [2006] EWHC 2006 (Comm); *Albon v Naza Motor Trading (No 3) SDN BHD* [2007] EWHC 665 (Ch).

[108] *Halki Shipping Corporation v Sopex Oils Ltd* [1998] 1 Lloyd's Rep. 49. The decision of the arbitrators on their own substantive jurisdiction is, however, subject to an appeal to the court under s.67 of the 1996 Act.

[109] *XL Insurance v Owens Corning* [2000] 2 Lloyd's Rep. 500. This power is available at any stage in the arbitral process, and may even be used where an award has been issued and the foreign action attempts to sidestep the award: *Noble Assurance Co v Gerling-Konzern General Insurance Co (UK)* [2008] Lloyd's Rep. IR 1.

[110] *American Speciality Lines Insurance Co v Abbott Laboratories* [2003] 1 Lloyd's Rep. 267.

[111] Under CPR PD 6.

[112] On the principle that the English courts will not recognise or enforce a foreign judgment which is contrary to an earlier English judgment. See: *Through Transport Mutual Insurance Association (Eurasia) Ltd v New India Assurance Co Ltd* [2005] 1 Lloyd's Rep. 67; *Markel International Co Ltd v Craft* [2006] EWHC 3150 (Comm).

[113] See generally: *Aggeliki Charis Compania Maritima SA v Pagnan SA, The Angelic Grace* [1995] 1 Lloyd's Rep. 87; *XL Insurance v Owens Corning* [2000] 2 Lloyd's Rep. 500; *Kallang Shipping SA v Axa Assurances Senegal, The Kallang* [2006] EWHC 2825 (Comm); *Noble Assurance Co v Gerling-Konzern General Insurance Co (UK)* [2008] Lloyd's Rep. IR 1.

injunction. While it is the case that "arbitration" is excluded from the Brussels Regulation by art.1.3, the European Court of Justice in *Allianz SpA (formerly Riunione Adriatica di Sicurta SpA) v West Tankers Inc*[114] ruled that if a court is seised (or capable of being seised) of a dispute, the fact that there is an arbitration clause does not take the dispute outside the Brussels Regulation[115] and the EU or EFTA court must be permitted to determine its own jurisdiction by ruling on the validity or otherwise of the arbitration clause without pre-emptive action by the English court in the form of anti-suit relief. The English courts have subsequently determined that they cannot grant negative declaratory relief as to the existence or otherwise of an arbitration clause.[116]

Applicable law: history

5–10 As a result of EU harmonisation measures, the rules which determine the law applicable to a marine insurance policy have been transformed in recent years. The common law principle of "proper law" was (with limited exceptions) replaced in 1991 by new rules. If the insurance risk was situated in the EU, the law applicable to the policy was to be found by application of the EU's Insurance Directives, which were designed to protect the assured as the weaker party to the transaction.[117] As far as marine insurance where the risk was situated within the EU was concerned, those rules were contained in the Second Non-Life Directive of June 1988,[118] and implementation in the UK was perfected by the Financial Services and Markets Act 2000 (Law Applicable to Contracts of Insurance) Regulations 2001.[119] However, if the risk was situated outside the EU, or if the policy was one of reinsurance, applicable law rules were contained in the Rome Convention 1980, implemented into English law by the Contracts (Applicable Law) Act 1990.[120] The 2001 Regulations and the Rome Convention remains applicable to insurance contracts entered into before December 17, 2009, but applicable law rules for contracts entered into after that date are now set out in the Rome I Regulation 2009.[121]

---

[114] Case C-185/07, [2009] 1 All E.R. (Comm) 435. This ruling overturned the English view of the matter: *Through Transport Mutual Insurance Association (Eurasia) Ltd v New India Assurance Co Ltd* [2005] 1 Lloyd's Rep. 67.

[115] See also *Youell v La Reuinion Aerienne* [2009] Lloyd's Rep. IR 405.

[116] *National Navigation Co v Endesa Generacion SA* [2009] EWCA Civ 1397.

[117] As a limited alternative to initial proposals, since dropped, to harmonise substantive insurance law in the EU.

[118] Council Directive 88/357/EEC. Life policies were subject to the Second Life Directive, 92/96/EEC, subsequently replaced by the Consolidated Life Directive, European Parliament and Council Directive 2002/83/EC. Existing Insurance Directives will be replaced in 2012 by the Solvency II Directive, European Parliament and Council Directive 2009/138/EC.

[119] SI 2001/2635.

[120] The Rome Convention was republished in consolidated form in 2005.

[121] European Parliament and Council Regulation 593/2008/EC. The Rome II Regulation, European Parliament and Council Regulation 864/2007/EC which, paradoxically, was adopted before the Rome I Regulation, is concerned with the law applicable to non-contractual claims, including claims in tort and restitution.

Applicable law: legal structure

The effect of this structure is as follows.   **5–11**

First, the common law proper law rules continue to apply to contracts which are excluded from the Rome I Regulation. Those contracts include, most importantly:[122] obligations arising under bills of exchange, cheques and promissory notes and other negotiable instruments to the extent that the obligations under such other negotiable instruments arise out of their negotiable character; arbitration agreements and agreements on the choice of court; the question whether an agent is able to bind a principal, or an organ to bind a company or other body corporate or unincorporated, in relation to a third party; and obligations arising out of dealings prior to the conclusion of a contract,[123] as these which are governed by the Rome II Regulation on non-contractual obligations. As regards arbitration agreements and agreements on the choice of court, any dispute in England as to the law applicable to an arbitration or jurisdiction clause—and thus which law determines the validity and interpretation of such a clause—is thus a matter for the pre-existing English common law. Arbitration and jurisdiction clauses are regarded as severable from the substantive contract to which they relate,[124] so that it is perfectly possible, although presumptively unusual, for different applicable laws to govern the arbitration or jurisdiction clause and the substantive contract.[125] The ascertainment of the law governing the procedure of an arbitral hearing is also outside the EU rules and, as far as English law is concerned, the curial law is that of the seat.[126]

Secondly, if the contract was entered into before December 17, 2009, applicable law rules are found in the Rome Convention and the Financial Services and Markets Act 2000 (Law Applicable to Contracts of Insurance) Regulations 2001 and the Rome Convention,[127] depending upon the situation of the risk. In summary: a marine policy insuring a risk situated within the EU is governed by the rules in the 2001 Regulations; a marine policy insuring a risk situated outside the EU is governed by the Rome Convention; and reinsurance contracts are governed by the Rome Convention.

Thirdly, if the contract was entered into on or after December 17, 2009, the choice of law rules to be applied by the English courts are found in the Rome I Regulation. The general rules on applicable law in arts 3 and 4 apply to all reinsurance contracts, large risks wherever situated are subject to art.7.2, non-large risks situated outside the EU are governed by arts 3 and 4, and non large risks situated inside the EU are governed by art.7.3–7.6. A large risk, as defined by art.5(d) of the First Non-Life Directive,[128] includes "all risks relating to railway

---

[122] Rome I Regulation, art.1.2.

[123] These are governed by the Rome II Regulation.

[124] This is statutory for arbitration: Arbitration Act 1996, s.7.

[125] For example, *Peterson Farms Inc v C & M Farming Ltd* [2004] EWHC 121 (Comm); *Tonicstar Ltd v American Home Assurance Co* [2005] Lloyd's Rep. IR 32.

[126] Arbitration Law 1996, ss.2 and 3.

[127] Law Applicable to Contractual Obligations (England and Wales and Northern Ireland) Regulations 2009, SI 2009/3064; Financial Services and Markets Act 2000 (Law Applicable to Contracts of Insurance) Regulations 2009, SI 2009/3075.

[128] Council Directive 73/239/EEC, applied to the Rome I Regulation by art.7.6.

rolling stock, aircraft, ships, liability for aircraft and liability for ships". This means that hull policies are large risks and the applicable law rules are those in art.7.2 of the Rome I Regulation. Cargo and other policies, however, may or may not constitute large risks. Much of the Rome I Regulation refers to the "habitual residence" of one or other of the parties. This concept, defined by art.19, means the place of a company's central administration or, in the case of a natural person, his principal place of business. If the contract is concluded in the course of the operations of a branch, agency or any other establishment, or if, under the contract, performance is the responsibility of such a branch, agency or establishment, the place where the branch, agency or any other establishment is located is the place of habitual residence.

Situation of risk

5–12 The situation of an insurance risk is significant for both the pre- and post-Rome I regimes. If the policy was entered into before December 17, 2009, a risk situated within the EU will attract the applicable law rules in the 2001 Regulations whereas a risk situated outside the EU will attract the applicable law rules of the Rome Convention. For contracts entered into on or after December 17, 2009, a large risk wherever situated is governed by reg.7.2 of the Rome I Regulation, any non-large risk situated outside the EU is governed by the ordinary rules in arts 3 and 4 and any non-large risk situated within the EU is governed by the special rules in arts 7.3 to 7.6.

The place in which a marine risk is situated is defined by art.2(d) of Council Directive 88/357/EEC (the Second Non-Life Directive): the risk is situated where the policyholder who is a natural person has his habitual residence or, in the case of a legal person, where the establishment to which the contract relates is situated.[129] The Rome Convention did not make any reference to two common situations: where the assured carried on business in a number of countries both inside and outside the EU so that the risks were situated in each of those countries; and where a policy covered a number of policyholders as co-assureds whose risks were situated a variety of EU and non-EU states. When faced with this question under the pre-2009 law, the courts confirmed that there has to be a single applicable law, and managed to avoid reaching a decision on the situation of the risk by holding that the test to be applied was the closest connection test,[130] generally pointing to the situation of the head office of the main policyholder.[131] The Rome

---

[129] This will generally be the place from which the business is carried on: *Evialis SA v SIAT* [2003] 2 Lloyd's Rep. 377.

[130] *American Motorists Insurance Co v Cellstar Corporation* [2003] Lloyd's Rep. IR 295; *Travelers Casualty & Surety Co of Europe Ltd v Sun Life Assurance Co of Canada (UK) Ltd* [2004] Lloyd's Rep. IR 846; *Travelers Casualty & Surety Co of Europe Ltd v Sun Life Assurance Co of Canada (UK) Ltd (No 2)* [2007] Lloyd's Rep. IR 619.

[131] *American Motorists Insurance Co v Cellstar Corporation* [2003] Lloyd's Rep. IR 295; *Travelers Casualty & Surety Co of Europe Ltd v Sun Life Assurance Co of Canada (UK) Ltd (No 2)* [2007] Lloyd's Rep. IR 619. In *Cellstar* the Court of Appeal doubted whether the Directives were intended to apply to a situation in which a policy issued outside the EU by non-EU insurers but covering some risks within the EU but noted that the 2001 Regulations did not expressly preclude that situation.

I Regulation has for the most part resolved these matters, by opting for a single set of rules for large risks wherever situated and, in the case of non-large risks, by providing for severability in recital 33:

"Where an insurance contract not covering a large risk covers more than one risk, at least one of which is situated in a Member State and at least one of which is situated in a third country, the special rules on insurance contracts in this Regulation should apply only to the risk or risks situated in the relevant Member State or Member States."

Equally, if the risk is situated in more than one Member Sate, art.7.5 provides that "the contract is to be considered as constituting several contracts each relating to only one Member State".

Significance of the applicable law

The English courts will apply the law applicable to a policy to all matters of **5–13** substance,[132] including: the existence of the agreement[133]; the legality of the obligations undertaken by the parties[134]; contractual capacity[135]; the existence of the terms of the agreement, by incorporation or otherwise[136]; vitiating elements, such

---

[132] Unless otherwise stated, the rules are the same under both the Rome Convention and the Rome I Regulation.

[133] If it is alleged that the parties have not entered into any agreement at all, art.10.1 of the Rome I Regulation provides that the question of validity is to be determined by the law which would be applicable if it were valid. In other words, the validity of the contract is presumed and validity is then tested by the applicable law. This was also the common law rule: *Mackender v Feldia AG* [1967] 2 Q.B. 590; *Britannia Steamship Insurance Association v Ausonia Assicurazioni SpA* [1984] 2 Lloyd's Rep. 98. There is, in art.10.2, an exception to art.10.1 which allows a party to rely upon the law of the country of his habitual residence to demonstrate that he had not consented to the making of the agreement, but this cannot be relied upon where it can be shown that the party in question had by his knowledge and conduct consented to the making of the agreement: *Egon Oldendorff v Libera Corporation (No 2)* [1995] 2 Lloyd's Rep. 64; *Welex AG v Rosa Maritime, The Epsilon Rosa* [2002] EWHC 2033.

[134] *Kahler v Midland Bank* [1950] A.C. 24. The English courts will refuse to enforce a contract valid under its applicable law if there is some overriding public policy reason for refusing enforcement (Rome I Regulation, art.21) or if it is unlawful in the place of performance (*Ralli Brothers v Compania Naviera Sota y Aznar* [1920] 2 K.B. 287—contract governed by English law; *Royal Boskalis Westminster NV v Mountain* [1997] 2 All E.R. 929—contract governed by foreign law).

[135] In a contract concluded between persons who are in the same country, a natural person who would have capacity under the law of that country may invoke his incapacity resulting from another law only if the other party to the contract was aware of this incapacity at the time of the conclusion of the contract or was not aware thereof as a result of negligence: Rome I Regulation, art.13.

[136] Rome Convention, art.8.1. If the existence of an exclusive jurisdiction or arbitration clause is in issue, the very existence of such a clause may be an important indication as to the applicable law. The English approach is to determine the validity of the clause under its putative applicable law and, if validity is established, then to use that clause to determine the law applicable to the agreement: *Egon Oldendorff v Libera Corporation* [1995] 2 Lloyd's Rep. 64; *Dornoch Ltd v Mauritius Union Assurance Co Ltd* [2006] Lloyd's Rep. IR 786.

as duress[137]; interpretation[138]; performance[139]; assessment of damages[140]; extinguishing of obligations most importantly by limitation periods[141]; and consequences of the nullity of the contract.[142] Matters of procedure, such as the rules for disclosure and inspection of evidence,[143] and the award of interest,[144] are governed by English law as the law of the forum. Any formal requirements imposed on the validity of a contract made between two parties in the same country are deemed to be satisfied if the contract complies either with the applicable law or the law of the country in which it was concluded, while if the parties are in different countries then it is enough if the formal requirements of the applicable law or of any of those countries are complied with.[145] Illegality committed in the performance of the contract will be relevant only if the conduct was illegal either under the applicable law or in the place of performance: a claim under a policy made in England, governed by English law and in respect of a loss while the subject matter was being used lawfully is unaffected by the fact that some other law rendered performance illegal.[146] In applying the applicable law, regard is to be had only to the substantive rules of that law and not its conflict of laws rules, so that if English choice of law rules point to a given applicable law, the substantive rules of that law govern the policy and it is irrelevant that the conflict of laws rules of that country might point to another applicable law.[147]

Where a policy has been assigned or there is contractual subrogation, the mutual obligations of the assignor and assignee are governed by the law applicable to the assignment,[148] whereas the assignability of the policy and the relationship between the assignee and the insurers are governed by the law applicable to the policy[149] as is the formal validity of the assignment.[150] The Rome

---

[137] *Dimskal Shipping Co SA v International Transport Workers Federation, The Evia Luck* [1991] 4 All E.R. 871.
[138] Rome I Regulation, art.12.1(a); *St Paul Fire and Marine Insurance Co v. Morice* (1906) 22 T.L.R. 449; *Rowatt Leaky & Co v Scottish Provident Institution* [1927] 1 Ch.55. Note that in *King v Brandywine Reinsurance Co (UK) Ltd* [2005] Lloyd's Rep. IR 509 the Court of Appeal found it difficult to accept that English and New York law would reach different conclusions on the interpretation of a commercial policy covering pollution risks. In *Halpern v Halpern* [2007] EWCA Civ 291 the Court of Appeal held that it was open to the parties to incorporate another law (including a system of law other than that as a country) in which case the incorporated law could be used as an aid to interpretation.
[139] Rome I Regulation, art.12.1(b).
[140] Rome I Regulation, art.12.1(c).
[141] Rome I Regulation, art.12.1(d); Foreign Limitation Periods Act 1984, which permits the limitation period under the applicable law to be disapplied by an English court in the case of "undue hardship".
[142] Rome I Regulation, art.12.1(e). This was a derogation which had been exercised by the UK under the Rome Convention: Contracts (Applicable Law) Act 1990, s 2(2).
[143] *South Carolina Insurance Co v Assurantie Maatschappij "de Zeven Provincien" NV and Al Ahli Insurance* [1987] 1 A.C. 24.
[144] *Midland International Trade Services Ltd v Sudairy* [1990] *Financial Times*, May 2; *Maher v Groupama Grand Est* [2009] EWCA Civ 1191.
[145] Rome I Regulation, art.11.
[146] *Euro-Diam v Bathurst* [1988] 1 Lloyd's Rep. 288.
[147] The approach of taking into account foreign choice of law rules, *"renvoi"*, was not recognised at common law (*Amin Rasheed Shipping Corporation v Kuwait Insurance Co* [1983] 2 All E.R. 884) and is excluded by art.20 of the Rome I Regulation.
[148] Rome I Regulation, art.14.1
[149] Rome I Regulation, art.14.2.
[150] *Raiffeisen Zentralbank Osterreich AG v Five Star General Trading LLC* [2001] Lloyd's Rep. IR 460.

I Regulation, art.15, provides that where the assured has a claim for breach of contract against a third party, and insurers have indemnified the assured for his loss, the law which governs the contract under which the claim arose also governs the existence or otherwise of a subrogated claim in favour of the insurers.

Where there is a right of set-off other than one agreed by the parties, art.17 of the Rome I Regulation states that the set-off shall be governed by the law applicable to the claim against which the right to set-off is asserted.

Express choice of applicable law: common law

Where the common law governs the position, i.e., in respect of those contracts **5–14** excluded from the Rome I Regulation, the parties are free to choose the applicable law, and their choice will be regarded as conclusive, even in the absence of any connection with England,[151] other than in the following exceptional cases: the law chosen must be that of a country and not that of a religion or general commercial law principles (e.g., *lex mercatoria*)[152]; the choice must not be contrary to public policy[153]; the parties' choice must not have been frustrated by events outside their control[154]; and the applicable law must be determined from the outset and not permitted to "float" by reference to the place in which proceedings are commenced.[155]

Express choice of applicable law: position prior to Rome I Regulation

A distinction has to be drawn between on the one hand risks situated outside the **5–15** EU and all reinsurance contracts, and on the other hand risks situated inside the EU.

If the risk is situated outside the EU or is one of reinsurance, the Rome Convention applies. The parties are free to choose the applicable law by art.3.1. The only limitations are those of public policy: the chosen law cannot oust the mandatory rules of the country in which all elements relevant to the situation are located if that country's law has not been chosen (art.3.3),[156] the parties cannot oust the mandatory principles of EU law if there is a choice of the law of a country outside the EU and all the elements relevant to the situation are located in one or more EU states (art.3.4); the mandatory laws of the forum are not to be deprived of effect even if another law is validly chosen (arts 7.2); and the courts may give effect to the mandatory laws of a third country, other than the forum and the country providing the applicable law, with which the contract has a close connection (art.7.1, a provision not adopted in England).

---

[151] *Vita Food Products Inc v Unus Shipping Co Ltd* [1939] A.C. 277.
[152] *Musawi v R E International (UK) Ltd* [2007] EWHC 2981 (Ch).
[153] *Vita Food Products Inc v Unus Shipping Co Ltd* [1939] A.C. 277.
[154] *Perry v Equitable Life Assurance Society of the United States of America* (1929) 45 T.L.R. 468.
[155] *Armor Shipping Co Ltd v Caisse Algerienne* [1981] 1 W.L.R. 207; *Amin Rasheed Shipping Corporation v Kuwait Insurance Co* [1984] A.C. 50; *CGU International Insurance plc v Szabo* [2002] Lloyd's Rep. IR 196; *Wasa International Insurance Co Ltd v Lexington Insurance Co* [2009] Lloyd's Rep. IR 675.
[156] *Caterpillar Financial Services Corporation v SNC Passion* [2004] EWHC 569 (Comm).

If the risk is situated within the EU, the Rome Convention does not apply and the rules are those laid down in the Second Non-Life Directive as implemented into English law by the 2001 Regulations. There are here important restrictions on choice. The assumption underlying the Second Non-Life Directive is that the policyholder is the weaker party to the transaction and accordingly merits a degree of protection. The relevant provisions therefore permit EU States to restrict party autonomy on choice of law. England, unlike a number of its EU counterparts, does not impose any such restrictions. The Directive does, however, recognise, that many commercial policies will, from the policyholder's point of view, be negotiated on at least equal terms, and all domestic restrictions on choice of law are removed. Regulation 4(7) of the 2001 Regulations states that "if the risk covered by the contract is a large risk the parties may choose any law as the applicable law." The definition of large risk was set out above, and may be repeated here for convenience: a large risk for present purposes means:

(i) all damage to or loss of river and canal vessels, lake vessels and sea vessels;

(ii) all damage to or loss of goods in transit or baggage; and

(iii) all liability arising out of the use of ships vessels or boats on the sea, lakes, rivers or canals (including carriers' liability).

It will be appreciated that most marine policies are large risks within these definitions, so that there is complete freedom of choice of the applicable law. Insofar as a marine policy is not a large risk, the 2001 Regulations distinguish three situations. In all cases the law of a country must be chosen.[157]

5–16   The first, in reg.4(2), is where the policyholder resides in the EU State in which the risk is situated. Where this is the case, the law applicable to the contract is that of the EU State in question, although the parties may choose some other law if the presumptively applicable law so permits. Residence for this purpose means, in the case of an individual, the country in which the policyholder has his habitual residence, and in any other case, the country in which the policyholder has its central administration.[158] The effect is that if the policyholder is an individual the situation of the risk and his residence are one and the same, so that the ability of the parties to choose some other law depends upon the law of his residence. If the policyholder is not an individual, then its residence is the country of its central administration whereas the risk may be situated in that country or in the country of any relevant branch or agency: once again, however, in most cases residence and situation of risk will coincide, so the law of that country determines whether or not the parties can choose some other law as the applicable law. As an alternative, if the risks covered by the contract are limited to events occurring in an EU State other

---

[157] *Shamil Bank of Bahrain v Beximco Pharmaceuticals Ltd* [2003] 2 All E.R. (Comm) 849; *Musawi v R E International (UK) Ltd* [2007] EWHC 2981 (Ch); *Halpern v Halpern* [2007] EWCA Civ 291, which also held that an express choice of a system of law other than that of a country does not render the contract void for uncertainty because in such a case the court would then be obliged to apply the relevant default choice of law rules under the Rome Convention.
[158] Regulation 1(3).

than that in which the risk is situated, the parties may choose the law of the former EU State.[159] *Evialis v SIAT*[160] illustrates the operation of reg.4(2). In this case the assured under a marine cargo open cover policy was resident in Italy and the risk was also situated in Italy. The open cover was stated to be governed by Italian law. The insurers issued a certificate of insurance in respect of a particular cargo, and this was stated to be governed by English law. The issue was whether there had been a valid choice of English law in respect of the certificate. Andrew Smith J. held that the effect of reg.4(2) was that Italian law—as the law of the country of the assured's residence and the situation of the risk—determined the validity of the choice of law clause in the certificate, and that under Italian law that choice was invalid as it was overridden by the choice of law clause in the policy itself.[161]

Secondly, if the policyholder does not reside in the EU State in which the risk **5–17** is situated (which is a remote possibility in the context of marine insurance), the parties to the contract may choose as the applicable law either:

(a) the law of the EEA State in which the risk is situated;

(b) the law of the country in which the policyholder resides;[162]

(c) if the law of either of those EU States so permits, any other law;[163] or

(d) if the risks covered by the contract are limited to events occurring in an EU State other than that in which the risk is situated, the parties may choose the law of the former EU State.[164]

Thirdly, if the policyholder carries on a business and the contract covers two or **5–18** more risks relating to that business which are situated in different EU States, the freedom of the parties to choose the applicable law conferred by this regulation extends to the law of any of those EU States and of the country in which the policyholder resides.[165] If the law of any of those EU States so permits, the parties may also choose any other law.[166] Further, if the risks covered by the contract are limited to events occurring in an EU State other than that in which the risk is situated, the parties may choose the law of the former EU State.[167]

Express choice of applicable law: Rome I Regulation

Under the Rome I Regulation, a distinction has to be drawn between: **5–19**

(a) reinsurance contracts and contracts which are not large risks and are situated outside the EU;

---

[159] Regulation 4(6).
[160] [2003] Lloyd's Rep. IR 377.
[161] The learned judge was of the view that, had English law been the relevant applicable law, the opposite conclusion would have been reached.
[162] Regulation 4(3).
[163] Regulation 4(5).
[164] Regulation 4(6).
[165] Regulation 4(4).
[166] Regulation 4(5).
[167] Regulation 4(6).

(b) large risks, wherever situated; and

(c) risks which are not large risks and which are situated inside the EU.

In case (a), the parties are free to choose the applicable law under art.3.1. The public policy limitations reflect those in the Rome Convention: the chosen law cannot oust the mandatory rules of the country in which all elements relevant to the situation are located if that country's law has not been chosen (art.3.3); the parties cannot oust the mandatory principles of EU law if there is a choice of the law of a country outside the EU and all the elements relevant to the situation are located in one more EU states (art.3.4); the mandatory laws of the forum are not to be deprived of effect even if another law is validly chosen (arts 9.2 and 21); and the court may give effect to overriding mandatory rules of law in the country of the place of performance insofar as those mandatory rules render performance unlawful (art.9.3).

In case (b) the relevant provision is art.7.2, which states that in the case of a large risk the parties may choose the applicable law in accordance with the principles set out in art.3.1. Cases (a) and (b) are, to this extent, thus treated in the same way.

In case (c), restrictions are imposed upon the parties' freedom of choice. Article 7.3, insofar as it is relevant to marine insurance, provides that the parties may choose the following.

(1) The law of any Member State where the risk is situated at the time of conclusion of the contract, although if that law permits greater freedom of choice then the parties may take advantage of that freedom. If that law is a law of any part of the United Kingdom, the parties to that contract may also choose as the law applicable to the contract: (i) the law of another country; or (ii) the law of another part of the United Kingdom.[168]

(2) The law of the country where the policy holder has his habitual residence although if that law permits greater freedom of choice then the parties may take advantage of that freedom. If that law is a law of any part of the United Kingdom, the parties to that contract may also choose as the law applicable to the contract: (i) the law of another country; or (ii) the law of another part of the United Kingdom.[169]

(3) For insurance contracts covering risks limited to events occurring in one Member State other than the Member State where the risk is situated, the law of that Member State.

(4) Where the policy holder of a contract pursues a commercial or industrial activity or a liberal profession and the insurance contract covers two or more risks which relate to those activities and are situated in different Member States, the law of any of the Member States concerned or the law of the country of habitual residence of the policy holder, although if that law permits greater freedom of choice then the parties may take advantage

---

[168] The Financial Services and Markets Act 2000 (Law Applicable to Contracts of Insurance) Regulations 2009, SI 2009/3075, reg.4.

[169] The Financial Services and Markets Act 2000 (Law Applicable to Contracts of Insurance) Regulations 2009, SI 2009/3075, reg.4.

of that freedom. If that law or any of those laws is a law of any part of the United Kingdom, the parties to that contract may also choose as the law applicable to the contract (i) the law of another country; or (ii) the law of another part of the United Kingdom.[170]

Where the contract covers risks situated in more than one Member State, the contract is to be considered as constituting several contracts each relating to only one Member State (art.7.5).

Express choice of applicable law: general principles

There are no formal requirements for express choice of law agreements in any of the three systems, and an agreement may be oral.[171] The incorporation of a choice of law clause from another contract is not likely to be sufficient to amount to a valid agreement.[172] **5–20**

All three systems recognise that a contract may be governed as to its divisible parts by different applicable laws. This principle was applied at common law[173] and is recognised by art.3.1 of the Rome Convention and art.3.1 of the Rome I Regulation. Although a floating choice of law is invalid at common law and probably under the Rome Convention and Rome I Regulation, there seems to be no objection to the parties agreeing to vary the applicable law once the contract has incepted (art.3.2 of the Rome Convention and art.3.2 of the Rome I Regulation) or to conferring upon one or both parties the right to opt for a new applicable law based upon the place in which proceedings are commenced.[174]

Implied choice of applicable law: common law

At common law, even where a marine policy was not expressly stated to be governed by English law, a choice of law could be implied. The English courts recognised the concept of the implied choice of law, so that in the absence of an express choice of law the courts could look to the other terms of the policy and the surrounding circumstances. **5–21**

Implied choice of applicable law: Rome Convention

Under the Rome Convention, art.3.1, the parties are taken to have chosen the applicable law, insofar as they are permitted to do so in accordance with the rules set out in para 5–15 above, if their choice is "expressed with reasonable certainty by the **5–22**

---

[170] The Financial Services and Markets Act 2000 (Law Applicable to Contracts of Insurance) Regulations 2009, SI 2009/3075, reg.4.

[171] *Oakley v Ultra Vehicle Design Ltd* [2005] EWHC 872 (Ch) (Rome Convention).

[172] *Gan Insurance Co Ltd v Tai Ping Insurance Co Ltd* [1999] Lloyd's Rep. IR 229; *AIG Group (UK) Ltd v The Ethniki* [1998] 4 All E.R. 301.

[173] *Forsikringsaktielskapet Vesta v Butcher* [1986] 2 All E.R. 588 (construction of the policy not subject to its applicable law).

[174] *Armadora Occidental SA v Horace Mann Insurance Co* [1977] 2 Lloyd's Rep. 406; *El Du Pont de Nemours & Co v Agnew* [1987] 2 Lloyd's Rep. 585; *Heath Lambert Ltd v Sociedad de Corretaje de Seguros* [2004] 1 Lloyd's Rep. 495; *King v Brandywine Reinsurance Co (UK) Ltd* [2004] Lloyd's Rep. IR 554 affirmed on other grounds [2005] Lloyd's Rep. IR 509; *Craft Enterprises (International) Ltd v Axa Insurance Co* [2005] Lloyd's Rep. IR 14.

terms of the contract or the circumstances of the case". The common law is all but replicated in art.3.1 of the Rome Convention, it being clear from the decided cases that the common law concepts of express and implied choice of law are encompassed by the Rome Convention's principle of choice of law expressed with reasonable certainty. An implied choice of law can arise in either of the two ways specified in art.3.1.[175] First, it can be derived from the other terms of the contract: relevant provisions for this purpose have been held at common law to include an arbitration clause nominating a particular country as the seat of the arbitration,[176] an exclusive jurisdiction clause[177] and a leading underwriter provision in which the following market agree to "follow London",[178] although not a non-exclusive jurisdiction clause.[179] Secondly, it can arise from the circumstances of the case, including for this purpose the negotiations leading to the conclusion of the policy.[180]

As far as insurance is concerned, the courts have held on a number of occasions that, under the Rome Convention, if a policy has been placed in the London market using London market wordings, the parties are to be taken to have intended their policy to be governed by English law.[181] Equally, if the policy is placed in an overseas market using local wordings, the parties will be treated as having impliedly chosen the law of that place.[182]

---

[175] *Marubeni Hong Kong and South China Ltd v Mongolian Government* [2002] 1 All E.R. (Comm) 873; *Dornoch Ltd v Mauritius Union Assurance Co Ltd* [1986] Lloyd's Rep. IR 786.

[176] *Norske Atlas Insurance Co Ltd v London General Insurance Co Ltd* (1927) 43 T.L.R. 541; *Maritime Insurance Co v Assecuranz Union von 1865* (1935) 52 Ll. L.R. 16; *James Miller & Partners Ltd v Whitworth Street Estates (Manchester) Ltd* [1970] A.C. 583; *Compagnie D'Armement Maritime SA v Compagnie Tunisienne de Navigation SA* [1971] AC 572; *Egon Oldendorff v Libera Corporation* [1995] 2 Lloyd's Rep. 64; *Egon Oldendorff v Libera Corporation (No 2)* [1996] 1 Lloyd's Rep. 380; *King v Brandywine Reinsurance Co (UK) Ltd* [2005] Lloyd's Rep. IR 509.

[177] *Royal Exchange Assurance Corporation v Sjoforsakrings Aktiebolaget Vega* [1902] 2 K.B. 384.

[178] *Armadora Occidental SA v Horace Mann Insurance Co* [1977] 2 Lloyd's Rep. 406.

[179] *Armadora Occidental SA v Horace Mann Insurance Co* [1977] 2 Lloyd's Rep. 406; *Cantieri Navali Riuniti SpA v NV Omne Justitia* [1985] 2 Lloyd's Rep. 428; *El Du Pont de Nemours & Co v Agnew* [1987] 2 Lloyd's Rep. 585; *King v Brandywine Reinsurance Co (UK) Ltd* [2004] Lloyd's Rep. IR 846 (Colman J.).

[180] *Dornoch Ltd v Mauritius Union Assurance Co Ltd* [2006] Lloyd's Rep. IR 127 (Aikens J.), affirmed [2006] Lloyd's Rep. IR 786; *Stonebridge Underwriting Ltd v Ontario Municipal Insurance Exchange* [2010] EWHC 2279 (Comm).

[181] *Tiernan v Magen Insurance Co Ltd* Unreported October 20, 1999 QBD (Comm); *Gan Insurance Co Ltd v Tai Ping Insurance Co Ltd* [1999] Lloyd's Rep. IR 229; *CGU International Insurance plc v Szabo* [2002] Lloyd's Rep. IR 196; *Assicurazioni Generali v Ege Sigorta AS* [2002] Lloyd's Rep. IR 480; *Tonicstar Ltd v American Home Assurance* [2005] Lloyd's Rep. IR 32; *Tryg Baltica International (UK) Ltd v Boston Compania de Seguros SA* [2005] Lloyd's Rep. IR 40; *Wasa v Lexington* [2009] Lloyd's Rep. IR 675; *Stonebridge Underwriting Ltd v Ontario Municipal Insurance Exchange* [2010] EWHC 2279 (Comm). In *Glacier Reinsurance AG v Gard Marine & Energy Ltd* [2010] EWCA Civ 1052 two marine reinsurance slips were prepared, both using London market wording. One was circulated in the London market, and the other was sent to Swiss reinsurers for their acceptance. The slip was duly scratched in Switzerland and returned to the London brokers. There was no dispute that the former was governed by English law, and the Court of Appeal held that the Swiss placement was also governed by English law: it was to be regarded not as a separate arrangement but rather as a part of the overall London market subscription, and that fact coupled with the use of London market language showed an implied intention to choose English law.

[182] *AIG Europe SA v QBE International Insurance* [2002] Lloyd's Rep. IR 22, where a French market placement was held to be governed by French law. Cf: *American Motorists Insurance Co v Cellstar Corporation* [2003] Lloyd's Rep. IR 359; *Travelers Casualty & Surety Co of Canada v Sun Life Assurance Co of Canada (UK) Ltd (No. 2)* [2007] Lloyd's Rep. IR 619.

Implied choice of applicable law: Rome I Regulation

As far as the Rome I Regulation is concerned, if the parties are free to choose the **5–23** applicable law in accordance with the principles discussed in para.5–16 above, art.3.1 refers to a choice of law "expressly or clearly demonstrated by the terms of the contract or the circumstances of the case", a test which is apparently stricter than that laid down by the Rome Convention. There is nevertheless no reason to believe that the courts will reach any different conclusion on implied choice of law for marine policies, so that the country of placement is likely in most cases to be regarded by implication as providing the law applicable to the policy.

Absence of choice: common law

At common law, if there is no express or implied choice of law, the courts have **5–24** applied a balancing test, weighing all relevant factors to determine the law with which the policy has the closest connection. Early marine cases arguably pointed to the insurers' head office.[183] However, there was an eventual shift to a "centre of gravity" test, which gave primacy to the law of the country in which the risk was placed.[184]

Absence of choice: position prior to Rome I Regulation

Again it is necessary to distinguish between policies where the risk is situated **5–25** in the EU and policies where the risk is situated outside the EU (including all reinsurance contracts).

As regards risks situated outside the EU, in the absence of any choice of law expressed with reasonable certainty, the law applicable to a marine policy is to be ascertained in accordance with the rules set out in art.4[185] of the Rome Convention.[186] This provides as follows:

1. To the extent that the law applicable to the contract has not been chosen in accordance with Article 3, the contract shall be governed by the law of the country with which it is most closely connected. Nevertheless, a severable part of the contract which has a closer connection with another country may by way of exception be governed by the law of that other country.

2. Subject to the provisions of paragraph 5 of this Article, it shall be presumed that the contract is most closely connected with the country where the party

---

[183] *Greer v Poole* (1880) 5 Q.B.D. 272; *Armadora Occidental SA v Horace Mann Insurance Co* [1977] 2 Lloyd's Rep. 406 in which, but for a "follow London" clause, the place of the insurer's residence would have prevailed; *Atlantic Underwriting Agents and David Gale (Underwriting) Ltd v Compagnia di Assicurazioni di Milano SpA* [1979] 2 Lloyd's Rep. 240; *El Du Pont de Nemours & Co v Agnew* [1987] 2 Lloyd's Rep. 585.

[184] *Amin Rasheed Shipping Corporation v Kuwait Insurance Co, The Al Wahab* [1983] 2 All E.R. 884; *Afia Worldwide Insurance Co v Deutsche Ruck Verischerungs AG* (1983) 133 N.L.J. 621; *Citadel Insurance Co v Atlantic Union Insurance Co SA* [1982] 2 Lloyd's Rep. 543; *Cantieri Navali Riunita SpA v NV Omne Justitia* [1985] 2 Lloyd's Rep. 428; *Islamic Arab Insurance Co v Saudi Egyptian American Reinsurance Co* [1987] 1 Lloyd's Rep. 315.

[185] Arts 4.3 and 4.4 apply to specific contracts and have been omitted.

[186] This is, by reg.5, subject to the application of the mandatory rules of the UK. There are apparently no such mandatory rules in the case of marine insurance.

who is to effect the performance which is characteristic of the contract has, at the time of conclusion of the contract, his habitual residence, or, in the case of a body corporate or unincorporate, its central administration. However, if the contract is entered into in the course of that party's trade of profession, that country shall be the country in which the principal place of business is situated or, where under the terms of the contract the performance is to be effected through a place of business other than the principal place of business, the country in which that other place of business is situated.

3. Paragraph 2 shall not apply if the characteristic performance cannot be determined, and the presumptions in [paragraph 2] shall be disregarded if it appears from the circumstances as a whole that the contract is more closely connected with another country.

The starting point in art.4.1 is that the applicable law is that of the country with which the policy is most closely connected. Article 4.2 then lays down a presumption. To apply this presumption it is necessary to identify the party who is to effect the performance which is characteristic of the contract: in the case of a contact of insurance, this is clearly the underwriter as the provider of the relevant services under the policy.[187] The applicable law is then presumed to be that of the country in which the insurer's principal place of business is situated, although if the contract is to be performed by a branch or agency then the applicable law is presumed to be the law of that country. In most cases the presumption will be in favour of the insurers' head office, and the English cases have taken the view that the art.4.2 presumption is to be regarded as ousted in exceptional circumstances only.[188] As seen above, insurance and reinsurance decisions have proceeded on the basis that a placement in a national market using wording employed in that market is to be regarded as having chosen with reasonable certainty the law of that country within the meaning of art.3, so that art.4 is not engaged at all. Those cases also decide that, if the ruling on art.3 is wrong, then the art.4.2 presumption in favour of the law of the country of the underwriter's head office provides the same solution. Accordingly, a placement in London with London market underwriters on terms generally used in the London market will be presumed to be governed by English law,[189] which reflects the position at common

---

[187] *American Motorists Insurance Co v Cellstar Corporation* [2003] Lloyd's Rep. IR 359; *Dornoch Ltd v Mauritius Union Assurance Co Ltd* [2006] Lloyd's Rep. IR 127, affirmed [2006] Lloyd's Rep. IR 786; *Stonebridge Underwriting Ltd v Ontario Municipal Insurance Exchange* [2010] EWHC 2279 (Comm).

[188] For example, *Ophthalmic Innovations International (United Kingdom) Ltd v Ophthalmic Innovations International Inc* [2004] EWHC 2948. See also *Glacier Reinsurance AG v Gard Marine & Energy Ltd* [2010] EWCA Civ 1052, in which the Court of Appeal held that there had been an implied choice of English law for a slip scratched in Switzerland because it was a part of a wider London market placement (see fn. 181 above) but, if that was wrong, then this was a case in which the presumption in favour of Swiss law would be ousted in order to secure that there was single applicable law for the entire placement.

[189] *AIG Group (UK) Ltd v The Ethniki* [1998] 4 All E.R. 301, affirmed [2000] Lloyd's Rep. IR 343; *Tiernan v Magen Insurance Co Ltd* 1998, unreported; *Gan Insurance Co v Tai Ping Insurance Co Ltd* [1999] Lloyd's Rep. IR 229; *Commercial Union Assurance Co plc v Simat Helliesen & Eichner Inc* [2001] Lloyd's Rep. IR 172; *Assicurazioni Generali SpA v Ege Sigorta AS* [2002] Lloyd's Rep. IR 480; *CGU International Insurance plc v Szabo* [2002] Lloyd's Rep. IR 196; *Tonicstar Ltd v American Home Assurance Co* [2005] Lloyd's Rep. IR 32; *Tryg Baltica International (UK) v Boston Compania de Seguros SA* [2005] Lloyd's Rep. IR 40; *Dornoch Ltd v Mauritius Union Assurance Co Ltd* [2006] Lloyd's Rep. IR 786.

law. The presumption will apply even if the policy is a global one covering risks in different jurisdictions.[190] In those cases where the head office is not the same as the country of placement, the latter may prevail. In *Gard Marine & Energy Ltd v Lloyd Tunnicliffe*[191] two slips were subscribed at more or less the same time in London and Switzerland, each using London market terms. Hamblen J. held that there was in effect a single placement rather than two separate placements, and that the case was one of "a Swiss reinsurer being invited to participate in a London market placement".

The presumption in art.4.2 can be ousted, in accordance, with art.4.5, in two situations: the characteristic performance cannot be determined; and the contract is more closely connected with some other country. The former possibility has been discounted in the context of insurance.[192] The latter possibility may arise where a policy is subscribed to by a number of insurers whose head offices are in different countries. In such a case it is plainly inappropriate for each subscription to be regarded as governed by a different law, and the approach adopted by the courts is to give the greatest weight to the country in which the risk was negotiated and placed.[193]

As regards EU risks, in the absence of any choice, or any valid choice, of applicable law, reg.4(8) of the 2001 Regulations lays down the principle that the applicable law is the law of the country with which the contract is most closely connected, and reg.4(9) states that the contract is rebuttably presumed to be most closely connected with the EU State in which the risk is situated. It will be noted that the default presumptions in the Rome Convention and the 2001 Regulations are different: the former points to the place of the insurers' place of business, whereas the latter points to the residence of the assured. This distinction was emphasised by the Court of Appeal in *Credit Lyonnais v New Hampshire Insurance Co*,[194] although in that case nothing turned on the point because the policy, covering risks situated in England, had been issued to a policyholder resident in England by the London underwriting agent of the insurers. The presumption in favour of the policyholder's EU's residence was held to have been rebutted[195] where the policy was issued in North America to North American parent company which happened to have a subsidiary in England.[196]

5–26

---

[190] *CGU International Insurance plc v Szabo* [2002] Lloyd's Rep. IR 196. Cf *American Motorists Insurance Co v Cellstar Corporation* [2003] Lloyd's Rep. IR 359. This was also the case at common law: *Cantieri Navali Riuniti SpA v NV Omne Justitia* [1985] 2 Lloyd's Rep. 428; *El Du Pont de Nemours & Co v Agnew* [1987] 2 Lloyd's Rep. 585.

[191] [2009] EWHC 2388 (Comm).

[192] *Dornoch Ltd v Mauritius Union Assurance Co Ltd* [2006] Lloyd's Rep. IR 127, affirmed [2006] Lloyd's Rep. IR 786.

[193] *Lincoln National Life Insurance Co v Employers Reinsurance Corporation* [2002] Lloyd's Rep. IR 853; *Travelers Casualty and Surety Co of Canada v Sun Life Assurance Co of Canada (UK) Ltd (No 2)* [2007] Lloyd's Rep. IR 619.

[194] [1997] 2 Lloyd's Rep. 1

[195] On the doubtful assumption that the Regulations could apply to a case of this type.

[196] *American Motorists Insurance Co v Cellstar Corporation* [2003] Lloyd's Rep. IR 395; *Travelers Casualty & Surety Co of Canada v Sun Life Assurance Co of Canada (No 2)* [2007] Lloyd's Rep. IR 619.

Absence of choice: Rome I Regulation

5–27 The drafting of art.4 of the Rome I Regulation departs from the structure of the Rome Convention in significant ways, although it may be that the same outcome is reached at least as regards marine insurance and that there is generally a presumption in favour of the insurers' principal place of business and thus the place in which the risk is placed. A number of situations have to be distinguished.

In the case of a non-large risk situated within the EU, art.7.3 provides that the contract is to be governed by the law of the Member State in which the risk is situated at the time of conclusion of the contract. This is an absolute rule.

In the case of a large risk, wherever situated, art.7.1 provides that:

> "To the extent that the applicable law has not been chosen by the parties, the insurance contract shall be governed by the law of the country where the insurer has his habitual residence. Where it is clear from all the circumstances of the case that the contract is manifestly more closely connected with another country, the law of that other country shall apply."

The use of the word "manifestly" strengthens the presumption in favour of the law of the country where the insurer has his habitual residence.

5–28 In the case of a reinsurance contract, or a non-large risk situated outside the EU, the position is governed by art.4 of the Rome I Regulation. In place of a single general presumption as to applicable law in the absence of choice, there is a series of presumptions based on particular classes of contract in art.4.1 and a sweeping up presumption for all other contracts in art.4.2. There is seemingly no reference to insurance, other than possibly art.4.1(b), which states that in the case of a contract for the provision of services the applicable law is presumed to be that of the habitual residence of the service-provider. However, it has yet to be determined whether insurance is a "service" for this purpose, and accordingly the rule applicable to insurance and reinsurance contracts is that in art.4.2, namely "the contract shall be governed by the law of the country where the party required to effect the characteristic performance has his habitual residence." The characterising performer is doubtless the underwriter, and his habitual residence is defined by art.19 points to central administration. So the head office test will generally operate.

The presumption can be ousted in two situations, as laid down by arts 4.3 and 4.4:

> "4.3   Where it is clear from all the circumstances of the case that the contract is manifestly more closely connected with a country other than that indicated in paragraphs 1 or 2, the law of that other country shall apply.
>
> 4.4   Where the law applicable cannot be determined pursuant to paragraphs 1 or 2, the contract shall be governed by the law of the country with which it is most closely connected."

The ouster in art.4.3 is unlikely to be relevant, given the strengthening of the presumption by the requirement of a manifest closer connection with some other country, and art.4.4 is not relevant to insurance.

CHAPTER 6

THE PREMIUM: PAYMENT AND RETURN

Timing of payment

Failure by the parties to agree on the timing of the payment of a premium will not **6–03** affect the validity of the policy. In *Allianz Insurance Co Egypt v Aigaion Insurance Co SA (No 2)*[1] a slip for reinsurance cover for a marine risk referred to a "Deferred Premium Clause" without specifying its actual terms. The reinsurers asserted that the entire policy was void for uncertainty. H.H. Judge Chambers Q.C., dismissing this argument, held that the phrase "Deferred Premium Clause" did not render the policy void for uncertainty, and in the circumstances was to be taken as a reference to a Deferred Premium Clause in the marine policy itself, which provided for quarterly instalments.

Timing of payment

A clause in these terms was adopted in *Allianz Insurance Company Egypt v* **6–04** *Aigaion Insurance Co SA (No. 2)*.[2]

Date on which premium is to be paid

The principle that the fiction which underlies s.53(1) is to be disregarded in deter- **6–09** mining whether there has been compliance with an express payment obligation was confirmed in *Allianz Insurance Company Egypt v Aigaion Insurance Company SA (No 2)*.[3] Here, a slip for a reinsurance agreement contained a "Deferred Premium Clause", which was held by the court to impose an obliga-tion for payment of the premium in quarterly instalments. After the acceptance of the slip, the reinsurers issued their own policy wording requiring payment of the premium within 60 days. Premium was duly forwarded by the reinsured to the broker within the 60 day period, but it was not transmitted to the reinsurers because the broker believed that the Deferred Premium Clause governed the rela-tionship. H.H. Judge Chambers QC. held that the governing provision was indeed the Deferred Premium Clause, so that the reinsurers had no right to treat the policy as terminated for non-payment, but the court added that the fiction under-lying s.53(1) that the premium had been paid by the broker would not have been of assistance had it been the case that there had been late payment. As was said by H.H. Judge Chambers QC:

---

[1] [2009] Lloyd's Rep. IR 533.
[2] [2009] Lloyd's Rep. IR 533.
[3] [2009] Lloyd's Rep. IR 533.

"I cannot imagine that an intelligent member of the Lloyd's marine insurance market looking at the [Marine Insurance Act] in 1906 could have been expected to read the fiction into the section with the consequence that, not only could an insurer obtain the premium from the broker but, without more, no policy could ever be treated as invalid for non-payment of the premium because the assured was always to be treated as having paid it."

Return of premium

6–30 *Note 142*: See also *Clydesdale Financial Services Ltd v Smailes* [2009] EWHC 3190 (Ch).

Arrest of vessel

6–31 The Supreme Court Act 1981 was redesignated as the Senior Courts Act 1981 by the Constitutional Reform Act 2005, s.59 and Sch.11.

Reform of the law

6–31A In July 2010 the English and Scottish Law Commissions published an Issues Paper (No 8) on the operation of ss.53 and 54. The Issues Paper sets out in some detail the law relating to the payment of premiums and the broker's lien where premiums are funded by the broker, and makes tentative recommendations for reform. Those recommendations have been sent out for consultation. The Issues Paper notes that the common law basis for the rule in s.53(1) is generally regarded as the fiction that the broker has paid the premium to the underwriter and the underwriter had loaned it back to the broker,[4] although there is an alternative view that the broker may be a principal in his own right.[5] The Issues Paper regards the operation of s.53(1) as unclear and anomalous, in that it has created confusion as to whether the common law fiction that the premium has actually been paid means that premium clauses are automatically complied with[6] or whether the fiction has in effect been repealed by s.53(1)[7] so that such clauses remain effective.[8] Particular problems with the law have been noted, namely that it is not clear whether s.53(1) depends upon the policy being governed by English law and whether the marine rule is of general application. The Law Commissions' proposal is to repeal s.53(1) and to replace it[9] with a provision which imposes the primary payment obligation on the assured but allowing the parties to agree that the broker accepts responsibility for payment. The Law Commissions felt that the

---

[4] *Universo Insurance Co of Milan v Merchants Marine Insurance Co Ltd* [1897] 2 Q.B. 93.
[5] *Power v Butcher* (1829) 10 B. & C. 329.
[6] So held in *Prentis Donegan & Partners Ltd v Leeds & Leeds Co Inc* [1998] 2 Lloyd's Rep. 326.
[7] The effect of the ruling in *Allianz Insurance Co Egypt v Aigaion Insurance Co SA* [2008] 2 Lloyd's Rep. 595.
[8] The ruling in *JA Chapman & Co Ltd v Kadirga Denizcilik Ve Ticaret* [1998] Lloyd's Rep. IR 377. See also *The Litsion Pride* [1985] 1 Lloyd's Rep. 437, where it was held that s.53(1) could not apply to a premium which was capable of being raised during the currency of the policy.
[9] Straight repeal without replacement was thought to give rise to the possibility that the common law, and the fiction of payment and loan, would be revived.

risk of the assured being required to pay the premium twice in the event that the broker, having received the premium, becomes insolvent, was a slight one, given that brokers are required to retain such sums in a separate client account for the benefit of assureds rather than general creditors.

The Law Commissions also examined the protection available to a broker to protect himself against non-payment by the assured. The broker's statutory lien over the policy, conferred by s.53(2), is regarded by the Law Commissions as operating satisfactorily, even though it was decided in *Eide UK Ltd v Lowndes Lambert Group Ltd*[10] that the assured can bring an action against the underwriters even though the broker is in possession of the policy and that the lien cannot operate where there are co-assureds who are not all in default.

Finally the Law Commissions were uncertain as to whether s.54 was any longer relevant in English practice, given that policies do not any longer state that the premium has been received by the underwriter when that is not the case.

Where the risk is entire and indivisible

Note 161: See also *Clydesdale Financial Services Ltd v Smailes* [2009] EWHC 3190 (Ch).

6–37

---

[10] [1998] 1 Lloyd's Rep. 389.

CHAPTER 7

THE ASSURED'S AGENTS: RIGHTS, DUTIES AND LIABILITIES

Disclosure of information

Note 71: See *Jones v Environcom Ltd (No 2)* [2010] EWHC 759 (Comm), where **7–10** David Steel J. noted that it did not suffice for the broker to issue a general warning or to rely upon terms of engagement:

> "I am not persuaded that it is sufficient simply to rely upon written standard form explanations and warnings annexed to proposals or policy documents . . . The broker must satisfy himself that the position is in fact understood by his client and this will usually require a specific oral or written exchange on the topic, both at the time of the original placement and at renewal (particularly if a new person has become that client's representative)."

See also Synergy Health (UK) Ltd v CGU Insurance Plc [2010] EWHC 2583 (Comm).
Note 73: See also *Yechiel v Kerry London Ltd* [2010] Lloyd's Rep. IR 295.

Content of policy

A useful summary of the scope of a broker's duties in this regard was provided in **7–11** *Dunlop Haywards (DHL) Ltd v Barbon Insurance Group Ltd*,[1] Hamblen J. holding that a placing broker was obliged:

(1) to exercise reasonable care and skill in the fulfilment of its instructions and the performance of its professional obligations;

(2) carefully to ascertain the client's insurance needs and to use reasonable skill and care to obtain insurance that met those needs;

(3) carefully to review the terms of any quotations or indications received;

(4) to explain to the client the terms of the proposed insurance; and

(5) to use reasonable skill and care to draw up a policy, or to ensure that a policy was drawn up, that accurately reflected the terms of the agreement with the underwriters and which was clear and unambiguous so that the client's rights under the policy were not open to doubt.

---

[1] [2010] Lloyd's Rep. IR 149. See also *Jones v Environcom Ltd (No 2)* [2010] EWHC 759 (Comm).

Producing and placing brokers

7–21 In the absence of an assumption of responsibility by the placing broker to the assured, which is probably the most likely situation, the producing broker faces liability to the assured but has a claim against the placing broker. That claim may be one for contribution under the Civil Liability (Contribution) Act 1978, or it may be one for breach of the sub-contract between the producing broker and the placing broker. In either case, the outcome will be that the court allocates responsibility between the two brokers in a manner which reflects their respective fault.[2] The duties owed by a placing broker to the producing broker were considered by Hamblen J. in *Dunlop Haywards (DHL) Ltd v Barbon Insurance Group Ltd*,[3] a case in which plainly incorrect instructions were given by the producing broker to the placing broker, but the placing broker took no steps to check the veracity of what he had been told and obtained quotes which were subsequently accepted by the producing broker. Hamblen J. ruled that a placing broker's duties were akin to those of a producing broker, and included the duties: to exercise reasonable care and skill in the fulfilment of its instructions and the performance of its professional obligations; carefully to review the terms of any quotations or indications received; to explain the terms of the proposed insurance; and to use reasonable skill and care to draw up a policy, and to ensure that a policy was drawn up, that accurately reflected the terms of the agreement with the underwriters and which was clear and unambiguous so that the insured's rights under the policy were not open to doubt. In particular, a placing broker is required to query instructions which are unclear, illogical or absurd, potentially disadvantageous to the assured or which appear not to meet the assured's requirements, and the placing broker had on the facts failed in that duty. The Court's allocation of responsibility was 80 per cent producing broker and 20 per cent placing broker.

Note 139: In *Dunlop Haywards (DHL) Ltd v Barbon Insurance Group Ltd* [2010] Lloyd's Rep. IR 149 it was assumed that the producing broker bore full liability to the assured even though the default was in part that of the placing broker.

Insurance would not have been obtainable

7–30 *Note 198*: See also *Jones v Environcom Ltd (No 2)* [2010] EWHC 759 (Comm), where the risk of fire was such that, had earlier fires been disclosed, it would have been impossible to place cover.

Contributory negligence

7–32 *Note 209*: See also *Dunlop Haywards (DHL) Ltd v Barbon Insurance Group Ltd* [2010] Lloyd's Rep. IR 149. Contrast the exceptional facts of *Synergy Health (UK) Ltd v CGU Insurance Plc* [2010] EWHC 2583 (Comm), where Flaux J. was

---

[2] *Dunlop Haywards (DHL) Ltd v Barbon Insurance Group Ltd* [2010] Lloyd's Rep. IR 149.
[3] [2010] Lloyd's Rep. IR 149.

of the view that the assured had itself been at serious fault by proffering information the accuracy of which had not been checked, so that that a deduction of 90 per cent would have been justified in the circumstances.

Duties owed by brokers to third parties

Where a broker is instructed by a company to obtain liability insurance for the **7–35** benefit of its directors, he is liable to the directors if he negligently fails to do so. That is so either because he owes them a duty of care on the basis that they are identifiable beneficiaries, or because they have a cause of action against the broker under the Contracts (Rights of Third Parties) Act 1999.[4]

Note 230: The Third Parties (Rights against Insurers) Act 2010 does not affect the proposition in this footnote

---

[4] *Crowson v HSBC Insurance Brokers* [2010] Lloyd's Rep. IR 441.

CHAPTER 8

PERSONS WHO MAY CLAIM ON THE POLICY

Who may benefit from a policy

The Third Parties (Rights against Insurers) Act 1930 is to be replaced, from a date **8–02** to be announced, by the Third Parties (Rights against Insurers) Act 2010. See para.8–49 *et seq* of this Supplement.

Rights of third party under marine liability cover

At common law, the insolvency of an assured vests any insurance moneys due to **8–49** him in his trustee in bankruptcy, liquidator or other successor in title, as the case may be. In the case of an assured who incurred liability to a third party and then became insolvent, the proceeds of the policy also belonged to the assured's successor in title for distribution to the assured's unsecured creditors in general and not just to the victim of the assured's negligence even though that victim's losses had triggered the claim against the insurers.[1] In the context of liability insurance, the common law rule was regarded as inappropriate and was modified by the Third Parties (Rights against Insurers) Act 1930. The Act was found not to operate in an altogether satisfactory fashion.[2] It was the subject of a detailed review by the English and Scottish Law Commissions from 1999 to 2002,[3] and a draft bill was prepared by the Commissions. The bill was amended in 2009 to reflect modern insolvency litigation, but otherwise without substantive change, and was introduced into Parliament at the end of 2009 under the special expedited procedure for uncontroversial Law Commission measures. The Third Parties (Rights against Insurers) Act 2010 became law in March 2010 but its implementation date has yet to be announced. The 2010 Act will apply in all cases from the day appointed for commencement, other than those in which either: (a) the assured both became insolvent and incurred liability before that day; or (b) the assured died before the appointed day (s.21 and Sch.3).

It is of interest to note that many of the changes suggested by the Law Commissions were adopted by the courts in a series of cases following the Law Commissions' report, so the 2010 Act will not have quite the dramatic effect that at one time seemed likely. The 1930 Act will remain effective for some time, so in the following paragraphs the both measures are considered.

---

[1] *Hood's Trustees v Southern Union General Insurance Co of Australasia* [1928] Ch. 793; *Re Harrington Motor Co* [1928] Ch. 105.
[2] For an influential critique of the 1930 Act, see Lord Mance, [1995] L.M.C.L.Q. 34.
[3] Law Commission No.272, Scottish Law Commission No.184, July 2001.

The general effect of the 1930 Act is stated in s.1(1), namely that the insolvent assured's "rights against the insurer under the contract shall . . . be transferred to and vest in the third party to whom liability was so incurred". The 2010 Act operates on much the same basis. Once the assured has become insolvent,[4] s.1(1)–(2) of the 2010 Act transfers the rights of the assured to a third party claimant and a direct action may be brought by him against the insurers. Equally, a judgment obtained against the third party who later becomes insolvent may be enforced against the insurers. Any judgment obtained against the insurers in respect of the policy cannot, however, be enforced against the insurers unless and until the third party has established and quantified the liability of the assured by means of a judgment, arbitration award or settlement (2010 Act, s.1(3)–(4)). The 2010 Act establishes a procedural advantage which was lacking from the 1930 Act. Under the earlier measure, if the assured was not insolvent, the third party had to commence an action against him and obtain judgment, which could then be enforced against the insurers following the assured's insolvency: it was not open to the third party to sue the insurers before establishing and quantifying the assured's liability.[5] Under the 2010 Act, although the third party may sue the insurers of an insolvent assured directly but cannot enforce the judgment until he has established and quantified the assured's liability, the third party may under s.2 of the 2010 Act seek a declaration in those proceedings as to the liability of the insurers under the policy. Coverage under the policy can, therefore, be dealt with as a preliminary issue, thereby dispensing with the need for a lengthy trial on the assured's liability in the event that the policy does not respond to the loss.

Proceedings against the assured

8–49A It has been suggested that the statutory transfer under the 1930 Act removes the right of the third party to proceed against the assured himself other than for any policy shortfall, although the point is unresolved.[6] Under s.14(1) of the 2010 Act, the third party cannot enforce his claim against the insolvent assured insofar as it is covered by the insurance. The effect is that the claim has to be brought against the insurers alone, and an action against the assured remains only for the uninsured sum, for the amount of any excess under the policy or for any sum which the insurers are unable to pay by reason of insolvency and which is not covered by the Financial Services Compensation Scheme (s.14(6)–(7)). Any agreement between the assured and his creditors dealing with insurance proceeds is not binding on the third party (s.14(2)–(3)).

---

[4] And has therefore become, in the terminology of the 2010 Act, a "relevant person".
[5] *Post Office v Norwich Union* [1967] 1 All E.R. 577.
[6] The suggestion was made by Chadwick L.J., but doubted by Arden L.J., in *Centre Reinsurance International Co v Freakley* [2005] Lloyd's Rep. IR 284. The point was left open in *Re T&N Ltd (No.4)* [2006] EWHC 1447 (Ch).

Policies within the legislation

The 1930 Act applies to all forms of liability insurance[7] including P&I and other **8–49B** mutual cover[8] insofar as the benefits are mandatory rather than provided at the option of the mutual association,[9] and also policies under which the assured has voluntarily assumed liability to a third party under contract whether by way of unliquidated damages or by way of debt.[10] The 1930 Act does not apply to reinsurance,[11] so that the policyholder of an insolvent insurer cannot seek recovery under the 1930 Act from that insurer's reinsurers.

The 2010 Act is to the same effect. The Act applies to rights under a contract of insurance (s.1(5)), a term which is not defined but which is assumed by the Act itself to extend to P&I and other mutual rules. The 2010 Act similarly applies to liabilities voluntarily incurred (s.16) and, as is the case with the 1930 Act, does not apply to reinsurance (s.15).

Jurisdiction and applicable law

It is uncertain whether the 1930 Act applies to all policies governed by English **8–49C** law or whether it is relevant only where the insolvency proceedings affecting the assured are opened in the UK, although the latter would appear to be the better view.[12]

The scope of the 2010 Act is expressly laid down, by s.18. This provides that if the assured has become insolvent under any of the UK insolvency procedures set out in the Act, then the Act applies irrespective of the place in which liability was incurred, the domicile of the parties, the law applicable to the policy and the place where payment has to be made. This does, however, beg two questions: do the English courts possess jurisdiction; and, if they do, what law is to be applied to the claim against the insurers. On the first point, if the insurers are domiciled within the EU, art.9 of the Brussels Regulation[13] allows the insurers to be sued by

---

[7] It was originally designed for use in motor claims cases alongside the introduction of compulsory motor liability insurance by the Road Traffic Act 1930. Shortly afterwards, the Road Traffic Act 1934 gave the victim of a negligent driver the right to enforce a judgment against the driver's liability insurers whether or not the driver was insolvent, thereby removing the operation of the 1930 Act in motor cases. The 1930 Act has since 1934, somewhat ironically, operated only outside the motor context.

[8] *Wooding v Monmouthshire and South Wales Mutual Indemnity Society Ltd* [1939] 4 All E.R. 570: *Firma C-Trade SA v Newcastle Protection and Indemnity Association, The Fanti* [1987] 2 Lloyd's Rep. 299: *Socony Mobil Oil Co Inc v West of England Shipowners Mutual Insurance Association Ltd, The Padre Island (No 1)* [1984] 2 Lloyd's Rep. 408; *Socony Mobil Oil Co Inc v West of England Shipowners Mutual insurance Association Ltd, The Padre Island (No.2)* [1987] 2 Lloyd's Rep. 529.

[9] There is authority for the proposition that a contract under which payments are not mandatory is not a contract of insurance at all, as there is a world of difference between a right to payment of a claim and a right to have a claim considered: *Medical Defence Union v Department of Trade* [1979] 2 All E.R. 421. See *CVG Siderugicia del Orinoco SA v London Steamship Owners' Mutual Insurance Association, The Vainqueur Jose* [1979] 1 Lloyd's Rep. 557, where it was recognised that such a contract entered into by a P&I Club might fall outside the 1930 Act.

[10] *Re OT Computers* [2004] Lloyd's Rep. IR 669.

[11] 1930 Act, s.1(5). See *Re OT Computers* [2004] Lloyd's Rep. IR 669.

[12] *Irish Shipping Ltd v Commercial Union Assurance Co plc, The Irish Rowan* [1989] 2 Lloyd's Rep. 144.

[13] Council Regulation 44/2001/EC. See Ch.5 of the main work and this Supplement.

the assured in the EU State of the assured's domicile or in the EU State of the insurers' domicile. Where there is a direct action brought against the insurers by a third party, art.11.2 says that the third party is to bring the action in the EU State of his own domicile[14] providing that the law so permits. It is unclear what law is being referred to here, but there is English authority for the proposition that the law governing the policy, rather than the law of the forum, must permit the direct action.[15] Accordingly, a claim can be brought in England against liability insurers under the 2010 Act only if either the insurers are domiciled in England, or if the third party is domiciled in England and the policy is governed by English law or another law which permits a direct action. A claim against insurers domiciled outside the EU is to be classified as contractual and thus is likely to be available only if the policy was made in, or governed by English law, or payment was due in England,[16] although if the English court has jurisdiction over the third party's claim against the assured then the insurers can presumably be joined to the proceedings on the basis that they are necessary and proper parties to such proceedings.[17]

Once jurisdiction has been established, the law applicable to the policy is of no significance. The 2010 is not triggered by reason of English law applying to the policy, but rather because the assured has become insolvent under a UK procedure.

Insolvency of the assured

8–50 Under the 1930 Act, the assured must have become subject to any of the insolvency procedures listed in s.1(1) of the Act. The relevant insolvency procedures are: bankruptcy[18]; composition with creditors; in the case of a corporate assured, the making of a winding up order, the passing of a voluntary winding up resolution,[19] administration, the appointment of a receiver, the taking of possession of property by debenture holders and the approval of a voluntary arrangement[20]; and in the case of a limited partnership[21] the position is as for companies with the reference to resolutions for voluntary winding up being substituted by a reference to a determination for voluntary winding up.[22] No express provision is made for ordinary partnerships, although it has been held that the insolvency of any one partner brings the 1930 Act into operation with respect to the partnership's policies.[23] Individual voluntary arrangements, unlike company voluntary arrangements, are not treated as insolvency events for the purposes of the 1930 Act, so

---

[14] *FBTO Schadeverzekeringen NV v Odenbreit* (C-463/06) [2008] Lloyd's Rep. IR 354.

[15] *Thwaites v Aviva Assurances* Unreported December 16, 2009, Mayors and City of London Court.

[16] CPR PD 6B, para.3.1(6).

[17] Under CPR PD 6, para.3.1(3).

[18] Whether or not the bankrupt has died: s.1(2). It was held in *Law Society of England and Wales v Shah* [2008] Lloyd's Rep. IR 442 that a claim against a bankrupt assured is not extinguished on the assured's subsequent discharge from bankruptcy, so that the third party may continue to press a claim against the assured's liability insurers even after such discharge.

[19] Other than solely for the purpose of reconstruction or amalgamation: s.1(6).

[20] Under Pt I of the Insolvency Act 1986.

[21] See the Limited Liability Partnership Act 2000.

[22] 1930 Act, s.3A, added by the Liability Partnerships Act (2000) (Commencement) Order, SI 2000/3316.

[23] *Re Greenfield, Jackson v Greenfield* [1998] B.P.I.R. 699.

that if an individual has entered into such an arrangement there is a moratorium on claims against him and it is not possible for the third party to pursue the claim against the insolvent individual so as to obtain a judgment enforceable under the 1930 Act: it is necessary for the third party to apply to have the individual voluntary arrangement set aside on the ground that he has been unfairly prejudiced by it,[24] although the third party cannot intervene in any settlement reached between the assured and the supervisor of the arrangement.[25] A third party who has not obtained a judgment cannot block a settlement reached between the assured (or at least the supervisor acting for him) and the insurers, because at that stage he has no rights under the 1930 Act given that the Act is not triggered by the assured entering into an individual voluntary arrangement.

The 2010 Act is more comprehensive in its definition, and seeks to catch all UK statutory insolvency procedures. As far as an individual is concerned, s.6 lists the following insolvency procedures:

(a) a deed of arrangement registered in accordance with the Deeds of Arrangement Act 1914;

(b) an administration order made under Part 6 of the County Courts Act 1984;

(c) an enforcement restriction order made under Part 6A of that Act;

(d) a debt relief order made under Part 7A of the Insolvency Act 1986;

(e) a voluntary arrangement approved in accordance with Part 8 of the Insolvency Act 1986; and

(f) a bankruptcy order made under Part 9 of the Insolvency Act 1986.

In addition, a deceased assured is within the 2010 Act (s.5). As far as a body corporate or an unincorporated body is concerned, the relevant procedures as listed in s.6 are:

(a) a compromise or arrangement between the body and its creditors (or a class of them) sanctioned in accordance with s.899 of the Companies Act 2006;

(b) dissolution under ss.100–1003 of the Companies Act 2006 without restoration to the register;

(c) a voluntary arrangement approved in accordance with Part 1 of the Insolvency Act 1986;

(d) an administration order made under Part 2 of the Insolvency Act 1986;

(e) the appointment of a receiver or manager under Part 3 of the Insolvency Act 1986;

(d) voluntary winding up under Part 4 of the Insolvency Act 1986;

(e) provisional liquidation under the Insolvency Act 1986;

---

[24] *Sea Voyager Inc v Bielecki* [1999] Lloyd's Rep. IR 356.
[25] *Re Greenfield, Jackson v Greenfield* [1998] B.P.I.R. 699.

(f) winding up by the court following the making of a winding-up order under the Insolvency Act 1986.

Establishing and quantifying the assured's liability

8–51 Under the 1930 Act, and subject to policy limits, the amount of such liability, along with any interest awarded against the assured if covered by the policy,[26] may be recovered by the third party directly from the insurers.[27] The third party has no cause of action against the assured's liability insurers until the liability of the assured has been established and quantified, these being the usual triggers for the right of the assured to claim under a liability policy. Liability may be established and quantified by a judgment or arbitration award in favour of the third party, or by a settlement which has become binding on the insurers in that it is based on legal liability or they have consented to it. This was so held in *Post Office v Norwich Union Fire Insurance Society*,[28] in which the Court of Appeal dismissed as premature an action by the third party against the assured's liability insurers in advance of any judgment having been obtained against the assured itself. It is thought that the insurers do not lose their rights under the policy simply by running the assured's defence[29] in the substantive proceedings in which the third party seeks to establish and quantify the assured's liability.[30]

The position under the 2010 Act is a little different. The third party has an action against the insurers under s.1 as soon as the assured has become insolvent, but the third party cannot enforce any judgment that he obtains against the insurers unless and until he has established and quantified the assured's own liability to him.

The third party's rights following insolvency

8–51A Under the 1930 Act, if it is simply the case that the assured has become insolvent but no liability has been established and quantified, the third party does not have any right to recover the policy moneys. He is, however, to be regarded as having inchoate or contingent rights running from the date of the assured's insolvency.[31] Accordingly, insurers cannot seek to vary the rights of the assured under the policy in accordance with its terms once the assured has become insolvent.[32] It

---

[26] *Cox v Bankside Members Agency Ltd* [1995] 2 Lloyd's Rep. 437.

[27] Along with any interest awardable against the insurers themselves for late payment: *Aluminium Wire and Cable Co Ltd v Allstate Insurance Ltd* [19851 2 Lloyd's Rep. 280. For the running of interest on insurance claims, see para.12–04A, below.

[28] [1967] 1 All E.R. 577.

[29] If the insurers do not participate in defending the assured, and the assured itself is insolvent and has no interest in doing so, the insurers face the greater risk of a default judgment which cannot later be set aside: *Rees v Mabco (102) Ltd* 1998 Unreported December 11, 1998 CA (Civ Div).

[30] The point was left open in *Wood v Perfection Travel Ltd* [1996] L.R.L.R. 233.

[31] *Cox v Bankside Members Agency Ltd* [1995] 2 Lloyd's Rep. 437; *Spriggs v Wessington Court School Ltd* [2005] Lloyd's Rep. IR 474; *Centre Reinsurance International Co v Freakley* [2005] Lloyd's Rep. IR 284; *Re OT Computers Ltd* [2004] Lloyd's Rep. IR 669.

[32] *Centre Reinsurance International Co v Freakley* [2005] Lloyd's Rep. IR 284.

is also arguable that the third party may have the right[33] to seek a declaration as to the insurers' liability to the assured in this interim period,[34] thereby forestalling the need for the third party to undertake a lengthy trial to establish and quantify the assured's liability once it has been shown that there is no prospect of an insurance recovery. The third party certainly has the right to seek to be joined to proceedings brought by the insurers against the assured for negative declaratory relief.[35] That the third party has a right to be joined to proceedings brought by the insurers against the assured to avoid the policy or otherwise to deny liability under it even though the third party has not at that stage established and quantified the assured's liability. As Langley J. has noted, the true beneficiary of the policy is the third party, and it is appropriate to allow him to be represented. The third party will also have the right to obtain an interim payment from the insurers if liability has been established but quantum remains disputed.[36]

The 2010 Act, by contrast, expressly recognises the right of the third party to commence proceedings for declaratory relief. Once the assured has become insolvent, the third party has the right under s.2 of the 2010 Act to seek a declaration against the insurers either as regards the liability of the assured to him or as regards the insurers' potential liability to the third party under the policy. In declaration proceedings the insurers are entitled to rely upon any policy defence open to them (s.2(4)), and any defence that the assured may have had against the third party. The assured may be joined to the proceedings under s.2(9) where his liability to the assured is in issue, so that if there is any claim for an uninsured sum the assured will be bound by any declaration in favour of the third party (s.2(10)).

Dissolved companies

In some cases the assured, if a company, will not merely have been dissolved but **8–52** also removed from the register of companies by the time that the third party seeks to bring an action against it. An action cannot as a matter of law be brought against a dissolved company.[37] In these circumstances, under the 1930 Act, it is necessary for the third party to establish and quantify the dissolved company's liability as a precondition to bringing an action against the insurers. The third party may apply to the Companies Court for the restoration of the company to the register purely so that it can be sued and its liability established and quantified.[38] There is no time limit for the application to the court if the action is one for

---

[33] The word "right" is misleading. The court always has a right to entertain proceedings for a declaration under CPR r.40.20: *Arbuthnot Pensions & Investments Ltd v Padden* [2004] EWCA Civ 582. The issue is whether its discretion to do so will be exercised in such circumstances.

[34] This has been denied: *Nigel Upchurch Associates v Aldridge Estates Investment Co Ltd* [1993] 1 Lloyd's Rep. 535; *Burns v Shuttlehurst* [1999] 1 W.L.R. 1449. However, these cases were decided before *Re OT Computers Ltd* [2004] Lloyd's Rep. IR 669, which fully recognised the contingent rights of the third party following the assured's insolvency.

[35] *Chubb Insurance Co of Europe SA v Davies* [2005] Lloyd's Rep. IR 1.

[36] Under CPR Pt 23. See *Cox v Bankside Members Agency Ltd* [1995] 2 Lloyd's Rep. 437.

[37] *Bradley v Eagle Star Insurance Co* [1989] 2 W.L.R. 568.

[38] Companies Act 2006, s.1029(2)(f).

damages for personal injury,[39] although in other cases the application may not be made more than six years from the date of dissolution.[40] In the case of an individual assured who has become bankrupt, the liability of the bankrupt can be established by the admission of the claim by the trustee in bankruptcy even in the absence of any judgment or other judicial ruling.[41] Once the limitation period for a claim against the assured has expired, it will no longer be possible for the third party to establish and quantify the assured's liability, assuming of course that the point is taken by way of defence in the proceedings against the assured. However, if the assured has become insolvent before the expiry of the limitation period, the third party's cause of action is replaced by a right to seek payment in the insolvency and the Limitation Act 1980 no longer applies. Thus any time bar defence will be removed if time had not expired at the date of the insolvency.[42]

The position under the 2010 Act is much simpler. The dissolution of a company is one of the statutory grounds upon which a direct claim can be brought against the insurers. Thus, the third party can initiate a single set of proceedings in which both the liability of the insurers under the policy and the liability of the assured are in issue, and the court can then, if necessary and appropriate deal with any policy disputes as preliminary issues before determining the liability of the assured. There is no need for the company to be resurrected.

Insolvency of assured after judgment against him

8–53   The 1930 Act may be used as a means of enforcing a judgment obtained by the third party against the assured. If the judgment remains unsatisfied, the third party may petition for the assured's winding up and if an order is granted the third party has access to the insures under the 1930 Act. This procedure may also be used against a company which is not registered in England under the Companies Act 2006 if the company has assets in England, and for this purpose an insurance claim against liability insurers is regarded as an asset.[43] It is indeed common for winding-up procedures to be initiated in England against an overseas shipowner

---

[39] Companies Act 2006, s.1030(1), although the court may refuse an application if it appears to the court that the action would fail under the Limitation Act 1980 or any other equivalent provision; s.1030(2). Given the power of the court to extend time under the Limitation Act 1980, s.33, for personal injury actions, it is unlikely that s.1030(2) will prevent a restoration order: *Re Workvale* [1992] All E.R. 627. The court may in making its restoration order direct that any period between dissolution and the making of the restoration order is not to count for limitation purposes: see ss.1030(3) and 1032(3), the predecessors of which were discussed in *Re Workvale* [1992] All E.R. 627 and *Smith v White Knight Laundry Ltd* Unreported May 11, 2001 CA (Civ Div).

[40] Companies Act 2006, s.1030(4). This was previously two years, under the superseded s.651 of the Companies Act 1985.

[41] *Financial Services Compensation Scheme Ltd v Larnell* [2006] Lloyd's Rep. IR 448; *Law Society of England and Wales v Shah* [2008] Lloyd's Rep. IR 442.

[42] *Financial Services Compensation Scheme Ltd v Larnell* [2005] EWCA Civ 1408, which holds that a potential claim against the assured's insurers under the 1930 Act is not a secured claim and thus is not outside the principle that insolvency does not stop time running in respect of a claim against trust assets or to enforce a security.

[43] *Re Compañia Merabello San Nicholas SA* [1973] Ch. 75; *Re Allobrogia Steamship Corporation* [1978] 3 All E.R. 423; *Re Eloc Electro-Optieck and Communicatie BV* [1982] Ch. 43; *Re A Company (No. 00359 of 1987)* [1987] 3 W.L.R. 339; *Irish Shipping Ltd v Commercial Union Assurance Co plc, The Irish Rowan* [1989] 2 Lloyd's Rep. 144.

whose only assets in England are the potential proceeds of a claim against his P&I Club or insurers.

The position is unchanged under the 2010 Act.

Defences available to insurers

The 1930 Act operates to transfer to the third party the assured's rights of suit **8–54** under the policy.[44] The third party's claim against the insurers is one under the policy, not one for damages for personal injury or property damage.[45] The third party gets no better rights against the insurers than were possessed by the assured, so that the insurers are entitled to rely upon all defences that would have been open to them in an action by the assured: the third party cannot "pick out the plums and leave the duff behind".[46] The third party is thus bound by limits on coverage and financial caps on liability,[47] including rateable proportion clauses[48] and restrictions on the recoverability of costs awarded against the assured.[49] Insurers may also rely as against the third party upon breaches of duty by the assured, including non-disclosure or misrepresentation, breach of warranty,[50] breach of policy conditions,[51] wilful misconduct,[52] late notification of claims,[53] failure to co-operate with the defence of the third party's claim[54] and admissions of liability.[55]

The 2010 Act operates in much the same way, but with some important exceptions. In general terms, any defence which the insurers have against the assured can be pleaded against the third party, whose rights are no better than those of the assured (s.9(1)). There are, however, three modifications under the 2010 Act:

(a) the third party is, if he can, entitled to satisfy the condition even though it may be personal to the assured (s.9(2));

(b) any obligation on the assured to provide information or assistance to the insurers is of no effect where the assured is a dissolved company or a deceased individual (s.9(3)); and

---

[44] It does not transfer rights which under the policy are transferred to the insurers on the assured's insolvency, e.g., the right to control claims: *Centre Reinsurance International Co v Freakley* [2005] Lloyd's Rep. IR 284.

[45] *Burns v Shuttlehurst* [1999] 1 W.L.R. 1449.

[46] *Post Office v Norwich Union Fire Insurance Society* [1967] 1 All E.R. 577, 581, *per* Harman L.J.

[47] See *Avandero (UK) Ltd v National Transit Insurance Co Ltd* [1984] 2 Lloyd's Rep. 613.

[48] *Phillips v Syndicate 992 Gunner* [2004] Lloyd's Rep. IR 418.

[49] *Centre Reinsurance International Co v Freakley* [2005] Lloyd's Rep. IR 284.

[50] *McCormick v National Motor & Accident Insurance Union Ltd* (1934) 40 Com. Cas. 76; *Cleland v London General Insurance Co* (1935) 51 Ll LR 156.

[51] *George Hunt Cranes Ltd v Scottish Boiler and General Insurance Co Ltd* [2002] Lloyd's Rep. IR 178.

[52] Although it has been held that a defence based on public policy merely imposes a personal bar on the assured's right to recover and does not affect a third party claim: *Total Graphics Ltd v AGF Insurance Ltd* [1997] 1 Lloyd's Rep. 599.

[53] See, e.g.: *Pioneer Concrete (UK) Ltd v National Employers Mutual General Insurance Association Ltd* [1985] 2 All E.R. 395; *Cox v Bankside Members Agency Ltd* [1985] 2 Lloyd's Rep. 437; *Total Graphics Ltd v AGF Insurance Ltd* [1997] 1 Lloyd's Rep. 599; *Alfred McAlpine v BAI (Run-off) Ltd* [2000] Lloyd's Rep. IR 352.

[54] *K/S Merc-Skandia v Certain Lloyd's Underwriters* [2001] Lloyd's Rep. IR 802.

[55] *Post Office v Norwich Union Fire Insurance Society* [1967] 1 All E.R. 577; *Total Graphics v AGF Insurance* [1997] 1 Lloyd's Rep. 599.

(c) any condition imposing an obligation on the assured to notify the insurers of any claim made by the third party, is ineffective (s.9(4)).

The position with regard to pay to be paid clauses is discussed separately at para.8.62 below.

Premiums and set-off

8–54A Where the 1930 Act is applicable, if the premium has not been paid, the insurers have a right of set-off against the policy moneys,[56] and insurers will also have a right of set off against any defence costs repayable to them by the assured.[57] A policy term which discharges, or has discharged, the insurers from liability in the event of unpaid premium is enforceable against the third party.

The position under the 1930 Act has been codified, in s.10 of the 2010 Act. Under that section, the insurers may exercise any right of set-off arising under the policy, which will in practice mean that the unpaid premium can be set off against any claim. The insurers may not set off against the claim sums owing by the assured under other contracts, e.g., previous years' premiums. As under the 1930 Act, policy terms relating to premium payment, including forfeiture, are binding on the third party.

Proceedings against the insurers

8–55 A claim against the insurers must, under s.5 of the Limitation Act 1980, be brought by the assured within six years from the date of the casualty. In a liability case, the casualty is taken as having occurred on the date on which the assured's liability to the third party was established and quantified. As the right of a third party to bring an action against insurers under the 1930 Act is derived from that of the assured, it would seem to follow that the third party itself has six years to bring an action against the insurers from the date of the judgment against the assured. The third party may face some difficulty here in a number of respects.

First, the third party's claim against the assured must be established and quantified before he can bring an action against the insurers under the 1930 Act, and the mere fact that the assured has become insolvent is not enough to allow an action to be brought. The third party must accordingly bear time limits in mind in making his own claim against the assured.

Secondly, the third party may have obtained a judgment against the assured at a time when the assured has not become insolvent, and if the assured subsequently becomes insolvent without having issued a claim form against the insurers the third party may find that the claim against the insurers is time-barred. This is an unlikely scenario, because if the assured delays in satisfying the judgment the third party may initiate an insolvency procedure against him and thereby obtain rights under the 1930 Act: the third party may then issue a claim form against the insurers immediately.

---

[56] *Cox v Bankside Members Agency Ltd* [1995] 2 Lloyd's Rep. 437, 451.
[57] *Cox v Bankside Members Agency Ltd* [1995] 2 Lloyd's Rep. 437.

Thirdly, the third party may have obtained judgment against the assured at a time when the assured has not become insolvent, and the assured has commenced proceedings against the insurers within the six-year period. If the assured becomes insolvent during the course of the action, the third party has an immediate right to issue proceedings under the 1930 Act. However, if the assured while pursuing a claim against the insurers becomes insolvent after the limitation period has expired, it has been held that the third party cannot take over the assured's own action but is time-barred from commencing his own action.[58] It is nevertheless arguable that the limitation period for the third party's action against the insurers cannot start to run until the assured has become insolvent, because until that point the third party has no cause of action,[59] and in any event it is possible under CPR Pt 19 for the court to order the third party to be substituted for the assured so that the original proceedings can continue in the third party's name.

The position under the 2010 Act is much the same, although it is modified in that the third party can bring a direct action against the insurers without having established and quantified the liability of the assured. The limitation period for proceedings relating to liability under the policy is six years from the date on which the assured's liability has been established and quantified, so that an action in advance of that plainly is unaffected by any limitation problem. The limitation period for a claim seeking to establish and quantify the assured's liability to the third party is the ordinary statutory limitation period relating to such a claim. In the latter case, if the third party has commenced an action against the assured within the limitation period then he may seek a declaration against the insurers to the effect that the assured has become insolvent and the limitation period has expired before the claim has been resolved (ss.2(5) and 12).

Dispute resolution provisions

Under the 1930 Act, the third party is bound by any choice of law, jurisdiction or **8–56** arbitration clause in the policy.[60] The separability of jurisdiction and arbitration clauses[61] from the substantive part of the policy does not restrict their operation against the third party. If it is the case that the limitation period for the third party's claim against the insurers runs from the date of the judgment against the assured rather than the date of the assured's insolvency, arbitration proceedings give rise to the problem of the assured becoming insolvent during the course of an arbitration against the insurers and after the expiry of the limitation period: fresh arbitration proceedings would appear to be necessary, but there is no power vested in arbitrators equivalent to CPR Pt 19 which permits them to substitute the third party for the assured in the proceedings against the insurers. It may be, however, that the solution is for the third party to take an assignment of the arbitration proceedings from the assured, the availability of assignment of this right

---

[58] *Lefevre v White* [1990] 1 Lloyd's Rep. 569; *Matadeen v Caribbean Insurance Co* [2002] UKPC 69.
[59] This was the approach adopted in *The Felicie* [1990] 2 Lloyd's Rep. 21, decided in 1987, which was not referred to in *Lefevre v White* [1990] 1 Lloyd's Rep. 569.
[60] *Montedipe SpA v JTP-RO Jugotanker, The Jordan Nicolov* [1990] 2 Lloyd's Rep. 11, although contrast the comments of Phillips J. in *London Steamship Owners' Mutual Insurance Association Ltd v Bombay Trading Co Ltd, The Felicie* [1990] 2 Lloyd's Rep. 21.
[61] Arbitration Act 1996, s.7.

having been confirmed by Hobhouse J. in *The Jordan Nicolov*.[62] An assignment can be effected by an agreement between the assured and the third party, and perfected by the third party giving notice of the assignment to the arbitrators and the third party. However, *The Jordan Nicolov* was not a case decided under the 1930 Act and there is no clear authority on the position under the Act.

The 2010 Act similarly recognises that the third party is bound by any choice of jurisdiction, choice of law or arbitration clause in the policy. If there is an arbitration clause, the third party will be required to proceed against the insurers in arbitration, although if the assured's liability to the third party has not at that point been resolved and any question of the assured's liability to the third party arises, then the arbitrators are given extended jurisdiction to resolve that question even though any claim by the third party against the assured would not have of itself been subject to arbitration (s.2(7)–(8)).

Right of third party to insurance information

8–57   Under s.2(1) of the 1930 Act, the assured is under a duty to provide to the third party

"such information as may reasonably be required by him for the purpose of ascertaining whether any rights have been transferred to and vested in him by this Act and for the purpose of enforcing such rights, if any . . ."

The third party may, therefore, demand from the assured information as to the identity of the insurers and as to the nature of the cover. The third party may, having obtained this information, then turn to the insurers, s.2(1) providing that the "insurer shall be subject to the same duty". The third party is to be permitted to inspect and take copies of all contracts of insurance, receipts for premiums and other relevant documents in the possession or power of the person upon whom the duty is imposed (s.2(3)). It is unclear whether the insurers are required to disclose any defences which they contemplate raising in respect of any policy claim. It was at one time thought that the right to obtain information could be exercised only after the assured had established and quantified the liability of the assured towards him, on the grounds that before that date no rights had been transferred to the third party as required by s.2(1)[63] or that it was impossible to know whether there was or was not any liability.[64] The earlier authorities were overruled by the Court of Appeal in *Re OT Computers*.[65] It was there held that the third party obtained contingent rights on the insolvency of the assured, and it was those rights which were referred to in s.2(1). The position is, therefore, that the third party may seek insurance information from the assured at any time after his insolvency and thereafter from the insurers. This right operates independently of the pre-action disclosure rules in CPR r.31.16.

---

[62] [1990] 2 Lloyd's Rep. 11.
[63] *Nigel Upchurch Associates v Aldridge Estates Investment Co Ltd* [1993] I Lloyd's Rep. 535.
[64] *Woolwich Building Society v Taylor* [1995] 1 B.C.L.C. 132.
[65] [2004] Lloyd's Rep. IR 669.

The problem of the absence of insurance information has been addressed in a comprehensive fashion by the 2010 Act. Under s.11 and Sch.1, once the assured has become insolvent[66] the third party has the right to obtain information as to the scope and validity of the assured's policy, and the policy may not contain any term which conflicts with this right (Sch.1, para.5). The third party has, under Sch.1, para.1(1), a right to obtain information from the assured where he reasonably believes that the assured has incurred liability and has become insolvent. In such a case, the third party may request information as to (Sch.1, para.1(3)):

(a) whether there is a contract of insurance that covers the supposed liability or might reasonably be regarded as covering it;

(b) if there is such a contract—

    (i) who the insurer is;

    (ii) what the terms of the contract are;

    (iii) whether the assured has been informed that the insurer has claimed not to be liable under the contract in respect of the supposed liability;

    (iv) whether there are or have been any proceedings between the insurer and the assured in respect of the supposed liability and, if so, relevant details of those proceedings;

    (v) in a case where the contract sets a limit on the fund available to meet claims in respect of the supposed liability and other liabilities, how much of it (if any) has been paid out in respect of other liabilities;

    (vi) whether there is a fixed charge to which any sums paid out under the contract in respect of the supposed liability would be subject.

As an alternative, the third party may by notice request the relevant information from another person who may be in possession of the relevant information, e.g., an insurer or broker (Sch.1, para.1(2)), as long as that information is under that person's control and is not protected by privilege. Information in respect of a dissolved company may also be sought from its ex-officers and any relevant insolvency practitioner (Sch.1, paras 3–4). Once a notice has been served, the recipient has 28 days to provide the requested information or, if he is unable to comply, to identify another person who can do so (Sch.1, para.2(1)–(2)). Failure to comply entitles the third party to apply to the court for an order (Sch.1, para.2(3)).

Removal or restriction of policy rights on insolvency

Section 1(3) of the 1930 Act states that: **8–58**

"In so far as any contract of insurance . . . purports, whether directly or indirectly, to avoid the contract or to alter the rights of the parties thereunder upon

---

[66] But not before the assured has become insolvent. The 2010 Act does not introduce any generalised process for obtaining disclosure of insurance information in civil proceedings. Any such measure was thought to be inappropriate in the context of the 2010 Act, although it may be that the matter will be addressed by amendment to the Civil Procedure Rules in due course. Schedule 1, para.6 recognises this possibility, by providing that information rights under the 2010 Act are without prejudice to any rights which may be conferred under the CPR.

the happening to the insured of any [insolvency event in section 1(1)], the contract shall be of no effect."

This provision seeks to prevent insurers from relying on any policy term which is triggered by a statutory act of insolvency within the 1930 Act and which removes or limits the rights of the assured, thereby prejudicing the statutory transfer. This encompasses a policy term which automatically terminates cover in the event of insolvency,[67] although the subsection does not affect the validity of a term which leaves the assured's legal rights unaffected but makes recovery under the policy impossible in practice.[68] It applies only to those terms which effect "an alteration in the enjoyment by the third party of his rights against the insurers by prejudicing or reducing those rights in some material way".[69] Thus a policy term which provides that, in the event of insolvency, the handling of claims against the assured is to be transferred to the insurers, is not one which can be regarded as adversely affecting the third party's right to establish the liability of the assured.[70] The protection of s.1(3) arises immediately upon the insolvency of the assured, whether or not the third party has established and quantified the liability of the assured at that date. Thus, a policy term which provides that on the insolvency of the assured the level of deductible borne by the assured is to be increased is outlawed by s.1(3) even though, at the date of the insolvency there is no liability under the policy.[71] The assured's insolvency must, in accordance with s.1(3), fall within one of the procedures listed in s.1(1),[72] although it has been held that a policy term which restricts the rights of the assured before the occurrence of a statutory insolvency event, e.g., on the exercise of contractual rights by a creditor in advance of insolvency, is nevertheless within s.1(3) if there is a sufficient connection between the contractual insolvency event and the subsequent statutory insolvency event.[73]

The 2010 Act similarly, by s.17, deprives of effect any policy term which directly or indirectly avoids or terminates a policy, or alters the rights of the assured, in the event that the assured becomes insolvent or an individual dies insolvent.

Settlement agreement between assured and insurers

8–59 Under s.3 of the 1930 Act,

"no agreement made between the insurer and the insured after liability has been incurred to the third party and after the [occurrence of a statutory insol-

---

[67] *Firma C-Trade SA v Newcastle Protection and Indemnity Society, The Fanti* and *Socony Mobil Oil Inc v West of England Shipowners Mutual Insurance Association, The Padre Island (No 2)* [1989] 1 Lloyd's Rep. 329, CA.

[68] As is the case with a "pay to be paid" clause: *Firma C-Trade SA v Newcastle Protection and Indemnity Society, The Fanti* and *Socony Mobil Oil Inc v West of England Shipowners Mutual Insurance Association, The Padre Island (No 2)* [1991] A.C. 7. See below.

[69] *Centre Reinsurance International Co v Freakley* [2005] Lloyd's Rep. IR 22, *per* Blackburne J.

[70] *Centre Reinsurance International Co v Freakley* [2005] Lloyd's Rep. IR 284.

[71] *Centre Reinsurance International Co v Freakley* [2005] Lloyd's Rep. IR 284.

[72] See para.8–50, above.

[73] This was the view of Blackburne J. in *Centre Reinsurance International Co v Freakley* [2005] Lloyd's Rep. IR 22. The point was held not to arise on appeal, [2005] Lloyd's Rep. IR 284.

vency event] ... nor waiver, assignment, or other disposition made by, or payment made to the insured after the commencement or day aforesaid shall be effective to defeat or affect those rights transferred to the third party under this Act, but those rights shall be the same as if no such agreement, waiver, assignment, disposition or payment had been made."

The section thus strikes down any settlement between the insurers and the assured which operates to remove the policy benefits from the third party. However, the section does not extend to settlements reached between the insurers and the assured which is made either before the insolvency event[74] or before the third party has established and quantified the liability of the assured towards him.[75]

The 2010 Act does not contain any equivalent provision, and there is no need for it to do so. Once the assured has become insolvent, s.1 effects an automatic transfer of the assured's rights to the third party, so the assured has no rights to negotiate away. As is the case under the 1930 Act, pre-insolvency agreements between the assured and the insurers are not affected.

Waiver by insurers of rights under the policy

Insurers may waive their rights under the policy by an unequivocal election not **8–60** to rely upon rights (waiver by affirmation) or by an unequivocal representation to that effect which is relied upon by the representee (waiver by estoppel). Waiver by affirmation is in principle binding only as between the assured and the insurers if it takes place before the assured has become insolvent and the third party has established and quantified the insurers' liability. Until these events have occurred the third party has only contingent rights under the policy and the original assured retains the legal right to pursue the insurers. Thus an alleged act of waiver cannot be relied upon by the third party if the assured was solvent at the time[76] or if the assured was insolvent but the third party had not at that stage established and quantified the assured's liability towards him.[77] One justification for this analysis is that if there are numerous third party claimants, an act of waiver in respect of one of them cannot be regarded as binding on the insurers as against the others. However, an unequivocal representation to one third party that the proceeds will be paid, and which is relied upon by him, is in principle capable of giving rise to an estoppel against the insurers although presumably only in respect of that particular claim.[78] The principles in this paragraph apply to the 1930 and 2010 Acts alike.

---

[74] *Normid Housing Association Ltd v Ralphs* [1989] 1 Lloyd's Rep. 265.

[75] *Re Greenfield, Jackson v Greenfield* [1998] B.P.I.R. 699.

[76] This was the view of Stanley Burnton J. in *Spriggs v Wessington Court School Ltd* [2005] Lloyd's Rep. IR 474.

[77] This was the holding in *Spriggs v Wessington Court School Ltd* [2005] Lloyd's Rep. IR 474. It was suggested in *Wood v Perfection Travel* [1996] L.R.L.R. 233 that insurers who defended the substantive proceedings against the assured thereby waived their right to rely upon policy defences, although the point was left open.

[78] This possibility was recognised in *Spriggs v Wessington Court School Ltd* [2005] Lloyd's Rep. IR 474 but no argument to that effect was put to the court.

Surplus insurance moneys

8–60A Any transfer under the 1930 Act is confined to the limits of the policy and to the extent that the policy moneys satisfy the claim. Any surplus, e.g., in respect of defence costs, reverts to the insolvent assured. Similarly, s.8 of the 2010 Act provides that any transfer is only for the amount of the assured's liability to the third party.

Insufficient insurance moneys

8–61 Because the 1930 Act confers upon the third party no better rights against the insurers than those possessed by the assured, the insurers can be liable only up to policy limits, so that if there is a shortfall the third party must submit a claim against the insolvent assured's estate for the balance of the claim.[79] Section 1(4) of the 1930 Act states that:

> "if the liability of the insurer to the insured is less than the liability of the insured to the third party, nothing in this Act shall affect the rights of the third party against the insured in respect of the balance."

The position is the same under the 2010 Act.

If there is more than one claim against the assured, and the value of those claims exceeds the sum payable under the policy, the priority of those claims is to be determined on a "first past the post" basis, so that as and when a claimant against the assured is able to establish and quantify the assured's liability then he has a claim against the insurers.[80] There is no basis for implying any form of apportionment between competing claimants, and there would be practical difficulties in operating apportionment given that claims may not be established for some time. There may accordingly be a race to judgment. The 2010 Act does not address this point, and it may therefore be assumed that the first past the post principle holds good.

Pay to be paid clauses

8–62 P&I Club rules normally make payment of the third party's claim by the member a condition precedent to the member's right of recovery from the Club. It has long been disputed whether this type of clause can operate under the 1930 Act, given that if the assured has become insolvent and is unable to pay then the clause if it is so construed[81] bars any claim under the policy and thus prevents any claim by the third party. In a joined appeal to the House of Lords, *Firma C-Trade SA v Newcastle Protection and Indemnity Society, The Fanti* and *Socony Mobil Oil Inc v West of England Shipowners Mutual Insurance Association, The Padre Island*

---

[79] 1930 Act, s.1(4))(b); *Avandero (UK) Ltd v National Transit Insurance Co Ltd* [1984] 2 Lloyd's Rep. 613.

[80] *Cox v Bankside Members Agency Ltd* [1995] 2 Lloyd's Rep. 437.

[81] Such a construction is not inevitable: *Charter Reinsurance Co Ltd v Fagan* [1996] 3 All E.R. 46.

(No.2),[82] in each of which third party cargo interests sought to recover under the 1930 Act from the P&I Clubs of insolvent shipowners, their Lordships ruled that the clause was effective. Staughton J. at first instance in *The Fanti*[83] had decided that the clause was ineffective because the assured's contingent right to be paid was transferred to the third party and the requirement of prepayment did not affect that right and was to be disregarded. By contrast, at first instance in *The Padre Island (No 2)*[84] Saville J. held that there was no contractual entitlement to payment by the Club without prepayment, so that the cargo owners did not obtain any right to recover by reason of the statutory transfer. The Court of Appeal[85] preferred the views of Staughton J., but the House of Lords was unanimously in favour of Saville J.'s approach and confirmed that the third party cannot by reason of the transfer under s.1(1) of the 1930 Act be in a better position than the assured. It was also held that there was no equitable principle which overrode the operation of the pay to be paid clause.

The 2010 Act addresses the problem of pay to be paid clauses. The general rule in s.9(5) is that such clauses will cease to be enforceable. However, special provision is made for marine insurance by s.9(6) (marine insurance being the main context in which such clauses are found). Under this provision, pay to be paid clauses are valid and enforceable unless the claim is one for death or personal injury. Accordingly, P&I Clubs can continue to insist upon prepayment for cargo and other property damage claims, but not for injury claims. This provision will not affect the validity of the pay to be paid wording under the standard collision liability clause in hull policies, as this clause expressly excludes liabilities for loss of life or personal injury (see para.23–25 below).

A further issue which arose in the pay to be paid cases was whether s.1(3) of **8–63** the 1930 Act, the restriction on the variation of the assured's rights on the happening of a statutory insolvency event, struck down a pay to be pay clause. At first instance in *The Fanti* Staughton J.'s view was that s.1(3) had that effect, in that although a pay to be paid clause did not alter the assured's legal right to make a claim against the insurers, the fact that the assured was insolvent meant that he could never satisfy the pay to be paid requirement so that his practical right to seek indemnity was removed. Saville J. in *The Padre Island (No.2)* disagreed with this analysis, and held that the rights referred to in s.1(3) were legal rights, and that after insolvency the assured retained the legal right to pursue the insurers. Saville J.'s view was confirmed by the Court of Appeal and ultimately by the House of Lords. Their Lordships held that the section referred to legal and not practical variations in the rights of the assured, and that a pay to be paid clause did not affect the assured's legal rights. The point remains a live one under the 2010 Act in respect of cargo and property damage claims under marine policies, but the 2010 Act does not seek to reverse the position reached under the 1930 Act.

---

[82] [1991] 2 A.C. 7.
[83] [1987] 2 Lloyd's Rep. 299.
[84] [1987] 2 Lloyd's Rep. 529.
[85] [1989] 1 Lloyd's Rep. 239.

Other direct actions against insurers

8–64   A series of international conventions confer direct actions upon third party victims against insurers.

In respect of oil pollution from vessels, the Merchant Shipping Act 1995 (as amended), which gives effect to the International Convention on Civil Liability for Oil Pollution Damage 1992 (the CLC Convention) and the International Convention on Civil Liability for Bunker Oil Pollution Damage 2001 (the Bunkers Convention),[85a] requires insurance to be taken out against oil pollution liabilities by any vessel carrying in bulk a cargo of more than 2,000 of persistent oil, in respect of that cargo[86] and by any ship having a gross tonnage greater than 1,000 tons in respect of bunker oil.[87] If liability has been incurred by the vessel's registered owner by reason of the discharge or escape of oil, or as a result of any threat of contamination, the victim may bring a direct action against the insurers.[88] The 2010 Act is disapplied where the claim is governed by the 1995 Act, although the 2010 Act continues to apply to pollution liability which is not required to be insured but in respect of which there is a policy in force.

The Civil Liability for Oil Pollution Damage resulting from Exploration for and Exploitation of Seabed Mineral Resources Convention 1977 requires the operator to possess liability insurance[89] and any claim for compensation for pollution damage may be brought directly against the operator's insurers.[90] This Convention is not yet in force.

The International Convention on Liability and Compensation in Connection with the Carriage of Hazardous and Noxious Substances by Sea 1996 requires liability insurance to be in place[91] and any claim for compensation for damage may be brought directly against the insurers.[92] This Convention is not yet in force, although a protocol agreed in April 2010 is designed to bring the Convention into force by the end of 2011.

The Nairobi Wreck Removal Convention 2007 requires the registered owner of a ship of 300 gross tonnage and above and flying the flag of a State Party to maintain insurance in respect of wreck removal costs,[93] and any claim may be brought

---

[85a] For the operation of Bunkers Convention, see the judgment of Beaston J. in *Islamic Republic of Iran Shipping Lines v Steamship Mutual Association (Bermuda) Ltd* [2010] EWHC 2661 (Comm).
[86] Merchant Shipping Act 1995, s.163; CLC, art.VII, para. 1.
[87] Merchant Shipping Act 1995, s.163A; Bunkers Convention, art.7, para.1. The Bunkers Convention came into force in November 2008.
[88] Merchant Shipping Act 1995, s.165; CLC, art.VII, para.8; Bunkers Convention, art.7, para.10. Every ship which is subject to the compulsory insurance regimes under CLC and the Bunkers Convention is required to hold a certificate attesting that the appropriate cover is in force. The right of direct action, which is subject to limits of liability under the respective Conventions, is against the insurer named in the certificate. The insurer cannot rely on policy defences, other than the owner's wilful misconduct; in some circumstances, even where the insurance cover has ceased or been terminated before the casualty, the named insurer will still be liable to meet direct action claims. Evidently, the scope of these direct action regimes is very different, and in many respects more onerous for insurers, than the regimes under the 1930 and 2010 Acts. A detailed discussion of these special regimes is outside the scope of this work.
[89] Exploration Convention, art.8, para.1.
[90] Exploration Convention, art.8, para.3.
[91] HNS, art.12, para.1.
[92] HNS, art.12, para.8.
[93] Nairobi Convention, art.12, para.1.

directly against the registered owner's insurers.[94] The Nairobi Convention is not yet in force.

The Athens Convention Relating to the Carriage of Passengers and their Luggage by Sea 1974 was amended by the 2002 Protocol to introduce compulsory insurance on the part of the carrier,[95] and also a direct claim by the passenger against the insurers.[96] The Athens Convention and the 2002 Protocol were implemented in part in the European Union by European Parliament and Council Regulation 392/2009/EC on the Liability of Carriers of Passengers by Sea in the Event of Accidents. The implementing Regulation applies to any international carriage and to carriage by sea within a single Member State by Class A and Class B passenger vessels[97] where:

the ship is flying the flag of or is registered in a Member State;

the contract of carriage has been made in a Member State;

or the place of departure or destination, according to the contract of carriage, is in a Member State.

For the sake of completeness, mention may be made of European Parliament and Council Directive 2009/20/EC on the Insurance of Shipowners for Maritime Risks, which requires each Member State to legislate, by January 1, 2010, to impose compulsory liability insurance upon any vessel of 300 gross tonnage or more flying its flag (other than warships, auxiliary warships or other State owned or operated ships used for a non-commercial public service). The Directive does not, however, specify that a direct cause of action against insurers is to be granted.

---

[94] Nairobi Convention, art.12, para.10
[95] Athens Convention, art.4bis, para.1.
[96] Athens Convention, art.4bis, para.10.
[97] As defined by Council Directive 98/18/EC on safety rules and standards for passenger ships.

CHAPTER 9

NAMING THE SHIP: FLOATING POLICIES AND OPEN COVERS

The importance of distinguishing types of open cover

Note 42: The Court of Appeal in *Limit No.2 Ltd v Axa Versicherung AG* **9–11**
[2009] Lloyd's Rep. IR 396 reversed in part the first instance ruling, but on other
grounds.

    Note 43: The Court of Appeal in *Limit No.2 Ltd v Axa Versicherung AG* [2009] **9–12**
Lloyd's Rep. IR 396 reversed in part the first instance ruling, but on other
grounds.

CHAPTER 11

INSURABLE INTEREST

There is a fourth reason why the Gambling Act 2005 has probably left the Marine **11–12** Insurance Act 1906 untouched, and that is that s.10 of The Gambling Act 2005 removes from its scope activities regulated under the Financial Services and Markets Act 2000, one of which is the carrying on of insurance business in the UK. Some marine policies are not regulated for this purpose, including those effected by an EEA firm from a branch outside the UK and under a co-insurance arrangement where the insurer is not the leading insurer,[1] and it would seem anomalous to draw a distinction of this type. The English and Scottish Law Commissions, in an Issues Paper on *Insurable Interest* published in January 2008, have tentatively recommended that there is no longer any need for an anti-gambling principle in insurance law, and that the indemnity principle should suffice. In other words, the only point at which the assured should be required to establish insurable interest is at the point of loss.

---

[1] See the Financial Services and Markets Act 2000 (Regulated Activities) Order 2001, SI 2001/544, arts 10 and 11.

CHAPTER 12

VALUATION OF INSURABLE INTERESTS

Nature of the assured's claim for non-payment

The principles discussed in this paragraph of the main work have been considered **12–04** by the English and Scottish Law Commissions in Issues Paper 6, entitled *Damages for Late Payment and the Insurer's Duty of Good Faith*, published in March 2010. Two main approaches to reforming the law in this area are identified in Issues Paper 6. The first approach, which would entail amendment of s.17 in the Marine Insurance Act 1906, would impose a specific non-excludable duty of good faith on insurers in relation to insurance claims and would make any breach of that duty actionable in damages. This approach would reverse the effect of the decision in *Banque Financiere de la Cité v Westgate*,[1] so far as the handling of claims by insurers is concerned. The second approach recommended by the Commissions, described as "the strict liability approach", would make it the primary obligation of insurers to pay valid claims within a reasonable time,[2] and an insurer who failed to meet that obligation would be liable for any loss that resulted from the late payment, subject to the usual limitations[3] of causation, remoteness,[4] and the assured's duty to mitigate.

Interest on the assured's claim

Under s.35A of the Supreme Court Act, 1981,[5] the Court has power to award **12–04A** interest[6] in proceedings for the recovery of a debt or damages from the date when

---

[1] [1991] 2 A.C. 249, affirming the judgment of the Court of Appeal [1990] 1 Q.B. 665.

[2] This appears already to be the position in Scots law. The position in English law is summarised in this paragraph (12–04) and at para.27–02 in the main work. The Law Commissions' proposal would reverse the effect of the decisions in *The Italia Express (No. 2)* [1992] 2 Lloyd's Rep. 216 and *Sprung v Royal Insurance (UK) Ltd* [1999] Lloyd's Rep. IR 111. The effect would be to be introduce a statutory implied term, similar to that which Mance J. had declined to imply in *Insurance Corp of the Channel Islands v McHugh* [1997] L.R.L.R. 94, 136. It is not clear whether, by their proposal to make payment within a reasonable time the insurer's *primary obligation*, the Commissions envisage that the present position whereby the assured's cause of action accrues at the time of loss (see e.g. *Chandris v Argo Ins. Co Ltd* [1963] 2 Lloyd's Rep. 65; *The Kyriaki* [1993] 1 Lloyd's Rep. 137) would cease to apply. The point was not addressed in Issues Paper No.6.

[3] The Commissions envisage that insurers would be free to exclude or limit their "strict liability" obligations, except in consumer contracts.

[4] The Commissions' proposals would not preclude arguments on remoteness of damage, which might well arise in the marine insurance context in the light of the decision of the House of Lords in *Transfield Shipping Inc v Mercator Shipping Inc (The Achilleas)* [2009] 1 A.C. 61.

[5] Now redesignated as the Senior Courts Act.

[6] Only simple interest can be awarded under s.35A. The Law Commission made proposals in 2004 to give the Court power to award compound interest but legislation has not been forthcoming. Arbitrators have the power to award compound interest, under the Arbitration Act, 1996, s.49.

the cause of action arose. In the present state of English law,[7] the assured's cause of action arises at the date of loss under a policy of indemnity insurance, in the absence of any contrary provision in the policy. It follows that the assured is *prima facie* entitled to interest on the judgment amount from the date of loss, subject to the Court's discretion.[8] The basic principle is that an award of interest is to compensate the claimant for being kept out of his money, not to penalise the defendant for delay in payment.[9]

Although the Court undoubtedly has power to award interest starting from the date of loss in insurance cases and is still likely to do so in straightforward cases, there are several instances in reported cases where interest has been awarded from a later date, so as to allow a reasonable time for investigation[10] by the insurer after notification of the assured's claim[11] before interest starts running. The practice in the Commercial Court in insurance cases which are unusual or are not straightforward is summarised in the following terms by Thomas J. in *Quorum AS v Schramm (No.2)*,[12] at para.8.

"In such cases, the Court usually exercises its discretion on the basis it is proper to allow insurers some time to consider the claim. The time varies accordingly to the nature of the loss, the way in which the claim is presented and the circumstances that require investigation. In many cases the time may be quite short. The Court will always have regard to the particular circumstances specific to that claim."

---

[7] See para.12–04 in the main work and above; also paras 26–87, 26–89 (general average), 27–01 (particular average), 29–03 (constructive total loss).

[8] *Rhesa Shipping Co SA v Edmunds (The Popi M)* [1984] 2 Lloyd's Rep. 555, per May L.J. at 562; *Kuwait Airways Corp v Kuwait Insurance Co S.A.K.(No.3)* [2000] Lloyd's Rep. IR 678, 689; *Seashore Marine SA v Phoenix Assurance Plc (The Vergina) (No.3)* [2002] 1 Lloyd's Rep. 238, paras 23, 29; *Quorum AS v Schramm (No.2)* [2002] 2 Lloyd's Rep. 72.

[9] See *BP Exploration Co (Libya) Ltd v Hunt (No.2)* [1979] 1 W.L.R. 783; *The Popi M*, above; *Kuwait Airways v Kuwait Insurance*, above; *Quorum v Schramm (No.2)* above. And see *Synergy Health (UK) Ltd CGU Insurance Plc* [2010] EWHC 2583 at para.263.

[10] See the cases cited in the preceding footnotes. In *The Popi M*, May L.J. expressed the view that the period of time to be allowed for consideration by insurers should be limited; the same view was taken by Aikens J. in *The Vergina* at paras 23, 29; see also the passage in *Quorum v Schramm*, quoted below.

[11] There is much to be said for the view that an assured is not being kept out of his money until he has made a claim or at least notified the insurers of the loss and his intention to claim under the policy; *Kuwait Airways (No.3)*, above, at 689.

[12] [2002] 2 Lloyd's Rep. 72, 75. Langley J. summarised the position in slightly different terms, but with similar effect, in *Kuwait Airways (No.3)* at 689, where he said that "generally the existence of and need to investigate a genuine dispute as to liability is not a material factor in postponing the running of interest", though the position is not so clear where there is a dispute or uncertainty about quantum; Langley J. went on to say that there is no difference in principle between disputes or uncertainties as to liability and as to quantum, and that the approach of asking the question in terms of when the claimant could reasonably and commercially have expected to be paid "has never been applied to extend the starting date beyond the date when a reasonable investigation would have been completed . . . and even then it has been used substantially in cases in which the claim can properly be viewed as sufficiently unusual as to inspire special investigation or where there is evidence of a commercial practice as to a later date of payment without an interest obligation." The approach to which Langley J. was referring was that suggested by Lord Wilberforce's dicta in *General Tire & Rubber Co v Firestone Tyre & Rubber Co* [1975] 1 W.L.R. 819, 836.

Under s.35A, the Court only has power to award simple interest. The House of Lords decision in *Sempra Metals Ltd v IRC*[13] has led to suggestions[14] that compound interest should now be recoverable in insurance cases, but in the present state of English law where the insurer's obligation is characterised as one for unliquidated damages for failure to hold the assured harmless not as a debt or obligation to pay a sum of money there would seem to be no basis upon which the reasoning in *Sempra* could be extended to the sphere of indemnity insurance. The only basis for an award of compound interest (in the absence of statutory provision) could be as damages for the insurer's breach, and the difficulties are the same as those discussed at para.12–04 in the main work and above.[15] Unless and until a separate obligation to pay valid claims is framed through the processes of litigation or as seems more likely by legislation,[16] we consider that *Sempra Metals* cannot be applied to claims under policies of indemnity insurance, either to justify claims for compound interest, or claims for damages in general.

---

[13] [2008] 1 A.C. 561.
[14] The editors are aware of insurance cases where a claim for compound interest has been pleaded, in the aftermath of *Sempra Metals*. The point has still to be judicially considered.
[15] See also para.27–02. The difficulties are particularly acute in the context of marine insurance since the measure of indemnity sections in the 1906 Act are "conclusively definitive", see *The Italia Express (No.2)* [1992] 2 Lloyd's Rep. 281, 291.
[16] Such as the proposals in Issues Paper No. 6 (see para.12–04 above). Amendment of s.35A to give the Court power to award compound interest may prove a more straightforward route.

CHAPTER 13

DURATION OF RISK: TIME POLICIES AND VOYAGE POLICIES

Practical considerations affecting the use of time and of voyage policies

Note 12: The rule enacted in s.44 of the Act is disapplied under cl.10.2 in **13–03** the Institute Cargo Clauses 1/1/09, in cases where, without the knowledge of the Assured or their employees, the ship sails for another destination. The purpose and effect of this amendment are discussed under paras 13–17 *et seq* below.

Loss within time—damage ascertained afterwards

The fundamental importance of the temporal limitations in a time policy is **13–08** highlighted by the decision of the House of Lords in *Wasa International Ins Co v Lexington Insurance*.[1] This was a case of reinsurance, but the principles stated are of general application to time policies, Lord Mance[2] and Lord Collins[3] both referring to the judgment of Lord Campbell C.J. in *Knight v Faith*[4] as the seminal decision in this area. The decision in *Wasa v Lexington* confirms the principles stated in this paragraph of the main work. As stated by Lord Collins[5]:

> "where an insurance or reinsurance contract provides cover for loss or damage to property on an occurrence basis, the insurer (or reinsurer) is liable to indemnify the insured (or reinsured) in respect of loss and damage which occurs within the period of cover but will not be liable to indemnify the insured (or reinsured) in respect of loss and damage which occurs either before inception or after expiry of the risk".[6]

---

[1] [2009] Lloyd's Rep. IR 675 at paras 15–16, 39, 74 and 77. See also *Municipal Mutual Ins Ltd v Sea Ins Co Ltd* [1998] Lloyd's Rep. IR 421 (cited in *Wasa v Lexington*, above) and *Loyaltrend Ltd v Creechurch Dedicated Ltd* [2010] Lloyd's Rep. IR 466.

[2] *Ibid*, para.39.

[3] *Ibid*, para.74.

[4] (1850) 15 Q.B. 649, 667 (cited at this point in the main work).

[5] The point at issue in *Wasa v Lexington* was whether losses occurring prior to inception were covered under the reinsurance, but the principles are stated more widely. Lord Mance added the necessary qualification (at para.39), in the light of *Knight v Faith*, placing the emphasis on the need for the peril insured against to occur during the continuance of the risk: "damage materialising or developing from it after the policy period would still be covered". The judgment of Bingham L.J. in *Kelly v Norwich Union Fire Ins Society Ltd* [1990] 1 W.L.R. 139 which (so far as the editors are aware) is the only case prior to *Wasa v Lexington* specifically to address the position with regard to losses caused by perils operating before inception would not appear to have been cited. There does not appear, however, to be any inconsistency between the statements of principle in these cases.

[6] Lord Collins went on (at para.77) to approve the statements of principle contained in *Municipal Mutual Ins Ltd v Sea Ins Co Ltd* (above) where Hobhouse L.J. observed that: "when the relevant cover is placed on a time basis, the stated period of time is fundamental and must be given effect to". Lord Mance also quoted and approved the same passage, at para.39.

Section 44: "Phantom Ships"

13–17 The "phantom ship" problem has been addressed in the new Institute Cargo Clauses 1/1/09[7] The effect of the revisions made to the Change of Voyage Clause, at cl.10.2 in the 2009 Clauses, is discussed under the paragraph headings which follow.[8]
Clause 10.2 in the 2009 Clauses reads as follows:

> "Where the subject-matter insured commences the transit contemplated by this insurance (in accordance with Clause 8.1), but without the knowledge of the Assured or their employees the ship sails for another destination, this insurance will nevertheless be deemed to have attached at commencement of such transit."

It is understood that the 2009 Clauses are already in widespread use,[9] no doubt in part because of this protection afforded against "phantom ship" losses. The "significant gap" in the cover afforded by standard cargo policies, referred to in this paragraph of the main work, has not been wholly eliminated,[10] but s.44 of the Act is of much less practical importance now that a standard alternative to and eventual replacement for the 1982 Cargo Clauses has become available.

Note 78: As indicated above the new Clauses in common use in insurances on cargo now provide a measure of protection against the application of s.44 of the Act. Clause 10 in the 2009 Cargo Clauses is in two parts. The first part of the Clause (10.1) deals with the position where there is a voluntary change of destination, by the Assured.[11] The second part of the Clause, quoted above, deals with the position where the vessel sails for a destination other than that specified in the policy, without the knowledge of the Assured or their employees. This solution (or partial solution) to the "phantom ship" problem which has been adopted under the 2009 Cargo Clauses may be contrasted with the technique used in the Hull and Freight Clauses where the "held covered" formula is employed both in relation to changes of voyage by the Assured and changes taking place without his knowledge or concurrence.

Application of s.44 to "warehouse to warehouse" cover

13–18 The Transit Clause has been revised in the 2009 Cargo Clauses, which provide for the risk to attach (under cl.8.1) from the time the goods are first moved in the warehouse or place of storage for the purpose of immediate loading, instead of the risk attaching upon leaving the warehouse or place of storage as had been the case under previous editions of the Institute Cargo Clauses. The revisions to the Transit Clause are discussed under later paragraph headings.[12]

---

[7] The Clauses are reproduced in the Appendix to this Supplement.
[8] Paras 13–18 to 13–23.
[9] See J. Dunt and W. Melbourne "Insuring Cargoes in the new millennium: The Institute Cargo Clauses 2009" in R. Thomas (ed), *The Modern Law of Marine Insurance*, Vol. 3 (2009), Ch.6.
[10] This was recognised by the draftsmen of the new clauses. It is an exaggeration to suppose that the "phantom ship" problem has been wholly exorcised by these amendments to the standard Clauses. See Dunt and Melbourne, *op. cit.* para.6.113; and see the present editors' comments at para.13–18 below.
[11] The new wording of cl.10.1 differs from that in cl.10 of the 1982 Clauses and is discussed below at paras 14–93 *et seq.*
[12] See at paras 13–39, 13–40 below.

The basic approach[13] to the construction of a cargo policy affording "warehouse to warehouse" cover is not affected either by the revisions made to the Transit Clause or by those made to the Change of Voyage Clause. The position will generally be (as it was before) that as a matter of construction the substance of the risk is delineated by the description of the voyage, to which the inland transit risks are to be regarded as supplementary. That position is modified only in the circumstances specified in the new cl.10.2 when the risk would otherwise not attach by virtue of s.44, owing to the Vessel's sailing for a non-contractual destination, but is to be "deemed" to have attached.

This revision to the Change of Voyage Clause disapplies s.44 only in defined circumstances and is designed to mitigate the practical consequences of the decision in *The Prestrioka*.[14] The amendment was aimed specifically at the perceived unfairness of an assured who becomes the victim of a "phantom ship" fraud being deprived of cover from the time of sailing and (arguably at least) retrospectively for any loss during the transit prior to shipment.[15] The revised wording would not affect any case involving shipment from the wrong port (the case provided for by s.43 of the Act). Nor would the revised wording appear to affect cases of the type illustrated by *George Kallis v Success Insurance*,[16] where the policy provided for shipment by a named vessel, without any provisions for substitution, and the voyage performed did not conform to that description. Nor would the revised wording affect breach of warranty issues in "phantom ship" cases arising from incorporation of the Institute Classification Clause.[17] It must also be noted that

---

[13] See *Simon Israel & Co v Sedgwick* (1892) 67 L.T.N.S. 352 (Wright J.); [1893] 1 Q.B. 303 (CA). Key passages from the judgments in this case are quoted and discussed at paras 13–19 and 13–20 in the main work. It may be that the approach to construction in *Simon Israel* is no longer appropriate in many contemporary insurances where the core of the policy cannot sensibly be regarded as the sea voyage; see para.13–22, fn.96 in the main work; *Dunt*, Marine Cargo Insurance (2009) para.12.22. However, there are no reported cases, as yet, in which the basic approach in *Simon Israel* has been challenged.

[14] *Nima SARL v Deves Insurance Public Co Ltd* [2003] 2 Lloyd's Rep. 327, discussed at paras 13–21 and 13–22 in the main work. The unpopularity of this decision can be judged from the following comment in Dunt and Melbourne, *op. cit.* at para.6.111: "*The Prestrioka* decision attracted criticism from leading academic commentators as being technical, unmeritorious, inconsistent with an assured's legitimate expectations . . . and generally out of step with modern multimodal transport."

[15] This last point was left open in *The Prestrioka*, and opinions are divided as to the correct answer to it; see Dunt and Melbourne, *op. cit.* para.6.110; Dunt, *op cit.* para.12.21. The present editors remain of the view stated at para.13–22. The 2009 amendment to the Change of Voyage Clause reduces the likelihood that this controversy will ever need to be resolved, but has not made the point academic. In cases where cl.10.2 applies, and where the only basis for holding that the risk has not attached would otherwise be the fact of the vessel's sailing for another destination, there will plainly be no question of retrospective loss of cover.

[16] [1985] 2 Lloyd's Rep. 8; *Dunt, op. cit.*, para.12.25 ("it must be doubted whether any clause could cover the situation in the *Kallis* case").

[17] "Phantom ships" are unlikely to have any valid classification. The assured's claim in *Nam Kwong Medicines and Health Products Ltd v China Ins Co Ltd (The Pacifica)* [2002] 2 Lloyd's Rep. 591 failed both on the ground that the assured was not entitled to be held covered under the Institute Classification Clause, as the risk of carriage on a "phantom ship" is uninsurable, and on the ground of non-attachment of risk under s.44. See also the similar decision in Singapore in *Everbright Commercial Enterprises v Axa Insurance Singapore Pte* Ltd [2001] 2 S.L.R. 316. The interpretation of the current (2001) version of this Clause is considered in this Supplement under paras 19–32A below. Where the Classification Clause is incorporated, as will very often be the case, the revised wording in cl.10.2 of the Cargo Clauses may well be of no assistance to the Assured, unless it can be argued on the facts of the particular case that the loss was complete before any breach occurred.

the revised wording only displaces s.44 where the vessel sails for a destination other than that specified in the description of the voyage in the policy *"without the knowledge of the Assured or their employees"* (emphasis added). This would not appear to provide any protection in a "phantom ship" case where, as might happen, the assured was the victim of a fraudulent conspiracy in which one or more of its employees participated[18] nor would it necessarily protect an assured in circumstances where his employee mistakenly books the cargo on a voyage to a destination other than that specified in the policy.[19]

Simon Israel & Co v Sedgwick

13–19 and 13–20 The amendment to the Change of Voyage Clause in the Institute Cargo Clauses 1/1/09 does not affect the basic approach to construction of a cargo policy incorporating warehouse to warehouse cover established in *Simon Israel v Sedgwick*. The starting-point from which cover is to commence under cl.8.1 in the 2009 Clauses is when the goods are first moved within the warehouse or place of storage for immediate loading, rather than when the goods leave the warehouse, and as noted above in the circumstances specified in cl.10.2 of the 2009 Clauses the risk will be deemed to have attached where it would not otherwise attach under the reasoning in *Simon Israel* and s.44. With those qualifications, the proposition at para.13–20 as to the usual requirements for attachment of risk is of continued relevance.

The Prestrioka

13–21 and 13–22 The revised wording of cl.10.2 in the Institute Cargo Clauses 1/1/09 which is intended to mitigate the consequences of *The Prestrioka* decision is discussed under para.13–18 above. The new Clause does not completely resolve the problems which may result from the analysis in *The Prestrioka*, either in "phantom ship" cases or in other types of cases where the statutory provisions on attachment of risk might be applied.

There is an ongoing controversy[20] as to whether s.44 has the effect of retrospectively invalidating cover in respect of a loss occurring during transit in the country of export, where the vessel sails for a destination other than that specified in the policy. The editors remain of the view stated in the main work, at para.13–22 and footnote 96.

---

[18] Given that this amendment to the Change of Voyage Clause was intended to mitigate the perceived unfairness of an assured who becomes the victim of a fraudulent conspiracy to steal the cargo being left without insurance cover, it is difficult to see why coverage should be denied because of an employee's involvement in such a conspiracy. The approach which was taken under cl.10.2 is decidedly less generous than that taken in relation to the Unseaworthiness and Unfitness Exclusion Clause, cl.5 in the 2009 Clauses; see para.20–41 below.

[19] It is not clear from the reports whether the mistake which led to the cargo in *Simon Israel v Sedgwick*, above, being shipped on a voyage to the wrong part of Spain was made by an employee or agent of the consignor. If such a mistake were to be made by an employee, it is questionable whether either part of cl.10 would afford any protection to the assured.

[20] See Dunt and Melbourne, *op. cit.* para.6.110.

When cover can be maintained despite s.44 of the Act

The editors' suggestion that an amendment to the Change of Voyage Clause in the **13–23** Cargo Clauses extending the "held covered" concept might obviate the problem of the assured being deprived of cover under s.44 when the ship sails for another destination without his knowledge or concurrence has become academic. An entirely different technique has been adopted in the revised Institute Cargo Clauses (the 2009 Clauses). As noted under paras 13–17, 13–18 above, when the 2009 Clauses are used and the carrying vessel sails for another destination without the knowledge of the Assured or their employees, the risk will be deemed to have attached (in derogation from s.44).

Note 99: The reference here is of course to the 1982 Cargo Clauses. The 2009 Clauses, when used, do afford a significant measure of protection in "phantom ship" cases.

Craft risk before loading

Note 114: See now the Institute War Clauses (Cargo) (1/1/09). The terms of the **13–27** Transit Clause (cl.5) are materially unchanged.

Warehouse to warehouse clauses

Some important changes of substance have been introduced under the latest **13–37** version of the standard Transit Clause, cl.8 in the 2009 edition of the Institute Cargo Clauses,[21] but in most respects the scheme of the Clause has not been altered. The new wording is discussed under paras 13–39, 13–40 below.

Decisions on clauses covering land risks under cargo policies

Note 150: See also the Australian decision in *Verna Trading Pty Ltd v New India* **13–38** *Assurance Co Ltd*,[22] for another important example of a case where a deliberate decision to leave the goods in an area at the discharging port for the assured's commercial convenience was held to take the consignment outside the course of transit (in that case, the "ordinary course of transit" in the 1982 Institute Cargo Clauses).

Notes 153 to 155: It is submitted that the amendments to the scope of cover under the Transit Clause in the 2009 Cargo Clauses would not affect the assured's position on facts similar to those in the case discussed in the text (*Bayview Motors Ltd v Mitsui Marine & Fire Ins Co*).

---

[21] It has been suggested that in the light of the major revision to some aspects of the Transit Clause, the 2009 Clauses can be better described as affording cover from "shelf to unloading" rather than "warehouse to warehouse" cover; Dunt and Melbourne, *op. cit.* para.6.59.

[22] [1991] 1 V.R. 129; Earlier decisions in Australia which raised similar issues were followed, *Leaders Shoes (Austr) Pty Ltd v Liverpool & London Globe Ins Co Ltd* [1968] 1 N.S.W.L.R. 299; *Wiggins Teape (Austr) Pty Ltd v Baltica Ins Co Ltd* [1970] 2 N.S.W.L.R. 77.

The Transit Clause in the Institute Cargo Clauses

13–39 The wording of the Transit Clause (cl.8) has been revised in some important respects in the most recent edition of the Institute Cargo Clauses (the 2009 Clauses). The 1982 version of this Clause was quoted in this paragraph of the main work, followed by a summary of what the editors consider to be the scheme of the relevant provisions in the 1982 Clauses. For convenience a similar approach is employed in this Supplement. The text of the new cl.8, in the 2009 Clauses, is set out below, and this is followed by a revised summary in similar form. The objective of the Clause remains unaltered, and it has also still to be read in conjunction with other relevant clauses[23] (cll.9, 10 and 18) and against the background of the general principles embodied in ss.42–49 of the 1906 Act.

The Transit Clause in the Institute Cargo Clauses 1/1/09 reads as follows:

"**8.1** Subject to Clause 11 below, this insurance attaches from the time the subject-matter insured is first moved in the warehouse or at the place of storage (at the place named in the contract of insurance) for the purpose of the immediate loading into or onto the carrying vehicle or other conveyance for the commencement of transit,

continues during the ordinary course of transit
and terminates *either*

8.1.1 on completion of unloading from the carrying vehicle or other conveyance in or at the final warehouse of place of storage at the destination named in the contract of insurance,

8.1.2 on the completion of unloading from the carrying vehicle or other conveyance in or at any other warehouse or place of storage, whether prior to or at the destination named in the contract of insurance, which the Assured or their employees elect to use either for storage other than in the ordinary course of transit or for allocation or distribution, or

8.1.3 when the Assured or their employees elect to use any carrying vehicle or other conveyance or any container for storage other than in the ordinary course of transit or

8.1.4 on the expiry of 60 days after completion of discharge overside of the subject-matter insured from the oversea vessel at the final port of discharge, whichever shall first occur.

8.2 If, after discharge overside from the oversea vessel at the final port of discharge, but prior to termination of this insurance, the subject-matter insured is to be forwarded to a destination other than that to which it is insured, this insurance, whilst remaining subject to termination as provided in Clauses 8.1.1 to 8.1.4, shall not extend beyond the time the subject-matter insured is first moved for the purpose of the commencement of transit to such other destination.

8.3 This insurance shall remain in force (subject to termination as provided for in Clauses 8.1.1 to 8.1.4 above and to the provisions of Clause 9 below)

---

[23] For the full text of the 2009 Clauses, see the Appendix below.

during delay beyond the control of the Assured, any deviation, forced discharge, reshipment or transhipment and during any variation of the adventure arising from the exercise of a liberty granted to carriers under the contract of carriage."

The scheme of the relevant provisions in the 2009 Clauses can, it is submitted, be summarised in the form of the following propositions:

(1) The basic concept is that the cover is to continue from the time of attachment[24] under cl.8.1 for the period during which the "ordinary course of transit" is continuing[25] up until the occurrence of one of the events specified in cll.8.1.1, 8.1.2 and 8.1.3[26] or the expiry of 60 days after completion of discharge overside from the oversea vessel at the final port of discharge under cl.8.1.4, whichever first occurs, or until the subject-matter insured is first moved[27] for the purpose of the commencement of transit to a destination other than that which it is insured, under cl.8.2, where the cover has not already terminated under cl.8.1.1 to 8.1.4.

(2) Subject to cll.8.1.1 to 8.1.4, the cover is to remain in force automatically in the circumstances set out in cl.8.3, even though those circumstances may involve an interruption of the ordinary course of transit, or a deviation which might not be excused under the general law as enacted in s.49 of the 1906 Act. The protection afforded by cl.8.3 is limited by cll.8.1.1 to 8.1.4,[28] in particular, the long-stop provision of the 60 day limit now to be found at cl.8.1.4[29] still applies. Clause 8.3 does not apply in those circumstances where cl.9 is applicable.

(3) The assured is given some further protection against loss of cover by cl.9 and cl.10. Clause 9 deals with premature termination of the contract of carriage or transit in circumstances outside the assured's control. Clause

---

[24] Under the 2009 Clauses, cl.8.1, the insurance is made to attach from the time the subject-matter is first moved in the warehouse or place of storage "for the purpose of the immediate loading into or onto the carrying vehicle or other conveyance for the commencement of transit". Under the 1982 Clauses, the insurance is made to attach from the time the goods leave the warehouse or place of storage "for the commencement of the transit". This important change to the scope of the standard cover is discussed at para.13–40 below. It should be appreciated that while the first movement of the goods (under the 2009 Clauses) or their leaving the warehouse (under the 1982 Clauses) is a necessary condition for the attachment of risk, it will not always be sufficient; see the discussion at para.13–20 in the main work and above in this Supplement.

[25] The relationship between the words "continues during the ordinary course of transit" and other provisions in the Transit Clause has been clarified under the 2009 Clauses. See the discussion at para.13–40 below.

[26] Clause 8.1.3 in the 2009 Clauses is a new provision. See para.13–40 below.

[27] The equivalent provision in the 1982 Clauses referred simply to "the commencement of transit" to a destination other than that to which the goods were insured, without defining what was to count as the commencement of transit. The new wording of cl.8.2 introduces the "first moved" test which is both much clearer and is consistent with the new scheme of cl.8.1. See para.13–40 below.

[28] The relationship between cl.8.3 and the preceding sub-clauses has been clarified, but has not been altered, under the 2009 Clauses. There is an additional sub-clause (the new cl.8.1.3). For further discussion, see at para.13–40 below.

[29] Clause 8.1.3 in the numbering of the 1982 clauses.

10.1 applies where, after attachment of the insurance, the destination is changed by *the assured*. Continuation of cover under cl.9 or cl.10.1 is conditional on prompt notice being given,[30] and is subject to an additional premium if required.[31] The new sub-clause at cl.10.2 protects the assured where, without his knowledge or that of his employees, the vessel sails for another destination. This sub-clause prevents the assured from being deprived of cover in such circumstances by the application of s.44 in the 1906 Act and the reasoning in *The Prestrioka*[32]; see the discussion at paras 13–17 to 13–22 above. For obvious reasons, there is no requirement for notice (or for an additional premium) under cl.10.2 which was specifically designed to protect assureds against the perceived injustice of their being deprived of cover in "phantom ship" cases.

(4) The assured is given some protection against loss of cover where there is a departure from the ordinary course of transit which is within his control, in circumstances where "any deviation" takes place (cl.8.3) and in circumstances where, after attachment of the risk, the destination of the vessel is changed by the assured (cl.10.1).[33] There is no such protection in the case of any unreasonable delay which is within the assured's control;[34] neither cl.8.3 nor cl.9 will apply in such circumstances, and the delay may well be a breach of condition under cl.18[35].

Interpretation of the Transit Clause[36]

Clause 8.1 (attachment of the Insurance)

13–40 The point at which the risk is to attach under the Institute Cargo Clauses 1/1/09 is when the goods are "first moved in the warehouse or at the place of storage (at the place named in the contract of insurance) for the purpose of the immediate loading into or onto the carrying vehicle or other conveyance for the commencement of transit". This represents an important change from the scheme of earlier editions of the Cargo Clauses, where the insurance was made to attach "from the

---

[30] The requirement for prompt notice is reinforced by the "NOTE" at the foot of the 2009 Clauses (a similar "NOTE" appears at the foot of the 1982 Clauses).

[31] Clause 10.1 cannot be invoked, should a loss occur prior to agreement on any amended rates and terms, unless cover would have been available at a reasonable commercial market rate on reasonable market terms; see further at paras 14–93 *et seq* and 19–42 below.

[32] [2003] 2 Lloyd's Rep.326.

[33] Subject to prompt notice and agreement on rates and terms, and subject to the risk being insurable on reasonable market terms; see para.14–93 below.

[34] The scheme of the 2009 Clauses is the same, in this respect, as that of the 1982 Clauses.

[35] The interpretation of cl.18 (unamended in the 2009 Clauses) is discussed at para.19–35 below in the light of the decisions of the Australian Courts in *Verna Trading Pty Ltd v New India Assurance Co Ltd* [1991] V.R. 129 and *Wiggins Teape (Austr) Pty Ltd v Baltica Ins Co Ltd* [1970] 2 N.S.W.L.R. 77, cited in Dunt, *op. cit.* para.11.38, Dunt and Melbourne, *op cit*, para.6.123.

[36] The commentary below relates to the new 2009 Clauses, drawing attention where appropriate to the changes from the previous wording in the 1982 Clauses (discussed in this paragraph of the main work).

time the goods leave the warehouse or place of storage at the placed named therein for the commencement of the transit".

The new wording appears to provide a straightforward test, which should not give rise to difficulty of interpretation, although it may lead to some hard cases;[37] Indeed, it appears already to have been common for cover of similar scope to be afforded in the London market.[38] The first movement of the goods may well be said to represent a more logical starting point for a policy of goods in transit insurance than that of their leaving the warehouse, when their journey may already have started.[39]

It will be noted that cl.8.1 in the 2009 Clauses refers to "commencement of transit", whereas cl.8.1 in the 1982 Clauses refers to "commencement of the transit". This change in language does not appear to have any significant consequences; it must still be a necessary condition for the attachment of risk that the movement of the goods for the purpose of loading should be in anticipation of commencing the transit contemplated by the insurance.[40]

Although the starting-point has been changed under the 2009 Clauses, the proposition at para.13–40 in the main work that the risk will not attach if the goods do not proceed on the contemplated transit remains valid, save only that the risk will be deemed to have attached under cl.10.2 and s.44 of the Act will be disapplied if without the knowledge of the assured or their employees the ship sails for another destination.[41]

The proposition that the policy will not attach if the insured adventure is for carriage by a named vessel and the goods are never appropriated by a contract of carriage to that insured voyage but are shipped by some other vessel[42] also remains valid in the context of the 2009 Clauses.

Clause 8.1 ("continues during the ordinary course of transit")

The relationship between this provision in cl.8.1 and other provisions in the Transit Clause has been clarified under the 2009 Clauses. It is submitted at this point in the main work that these words in the 1982 Clauses ought to be construed as imposing a limit on the duration of cover, which is separate from the specified events of termination in later sub-clauses, but that a mere interruption to the ordinary course of transit under cl.8.1 should not be construed as resulting in the

---

[37] "Immediate" is to be read as meaning as quickly as is reasonably possible, without any unreasonable delay. Although the word "immediate" is used in relation to loading, it is submitted that cl.8.1 is to be read as contemplating also that loading will be for the immediate commencement of the transit. Hence, it may be the case (as one commentator has suggested) that goods loaded onto a carrying vehicle on a Friday afternoon for despatch from the warehouse on Monday morning would be uninsured (under the Transit Clause) over the weekend; Dunt, *op. cit.* para.11.22.

[38] See Dunt and Melbourne, *op. cit.*, para.6.62.

[39] In the absence of a precise definition, the term "transit" might well extend to operations of loading and unloading; see the commentary on cl.8.1 and cl.8.2 in the 1982 Clauses and fn.178, at para.13–40 in the main work.

[40] Clause 10.2 in the 2009 Clauses operates where the subject matter insured "commences the transit contemplated by this insurance (in accordance with Clause 8.1)".

[41] See the discussion at paras 13–17 to 13–22 above in this Supplement.

[42] This proposition was based on *George Kallis v Success Insurance* and was approved in *The Prestrioka* (both cited at para.13–40 in the main work). See also the discussion of the conditions for attachment of risk at para.13–20 in the main work and above in this Supplement.

termination of cover in the circumstances where it is provided that the insurance shall remain in force under cl.8.3, such as deviation.

The Transit Clause in the 2009 Clauses now makes it clear that "continues during the ordinary course of transit" is to be treated as a free-standing provision[43] which may result in the cessation of cover, if some discontinuity occurs before any of the terminating events at cll.8.1.1 to 8.1.4 or 8.2. At the same time, cl.8.3 has been amended so as to make it clear that there will be no loss of cover in the circumstances provided for in this sub-clause merely because those events also mean that the ordinary course of transit has ceased or been interrupted. Clause 8.3 is now expressed to be "subject to termination as provided for in Clauses 8.1.1 to 8.1.4 above. . .", where previously cl.8.3 in the 1982 Clauses was "subject to termination as provided for above. . . .".

There has been one judicial decision on the interpretation of this part of the Transit Clause in the 1982 Clauses: *Verna Trading Pty Ltd v New India Assurance Co Ltd*,[44] a decision of the Supreme Court of Victoria (Appellate Division). The insured cargo was left in storage in the stevedores' bond area at Melbourne for over a month following discharge, as a matter of deliberate decision for the insured's commercial convenience. The claim failed (amongst other reasons)[45] on the ground that the storage was not in the "ordinary course of transit". The Court followed and applied the "reasonable furtherance" test proposed by Ackner J. In *SCA v Gibson*.[46] As is made clear by the judgment of Ormiston J. this was not a case where the election to store the goods fell within any of the terminating events in cl.8.1.1 or 8.1.2; the stevedores' area was "a true transit area", and it was only the deliberate decision to store the cargo there as a matter of convenience which took the goods out of the ordinary course of transit.[47]

The decision in *Verna Trading* also serves to highlight the potential importance of the burden of proof, in the context of the Transit Clause. The insured had the burden of proving that the loss had occurred while the ordinary course of transit was continuing, which he was unable to discharge.[48]

---

[43] The layout of the Transit Clause has been altered, so that this provision is no longer embedded in the same paragraph at cl.8.1 but appears in a separate line at the end of the sub-clause. These words "impose a self-standing, over-arching termination provision which applies in addition to the most common examples of circumstances which trigger termination, as set out in clause 8.1.1 to 8.1.4": Dunt & Melbourne, *op. cit.* para.6.72.

[44] [1991] I.V.R. 129.

[45] The claim also failed on the ground that the insured was in breach of the Reasonable Despatch Clause at cl.18 in the 1982 Clauses (Kaye and McGarvie JJ.) or by reason of s.54 in the Marine Insurance Act 1909 (Commonwealth), which is in identical terms to those of s.48 in the 1906 Act (Ormiston J.). These aspects of the decision are discussed at paras 14–53 and 19–35 below.

[46] [1974] 2 Lloyd's Rep. 533, cited above in the main work. The judgments in *Verna Trading*, particularly that of Ormiston J., contain a detailed analysis of the Transit Clause and review of the limited number of cases in point.

[47] *Safadi v Western Assurance*, which is cited above in the main work, is an earlier illustration of the same point, albeit in the context of different language in the policy. See also *Wiggins Teape (Austr) Pty Ltd v Baltica Ins Co Ltd* [1970] 2 N.S.W.R. 77; *Fedsure Gen Ins v Carefree Investments (Pty) Ltd* [2001] 2 A.S.C.A. 88 (Sup Ct CA South Africa).

[48] Not surprisingly, since the goods were containerised. Both Kaye and Ormiston JJ. also considered that the assured had the burden of proof on the issue of unreasonable delay under cl.18 in the Cargo Clauses or s.54 of the Australian Act. That seems more questionable, from an English law perspective; cf *Bond Air Services Ltd v Hill* [1955] 2 Q.B. 417; para.19–14 in the main work.

Clauses 8.1.1 to 8.1.3[49]

These sub-clauses in the 1982 version of the Transit Clause have been expanded by the addition of a further sub-clause at 8.1.3 in the 2009 Cargo Clauses. The basic scheme and structure of these provisions in the 2009 Clauses and their relationship with other parts of the Transit Clause and other provisions in the Institute Cargo Clauses are unchanged. With the necessary modifications to take account of the amendment adding the new cl.8.1.3, this paragraph in the main work which was addressed to the 1982 Clauses applies equally to the 2009 Clauses.

Clause 8.1.1. ("delivery to the Consignees' or other final warehouse or place of storage")

The wording of this sub-clause in the 1982 Clauses has been amended under the 2009 Clauses, where cl.8.1.1 now provides for termination "on completion of unloading from the carrying vehicle or other conveyance in or at the final warehouse or place of storage at the destination named in the contract of insurance". The substitution of "the completion of unloading" for "delivery", under the new wording, may make a material difference in some cases. The construction of this expression does not appear likely to cause difficulty in its practical application. The process of unloading will be complete when the goods are landed. The omission of any reference to the Consignees' final warehouse or place of storage does not appear to be a change of any real substance.

The key feature of this sub-clause, both under the 1982 Clauses and the new 2009 Clauses, is that the delivery or completion of unloading only operates as a terminating event at the "final" warehouse or place of storage at the named destination. It is the meaning of this concept of finality, in the context of an insurance under the Institute Cargo Clauses, which has occasioned most difficulty. The matter is discussed at this point in the main work at para.16–40, which is of continuing relevance in the context of the new Clauses.[50]

Clause 8.1.2.1 ("storage other than in the ordinary course of transit")

This heading refers to the 1982 Clauses, where cl.8.1.2 was in two parts, which provided for termination of the cover on delivery to any other[51] warehouse or place of storage, whether prior to or at the stipulated destination, which the assured elect to use either for storage other than in the ordinary course of transit (8.1.2.1) or for allocation of distribution (8.1.2.2). Under the 2009 Clauses, these two limbs of the former 8.1.2 have been combined into a single sub-clause 8.1.2

---

[49] This heading in the main work at para.13–40 refers to the numbered sub-clauses in the 1982 Cargo Clauses. There is now an additional sub-clause at cl.8.1.3 in the 2009 Clauses, under which the insurance is to terminate "where the Assured or their employees elect to use any carrying vehicle or other conveyance or any container for storage other than in the ordinary course of transit" and the longstop provision whereby the insurance terminates on the expiry of 60 days after the completion of discharge, previously at cl.8.1.3, now appears at cl.8.1.4.

[50] See also, Dunt, *op. cit.*, paras 11–43 to 11–47.

[51] Meaning other than the Consignees' or other final warehouse or place of storage at the destination (to which cl.8.1.1 referred).

which is in materially the same terms, except that it refers to the election of the Assured or their employees and that the terminating event under the 2009 Clauses is now the "completion of unloading from the carrying vehicle or conveyance" in or at the relevant warehouse or place of storage, rather than "delivery". At the same time, a new sub-clause 8.1.3 has been added under the 2009 Clauses, which provides for termination "when the Assured or their employees elect to use any carrying vehicle or other conveyance or any container for storage other than in the ordinary course of transit". The evident purpose of this new sub-clause is to prevent assureds from taking advantage of the revised wording in 8.1.1 and 8.1.2 which refers to "completion of unloading".

The common feature of the two limbs in cl.8.1.2 and of the new cl.8.1.3 is that these all refer to an election made by the Assured or their employees.[52] When such an election is implemented, this will usually[53] mean that the ordinary course of transit is interrupted. Hence, as was noted at this point in the main work (at p.462), it is difficult at first sight to see what additional purpose is served by specifying these events as terminating events, when the general words "continues during the ordinary course of transit" in cl.8.1 would usually achieve the same result. The reason why the distinction is important is to be found in the context of cl.8.3, as is noted at this point in the main work. It is now specified expressly that cl.8.3 is subject to 8.1.1 to 8.1.4, in the 2009 Clauses, making it clear beyond argument that cl.8.3 has precedence over a mere interruption in the ordinary course of transit (cl.8.1) which does not bring any of the terminating provisions in 8.1.1 to 8.1.4 into play.

The scheme of the Transit Clause remains essentially unchanged under the 2009 clauses, so far as the provisions relating to termination are concerned. Typical terminating events are specified in 8.1.1 to 8.1.3, with a long-stop provision in 8.1.4 for termination 60 days after completion of discharge. If any of those provisions apply, whichever of them first occurs will have the effect of terminating the cover taking precedence over cl.8.3. A mere discontinuity in the ordinary course of transit which does not also fall within 8.1.2 or 8.1.3 may bring the cover to an end (under cl.8.1), but that provision will not prevail where the assured is able to rely on cl.8.3.

There has been one decision in Australia on the interpretation of an earlier version of the "allocation or distribution" sub-clause[54].

Clause 8.2 ("transit to such other destination")

Under the 1982 Clauses, the terminating event under this sub-clause was the "commencement of transit" to a destination to which the goods were to be

---

[52] It is not clear what, if any, practical effect should be given to the addition of the words "or their employees", which did not appear in the previous version of the Transit Clause.

[53] An election for purposes of "allocation or distribution" might not take the goods out of the ordinary course of transit. Implementation of an election within the first limb of 8.1.2 or within the new 8.1.3 necessarily involves or gives rise to an interruption of the ordinary course of transit.

[54] *Leaders Shoes (Austr) Pty Ltd v Liverpool & London & Globe Ins Co Ltd* [1968] 1 N.S.W.R. 279; see also the subsequent decisions in Australia where the assured's election to store the goods for his commercial convenience took them out of the ordinary course of transit, *Wiggins Teape (Austr) Pty Ltd v Baltica Ins Co Ltd* [1970] 2 N.S.W.R. 77; *Verna Trading Pty Ltd v New India Ass Co Ltd* [1991] 1 V.R. 129.

forwarded other than that to which they were insured under the policy. In cl.8.2 of the 2009 Clauses, the trigger event is when the goods are "first moved" for the commencement of such transit. This change in wording removes the uncertainties to which the previous version appeared to give rise (noted at this point in the main work, (at p.463), and is consistent with the approach now taken to the attachment of risk in cl.8.1 of the 2009 Clauses.

Clause 8.3 (delay, deviation etc)

The function of this important provision in the overall scheme of the Institute Cargo Clauses as regards the duration of cover has not been altered under the 2009 Clauses. As already noted, the revised cl.8.3 is expressed as having effect subject to termination as provided in cll.8.1.1 to 8.1.4, whereas the equivalent provision in the 1982 version of the Transit Clause (discussed at this point in the main work) was "subject to termination as provided for above." This revision makes it clear that cl.8.3 is to prevail where there is an interruption in the ordinary course of transit (within the general words in cl.8.1) which does not also fall within any of cll.8.1.1 to 8.1.4, but this does not amount to a change of substance since (it is submitted) cl.8.3 in the 1982 Clauses was in any event to be construed in the same manner.

In other respects, the wording of cl.8.3 is unchanged in the 2009 Clauses, and the discussion at pp. [463–464] in the main work remains apposite.

Duration of risk under the Institute War Clauses

The wording of the Transit Clause (cl.5) in the 2009 Clauses does not differ **13–41** materially from the wording in the 1982 Clauses which is discussed at this point in the main work. The terms of the relevant clause are reproduced in the Appendix below.

Insurable interest and duration of risk

Note 190: The wording of the Insurable Interest Clause (cl.11) is unchanged, under **13–42** the Institute Cargo Clauses 1/10/09. The present form of the Clause, first introduced in the 1982 Cargo Clauses, appears to have been purposely drafted with a view to affording narrower cover than was provided by the "lost or not lost clause" under the reasoning in *Sutherland v Pratt*; see Dunt, *op. cit.* paras 4.18 to 4.21.

CHAPTER 14

CHANGE OF VOYAGE, DEVIATION AND DELAY

Insuring "from" and "at and from" the terminus a quo

Note 14: The Transit Clause has been revised, under the Institute Cargo Clauses **14–05** 1/1/09. The new wording is discussed at paras 13–39 and 13–40 above in this Supplement.

Attachment of risk, change of voyage and deviation

Note 18: Section 44 of the Act is disapplied under cl.10.2 of the 2009 Cargo **14–06** Clauses in cases where the ship sails for another destination, without the knowledge of the Assured or their employees. This provision, which was designed to protect cargo assureds in "phantom ship" cases, is discussed at paras 13–17 *et seq* above in this Supplement.

    The conceptual problems discussed at this point in the main work are now of **14–09 to** less practical importance, following the introduction and widespread adoption of **14–12** the revised Institute Cargo Clauses (the 2009 Clauses). The new wording at cl.10.2 in the 2009 Clauses is discussed at paras 13–17 *et seq* above. This amendment was designed to protect cargo assureds against the adverse consequences of *The Prestrioka* decision in "phantom ship" cases, but has not made the controversies discussed in these paragraphs of the main work academic. The editors remain of the view that the fact of sailing to a destination other than that specified in the policy has the result that the risk may disattach retrospectively under s.44 of Act, in the absence of an effective Change of Voyage Clause. Where cl.10.2 in the 2009 Clauses can be invoked, the risk will be deemed to have attached, and no question of retrospective loss of cover can arise.

Deviation

Note 60: See now the Institute Cargo Clauses 1/1/09, cl.9 and cl.10.1 below. The **14–26** wording of the Change of Voyage Clause (cl.10) has been revised in the 2009 Cargo Clauses; see paras 13–17 *et seq* above for discussion of cl.10.2 and paras 14–93 *et seq* below for discussion of cl.10.1 The wording of the Transit Clause (cl.8) in the 2009 Clauses does not differ materially from that in cl.8 of the 1982 Clauses, so far as preserving the cover in the event of any deviation is concerned; see paras 13–39 and 13–40 above.

Delay

It will be noted that the two Sections in the 1906 Act which deal with delay (ss.42 **14–53** and 48) both refer to "the adventure" or "the adventure insured". The equivalent section to s.48 has been construed in one case in Australia[1] as applying only to the sea voyage and as having no application to periods of land transit under a policy affording warehouse to warehouse cover. It is submitted, however, that the dissenting judgment of Ormiston J. on that question is more consonant with English law,[2] and that an unreasonable delay on the part of the assured in prosecuting the land transit leg before shipment or after discharge under a cargo policy on warehouse to warehouse terms would in an appropriate case result in underwriters being discharged from liability under s.48 of the Act.[3]

14–59   See now cl.8 in the Institute Cargo Clauses 1/1/09. There is no material difference between the 1982 Clauses and the 2009 Clauses, so far as the maintenance of cover in the event of delay is concerned, and as regards the distinction made under these Clauses between deviation and delay. Under both the 1982 Clauses and the 2009 Clauses, cover will be preserved in the event of a delay which is beyond the control of the assured (even if that delay is such as to take the goods outside the "ordinary course of transit"). In the event of a delay which is within the assured's control, the saving provisions in the relevant part of the Transit Clause (cl.8.3) do not apply; in that situation, it is likely that the goods will cease to be covered, on the ground of discontinuance of the "ordinary course of transit"[4] and/or pursuant to s.48 of the 1906 Act[5] or (arguably) cl.18 in the Cargo Clauses.

Deviation or delay authorised by a special term

14–64   *Note 130*: See now cl.8.3 in the 2009 Clauses discussed at para.13–40 above. There is no material difference between the 1982 Clauses and the 2009 Clauses, so far as the effects of deviation and of delay in prosecuting the adventure are concerned.

---

[1] *Verna Trading Pty Ltd v New India Assurance Co Ltd* [1991] V.R. 129. The claim failed both on the ground that the insured goods were no longer in "the ordinary course of transit" when they were left in storage after discharge at Melbourne for the assured's commercial convenience, and on the ground that this was an unreasonable delay. The "ordinary course of transit" point is discussed at para.13–40 above. Conflicting views were expressed by the Appellate Division in the Supreme Court of Victoria on the question of delay. The majority view, set out in the judgment of Kaye J., was that s.54 of the Marine Insurance Act 1909 (Commonwealth) would not apply to delay in prosecuting a transit by land, and that cl.18 in the Institute Cargo Clauses was designed to cover such delays. Ormiston J. dissented on this point, holding that the land transits under a warehouse to warehouse policy are part of "the adventure" and that s.54 did apply to such transits. Having decided that the claim stood to be defeated on the ground that the cargo was no longer covered under the Transit Clause (the "ordinary course of transit" point) and on the ground of unreasonable delay under s.54 (the equivalent of s.48 in the 1906 Act) Ormiston J. declined to express a concluded view on "the difficult question as to the operation and effect of Clause 18 of the Institute Cargo Clauses." That question is further discussed at para.19–35 below.
[2] The wording of s.48 ("the adventure insured") would not seem to be open to a construction that is confined to the sea voyage, notwithstanding that it is one of a group of sections in the Act under the general heading of "The Voyage", that s.48 itself is headed by the words "Delay in voyage" and that the Excuses in s.49 apply to delay in prosecuting the voyage. Several of the reported cases cited at paras 14–53 *et seq* in the main work related to delays in port.
[3] The point will almost always be academic, because an unreasonable delay which is within the control of the Assured will usually take the goods outside the "ordinary course of transit" so that they will no longer be covered under the Transit Clause (cl.8) in the Institute Cargo Clauses, discussed above at paras 13–39 and 13.40 in the main work and in this Supplement.
[4] As in the *Verna Trading* case (above); see also paras 13–39 and 13–40 above.
[5] See at para.14–53, in the main work and above.

Causes short of actual force or constraint which justify deviation

Note 145: It is submitted that the view expressed in Halsbury's *Laws of England* **14–73** is correct. As a result of the recent upsurge in the number of piracy incidents in the Gulf of Aden and the Indian Ocean, there may well be cases of deviation or delay taking place for the reasonable purpose of avoiding seizure which would not fall precisely within the ambit of the "excuses" in s.49 of the 1906 Act, but it is unlikely that the Courts would construe the provisions of s.49 restrictively, should the point ever arise for decision, so as to deprive the assured of continuing insurance cover.

The Transit Clause

Clause 8.3 in the Institute Cargo Clauses 1/1/09 is in materially the same terms **14–92** as the clause discussed in the text (cl.8.3 in the 1982 Clauses). See para.13–40 above where the revisions to the Transit Clause under the 2009 Clauses are discussed.

"Held Covered" Clauses

The revised Institute Cargo Clauses 1/1/09 continue the practice from the 1982 **14–93** version of these Clauses whereby the only events to which provisions of the kind **and** commonly known (at least to lawyers) as "held covered" clauses apply are **14–94** Change of Voyage (cl.10) and Termination of the Contract of Carriage (cl.9). However, the "held covered" formula is no longer used in these clauses. Instead, the same effect is achieved without resort to technical jargon, with a view to making the position more readily understandable to potential assureds.[6]

As already explained at paras 13–17 *et seq* above, the Change of Voyage Clause (cl.10) in the 2009 Clauses is in two parts. Clause 10.2, which is discussed in those earlier sections (paras 13–17 *et seq*) deals with the position where the vessel sails for another destination without the knowledge of the Assured and their employees. This sub-clause addressed the perceived injustice of assureds being deprived of cover by virtue of s.44 of the 1906 Act in "phantom ship" cases. Under cl.10.2, the risk is to be deemed to have attached, and no question of the assured being required to give notice or of an additional premium being required will arise. Clause 10.2 is not a "held covered" clause.

The first part of the revised Change of Voyage Clause (cl.10.1 in the 2009 Clauses) deals with the position where the destination is changed "by the Assured." The previous version of the Clause (cl.10 in the 1982 Clauses) was of similar scope. The new wording differs in that, instead of using the hallowed "held covered" formula, cl.10.1 goes on to stipulate[7]:

---

[6] See *Dunt*, Marine Cargo Insurance, para.12–17. A similar drafting decision had already been made in relation to the Institute Classification Clause (2001); see *ibid* paras 8.77 to 8.79. See also cl.11 in the International Hull Clauses where, similarly, the traditional "held covered" formula has been abandoned.

[7] The passages quoted here appear in italics in the printed Clauses.

". . . this must be notified promptly to Insurers for rates and terms to be agreed. Should a loss occur prior to such agreement being obtained cover may be provided but only if cover would have been available at a reasonable commercial market rate on reasonable market terms."[8]

A slightly different formula[9] is used in the Termination of Contract of Carriage Clause (cl.9) in the 2009 Clauses. Instead of the "held covered" formula being used, the revised cl.9 now provides for termination of the insurance where owing to circumstances beyond the control of the Assured, either the contract of carriage is terminated at a port or place other than the named destination or the transit is otherwise terminated before unloading as provided for in cl.8 (The Transit Clause)[10]

"unless prompt notice is given to the Insurers and continuation of cover is requested when this insurance shall remain in force, subject to an additional premium if required by the Insurers."

The Clause then goes on to stipulate the duration of any such extended cover; the full text will be found in the Appendix to this Supplement, and need not be quoted here.

Both these Clauses are to be read in conjunction with the "NOTE" at the foot of the 2009 Clauses,[11] which is in the following terms:

"Where a continuation of cover is requested under Clause 9, or a change of destination is notified under Clause 10, there is an obligation to give prompt notice to the Insurers and the right to such cover is dependent on compliance with this obligation."

It is submitted that these new provisions are to be construed in the same manner as clauses using the traditional "held covered" formula. The usual incidents of such clauses are discussed at this point and at Chapter 19 (Express Warranties) in the main work. The proviso to cl.10.1, stipulating for cover to be provided only where this would have been available at a reasonable commercial market rate on reasonable market terms spells out the effect of earlier cases recognising this limitation on the right to be "held covered" under such clauses, see for example, *Liberian Insurance Agency Inc v Mosse.*[12]

---

[8] The proviso spells out the implied limitation on the efficacy of "held covered" clauses which was recognised in *Liberian Insurance Agency v Mosse*, below. Although cl.10.1 stipulates that cover "may" be provided, the "NOTE" appended the 2009 clauses refers to the Assured having the "right" to such cover. Clause 10.1 and the "NOTE" should be read together.

[9] As can be seen, cl.9 only envisages an additional premium, unlike cl.10.1 which contemplates that amended rates and terms may be required. There is also no express limitation under cl.9, limiting its scope to where the extended cover can be insured at a reasonable market rate; that limitation ought probably still to be implied.

[10] See paras 13–39, 13–40 above, where the Transit Clause is analysed. Clause 9 takes precedence over the saving provisions at cl.8.3, which are made "subject to . . . the provisions of Clause 9 below."

[11] A similar "NOTE" appeared at the foot of previous editions of the Institute Cargo Clauses. It was stated in *Liberian Insurance Agency v Mosse* [1977] 2 Lloyd's Rep. 560, at 566, that the similar "NOTE" in the 1963 Clauses accurately stated the law, whether or not it was strictly contractual.

[12] [1977] 2 Lloyd's Rep. 560 at 567–568, and see para.19–44 in the main work.

Note 204: The revised wording of the Change of Voyage Clause (cl.10.1) in **14–98** the Institute Cargo Clauses 1/1/09 makes it clear that the assured can only invoke the right to be held covered in circumstances where cover for the voyage to the changed destination would have been available at a reasonable commercial rate and on reasonable market terms thereby giving express recognition to the implied limitation on the efficacy of "held covered" clauses established by the authorities cited. See the discussion under paras 14–93 and 14–94 above.

CHAPTER 15

PRE-CONTRACTUAL DUTY OF UTMOST GOOD FAITH:
GENERAL PRINCIPLES

The proposals for reform

The English and Scottish Law Commissions published their much anticipated **15–07** proposals for reform on December 15, 2009, in the form of the Consumer Insurance (Disclosure and Misrepresentations) Bill.[1] Commercial insurance is to be dealt with in a separate bill, which is expected to be published in the latter part of 2010. The 2009 Bill applies only to individuals, although it may at some later point be extended to "micro-businesses" (as yet undefined). The main effect of the Bill, if enacted, will be to abolish the duty of disclosure, and to replace it with a duty to take reasonable care to avoid misrepresentation. An assured who without fault makes a false statement will be entitled to enforce the policy. By contrast, if the assured's misrepresentation is deliberate or reckless, the insurers, will—as at present—be entitled to avoid the policy and to retain the premium. Where the misrepresentation is negligent, the insurers will be permitted to avoid the policy but only if they can show that, but for the misrepresentation, they would not have entered into it on any terms. It will not be open to insurers (if the Bill is enacted) to convert all statements into warranties by means of a "basis of the contract" clause, although specific warranties may be created. Accordingly, it will be necessary to apply the rules on misrepresentation to all statements other than those which are specifically warranted.

Relevance of the origin of utmost good faith

The reference to CPR r.6.20 should now be to CPR PD 6B.   **15–25**

Overlap between misrepresentation and non-disclosure

Note 108: The relevant holding at first instance in *Limit No.2 Ltd v Axa Versicherung* **15–53** *AG* was reversed on appeal[2]; the case no longer illustrates the point made in the text and in this footnote. In most cases, it is of little or no significance whether there has been a non-disclosure or a misrepresentation but in some circumstances the distinction will matter; see e.g. *Synergy Health (UK) Ltd v CGU Insurance Plc* [2010] EWHC (Comm) 2583 at paras 153, 154. This was again a case involving a renewal where the insurers sought to avoid the policy on both grounds.

---

[1] Law Commission Report No.319.
[2] [2009] Lloyd's Rep. IR 396.

The burden of proof and discharge of the burden of proof with regard to inducement

15–75 For further examples of cases where the insurers' failure to call evidence from available witnesses to prove inducement was fatal to an avoidance defence see *Laker Vent Engineering Ltd v Templeton Insurance Ltd*[3] and *Lewis v Norwich Union Healthcare Ltd.*[4]

15–80 The proposition that there will be few cases in which any "presumption" will be of relevance is borne out by the most recent decisions on inducement. The "presumption" did not avail the insurers in *Laker Vent Engineering* (above), or in *Lewis v Norwich Union Healthcare* (above).

Although it has been said that the test of inducement is not a heavy one,[5] the evidence of the underwriters as to whether they were induced is likely to be subjected to close scrutiny in doubtful cases, bearing in mind that such evidence is necessarily hypothetical, and that it is very easy for an underwriter to convince himself after the event that he would have declined a risk or imposed special terms.[6]

Materiality a question of fact

15–89 Although it is now the general practice to call expert evidence on the question of influence on the prudent underwriter (materiality), as well as to call the actual underwriter on the question of inducement, expert evidence on materiality is not, in principle, essential in all cases. In *A.C. Ward & Son Ltd v Catlin (Five) Ltd (No.2)*,[7] where expert evidence was in fact called on behalf of the defendant underwriters, and was accepted, Flaux J. observed[8] that even without the assistance of such evidence he would still have concluded that the matters misrepresented were material. This was one of those cases where (in the opinion of Flaux J.) the Court can and should adopt "the robust approach" taken by Scrutton L.J. in *Glicksman v Lancashire and General Assurance Co.*[9] While *Ward v Catlin (No.2)*, above shows

---

[3] [2009] Lloyd's Rep. IR 704.
[4] [2010] Lloyd's Rep. IR 198.
[5] *WISE (Underwriting) Agency Ltd v Grupo Nacional Provincial SA* [2004] 2 Lloyd's Rep. 483, per Rix L.J. at para.99.
[6] See *Synergy Health (UK) Ltd v CGU Insurance Plc* [2010] EWHC 2583 (Comm) at para.186; *North Star Shipping Ltd v Sphere Drake Insurance Plc* [2005] Lloyd's Rep. 76, para.254.
[7] [2009] EWHC 3122 (Comm). See also *Synergy Health (UK) Ltd v CGU Insurance Plc* [2010] EWHC 2583 (Comm), where Flaux J. again held that materiality was a matter for the Court and could, in appropriate cases, be determined without expert evidence.
[8] *Ibid*, at para.218.
[9] [1925] 2 K.B. 593, 609. The relevant passage is quoted in *Ward v Catlin*, above, at para.218. Referring to the argument that you cannot find that a fact was material unless somebody gave evidence of the materiality, Scrutton L.J. said "That is, in my view, and I agree with Mr Justice Roche [the trial Judge], entirely contrary to the whole course of insurance litigation. It is so far contrary that it is frequently argued that you are not entitled to call other people to say what they think is material. That is a matter for the Court on the nature of the facts. I entirely agree with Mr Justice Roche that the nature of the facts may be such that you do not need anyone to come and say: 'This is material'." The practice nowadays is of course very different from that in 1925, and it could no longer be suggested that a party was not entitled to call evidence on materiality, indeed the usual expectation would be that he would and should do so, but the proposition that the nature of the case may be such that evidence of materiality is unnecessary is plainly correct in principle.

that expert evidence on materiality may not always be essential, recent cases on inducement continue to bear out the statement in this paragraph that it would be an unwise insurer who relied on a presumption of inducement where the actual underwriter was available and willing to give evidence.[10]

Time at which the s.18 and s.20 duty attaches

Failure to correct a representation made during the placing of a previous years's **15–114** cover or made during the currency of an existing cover may amount to a misrepresentation or material non-disclosure at the time when the policy comes to be renewed.[11] The proposition in the text of the main work, that a representation to have any effect upon the policy must have been made "during the negotiations for the contract", based on the wording of s.20(1) in the Act, is to be understood in that light; see the discussion at paras 15-137 and 138 in the main work and below ("Renewals"). In *Synergy Health (UK) Ltd v CGU Insurance Plc* (above) by not correcting a misrepresentation made some three months prior to negotiations for renewal of an existing policy, the insured was held to have impliedly repeated that misrepresentation at the time of renewal.

Variations to the original cover

The reasoning of Mr Hirst QC in *Limit No.2 Ltd v Axa Versicherung AG* with **15–134** regard to the endorsement to the 1996 treaty was upheld on appeal[12]; his decision with regard to the 1998 renewal was reversed (see below).

Renewals

The decision of the Deputy Judge with regard to the 1998 renewal of the treaty in **15–138** *Limit No.2 Ltd v Axa Versicherung AG*[13] was reversed on appeal.[14] The Deputy Judge's characterisation of the syndicates' representation in the previous year as having been a representation of the reassured's "policy" or "practice" was held by the Court of Appeal to be inaccurate. This had been a representation of intention. The relevant question was therefore whether the syndicates' representation of their intention was a continuing one, and the Court of Appeal held that it was not. It could not be supposed that a statement of intention relating to deductibles was to be taken as still operative after a lapse of 19 months. Whatever the Syndicates' intention as to deductibles was in 1996 had become irrelevant in 1998 and no statement as to the Syndicates' 1998 intention was ever made. *The Moonacre*[15] and *Hill v Citadel*,[16] on which the Deputy Judge had relied, were distinguishable.

---

[10] See *Laker Vent Engineering Ltd v Templeton Ins Ltd* above; *Lewis v Norwich Union Healthcare Ltd*, above.

[11] See *Synergy Health (UK) Ltd v CGU Ins Plc* [2010] EWHC 2583 (Comm) at paras 159-163; *Glencore Intl AG v Alpina Ins Co Ltd* [2004] 1 Lloyd's Rep. 111, at 131–2.

[12] [2009] Lloyd's Rep. IR 396, para.20.

[13] [2008] Lloyd's Rep. IR 330. The Deputy Judge's decision with regard to the earlier treaty years was upheld.

[14] [2009] Lloyd's Rep. IR 396.

[15] [1992] 2 Lloyd's Rep. 501, discussed at para.15–137 in the main work.

[16] [1995] L.R.L.R. 218; see para.15–137 in the main work.

The decision of the Court of Appeal in *Limit No.2 v Axa* (above) turned on the nature of the representation made by the Syndicates having been one of intention rather than of fact. In *Synergy Health (UK) Ltd v CGU Insurance Plc*,[17] a similar issue arose as to the nature of a representation, made some months prior to renewal of an existing policy and not as part of any negotiations. The insured had requested that an improved intruder alarm system would be installed at one of the insured premises by the end of December 2005, but this representation was only relayed to the insurers on December 28. In those circumstances, Flaux J. held that it was properly to be regarded as a respresentation of fact, not intention, and that when it was not corrected on renewal there was an implied representation that the improvement had been implemented. Had he considered the representation to be one of intention, Flaux J. would have held that it had no effect at renewal.

---

[17] [2010] EWHC 2583 (Comm); see also *Glencore International AG v Alpina Ins Co* Ltd [2004] 1 Lloyd's Rep. 111 at 131–2.

CHAPTER 16

NON-DISCLOSURE

Proposals for reform

The English and Scottish Law Commissions have put forward wide-ranging **16–01A**
proposals for reform in this branch of the law, which are at present confined to
consumer insurance and will therefore have relatively little effect in the sphere of
marine insurance. Under the proposals contained in the draft Consumer Insurance
(Disclosure and Misrepresentations) Bill, published in December 2009, the duty
of disclosure will be abolished where the insured is an individual consumer. A
draft Bill dealing with commercial insurance is expected to follow in the near
future. See para.15–07 above in this Supplement.

Every material circumstance known to the assured

Note 13: The House of Lords by a 3:2 majority affirmed the decision of the Court **16–07**
of Appeal in *Stone & Rolls v Moore Stephens* [2009] UKHL 39.

Partnerships

Note 16: This decision was reversed in part on appeal, but on other grounds: *HLB* **16–10**
Kidsons v Lloyd's Underwriters [2009] Lloyd's Rep. IR 178.
   Note 16: This decision was reversed in part on appeal, but on other grounds: **16–19**
HLB Kidsons v Lloyd's Underwriters [2009] Lloyd's Rep. IR 178.

Multiple assureds

Note 89: The decision in *Kidsons* was in part reversed by the Court of Appeal, **16–48**
[2009] Lloyd's Rep. IR 178, without reference to this point. The House of Lords
by a 3:2 majority upheld the decision of the Court of Appeal in *Stone & Rolls v
Moore Stephens* [2009] UKHL 39, but the majority judgments cast no light on
the correctness or otherwise of *Arab Bank v Zurich Insurance* [1999] 1 Lloyd's
Rep. 262 on the imputation issue.

The fraud exception: the Hampshire Land principle

Note 141: On appeal, in *Stone & Rolls v Moore Stephens* [2009] UKHL 39, the **16–67**
House of Lords inconclusively discussed the nature of the *Hampshire Land* principle. The view of Lord Brown (and also, seemingly, Lord Phillips) was that *Re
Hampshire Land* applied only to attribution of knowledge from agent to principal,
and operated to allow the principal to assert that he was unaware of acts of fraud
committed by the agent. Lord Walker, for the majority, and Lords Scott and
Mance (both dissenting in the outcome) preferred a wider view of *Re Hampshire*

Land, holding that it prevented the fraudulent acts of the agent being imputed to the principal. It is the view of the editors that *Re Hampshire Land* is a limited exception which is confined to knowledge, and has nothing to do with acts.

16–69   The Third Parties (Rights against Insurers) Act 1930 is to be replaced, from a date to be announced, by the Third Parties (Rights against Insurers) Act 2010. The point made in the text is unaffected by the new Act.

16–70   The House of Lords in *Stone & Rolls v Moore Stephens*[1] by a 3:2 majority upheld the decision of the Court of Appeal, although the reasoning was quite different. The issue in this case was whether the fraudulent acts of the company's controller were to be imputed to the company itself so as to preclude an action by the company against third parties on *ex turpi causa* principles. The majority, dismissing the action, did not need to decide whether Rix J. had been right to express the view in *Arab Bank v Zurich Insurance* that fraud by the assured's agent which was targeted against the insurers, with the assured being merely a "secondary victim", was enough to attract the principle in *Re Hampshire Land* that the knowledge of an agent is not attributed to the principal. In *Stone & Rolls* the question was not whether information of the agent's fraud was attributed from the agent to the principal, but whether the agent's fraudulent conduct was attributed to the principal. Lord Brown (and, apparently, Lord Phillips) was of the view that *Re Hampshire Land* had no application to conduct at all, so that the point did not arise. That had been the approach of Rimer L.J. in the Court of Appeal, when he expressed surprise that *Re Hampshire Land* had been relied upon at all. Lord Walker, the third member of the majority, held that *Re Hampshire Land* did apply to conduct as well as to knowledge, but that on the facts the fraudulent agent was the alter ego of the company and that *Re Hampshire Land* did not extend to "one-man" companies. On either view, the decision in *Arab Bank* did not fall to be considered. The minority, Lords Scott and Mance, by contrast, were both of the view that *Re Hampshire Land* applied to conduct, so that it was relevant to the present case and they further held that *Arab Bank* was correctly decided and that an agent's fraud directed against a third party was not to be imputed to the principal even though directed primarily against a third party. It is the view of the editors that *Arab Bank* survives the appeal in *Stone & Rolls*, albeit on the narrow ground that the majority were not concerned with its correctness, so that the question of its correctness remains open.

16–71   The Court of Appeal upheld in part an appeal from the decision of Gloster J. in *Kidson's v Lloyd's Underwriters*.[2] The point discussed in the text did not arise on appeal.

Multiple assureds

16–76 *Note 163*: The Court of Appeal partially reversed the decision in *Kidsons* [2009] Lloyd's Rep. IR 178, without reference to this point.

---

[1] [2009] UKHL 39.
[2] [2009] Lloyd's Rep. IR 178.

Non-disclosure of the national character of the subject insured, or of other facts that may aggravate the risk

Note 241: See also *Garnat Trading & Shipping (Singapore) Pte Ltd v Baominh* **16–128** *Insurance Corp* [2010] EWHC 2636 (Comm), where it was found that a towage plan which indicated the potential instability of the tugs to be used to transport a floating dock was a material fact.

The Race Relations Act 1968 has been prospectively repealed and replaced by **16–130** the Equality Act 2010. The effect of the 1968 Act as stated in the text is retained.

Characteristics of the subject matter insured

Note 309: See also *Garnat Trading & Shipping (Singapore) Pte Ltd v Baominh Ins* **16–182** *Corp* [2010] EWHC 2578 (Comm) which is another classic example of a case where the underwriters were put on inquiry as to the characteristics of the subject matter insured. This was again a case involving the insurance of a floating dock for an ocean voyage. The underwriters were content to insure the dock without themselves scrutinising the towage plan provided that it was approved by the Classification Society, although they recognised that this was a very important document which was likely to contain material information from an underwriting perspective.

Any circumstance as to which information is waived by the insurer

Similarly, the underwriters in *Garnat Trading & Shipping (Singapore) Pte Ltd v* **16–202** *Baominh Ins Corp*[3] were put on inquiry as to the seaworthiness of a floating dock for an ocean voyage under tow, which they were content to insure without themselves scrutinising the detailed towage plan provided it was approved by the Classification Society. The underwriters did not have the technical knowledge that would enable them to assess the contents of the towage plan, but a reasonable underwriter in their position would have realised that it was likely to contain wave height restrictions. Christopher Clarke J. held that the relevant information was disclosed, and that in any event the underwriters waived its disclosure by failing to make any inquiry about wave height restrictions, when a reasonably careful underwriter would have asked if it was a matter which concerned him.

General principles

The analysis of the law on waiver of disclosure contained in the judgment of **16–225** Longmore L.J. in *WISE Underwriting Agency Ltd v Grupo Nacional Provincial SA*[4] was considered and applied in *Synergy Health (UK) Ltd v CGU Insurance Plc*,[5] where Flaux J. noted that Rix L.J. took a somewhat different view as to the law in waiver "but the decisions of the majority of the Court of Appeal in both *CTI v Oceanus* and *Grupo Nacional* are binding on this Court."[6]

---

[3] [2010] EWHC 2578 (Comm) at paras 142–151.
[4] [2004] Lloyd's Rep. IR 764.
[5] [2010] EWHC 2583 (Comm).
[6] *Ibid*, para.74.

Note 405: See also *Sugar Hut Group Ltd v Great Lakes Reinsurance (UK) Plc* [2010] EWHC 2636 (Comm).

Waiver by asking some questions but not others

16–238   The test set out in *MacGillivray on Insurance Law* at paras 17–17 to 17–19 and approved by Woolf J. in *Hair v Prudential Ass Co Ltd*[7] and (*obiter*) by the Court of Appeal in *Doheny v New India Ass Co*[8] was again applied in *R & R Developments Ltd v Axa Insurance UK Plc*.[9]

16–239   The issue which arose in *R & R Developments* (above) was very similar to the issue which would have arisen in *Doheny* if the Court of Appeal had taken a different view on the construction of the questions in the proposal form. Although he was not bound by the tentatively expressed opinions[10] in *Doheny*, Mr Strauss QC took the same view (sitting as Deputy Judge) in *R & R Developments v Axa*[11] and held that by asking questions relating to the insured and its directors alone, the insurers waived any enquiry relating to similar questions with regard to companies with which the directors were involved. The inference of waiver was not displaced by the declaration at the foot of the proposal form in *R & R Developments*, which was said by the insurers to be an effective anti-waiver clause.[12]

16–240   In *Garnat Trading & Shipping (Singapore) Pte Ltd v Baominh Insurance Corp*[13] underwriters who had insured a floating dock to be towed from Russia to Vietnam asserted that the assured had failed to disclose data set out in the towage plan which related to ability of the tugs to withstand swell. Christopher Clarke J. found that there had been disclosure, but chose to deal, obiter with the assured's argument that the underwriters had in any event waived disclosure by agreeing to accept the plan as long as it had been approved by a Classification Society, which was the case on the facts.

Any circumstance which is superfluous to disclose by reason of any express or implied warranty

Seaworthiness

16–251   The wording of the Unseaworthiness and Unfitness Exclusion Clause (cl.5) has been substantially revised in the new Institute Cargo Clauses (the 2009 Clauses, reproduced in the Appendix to this Supplement). Under the new wording, the exclusion

---

[7] [1983] 2 Lloyd's Rep. 667.
[8] [2005] Lloyd's Rep. IR 251.
[9] [2009] EWHC 2429 (Ch). See also *Synergy Health (UK) Ltd v CGU Insurance Plc* [2010] EWHC 2583 (Comm), at paras 165–168.
[10] Summarised in this paragraph of the main work. See per Longmore L.J. at para.21, per Sir Christopher Staughton at para.29 and per Potter L.J. at paras 37–8, in *Doheny v New India*, above.
[11] [2009] EHWC 2429 (Ch), at para.42.
[12] *Ibid* at para.43. This is a question of construction. A differently-worded declaration might have been effective. In *R &R Developments*, the declaration required disclosure of all material information which "may influence" the insurer; *ex hypothesi*, if an insurer has indicated by the wording of his questions that he is not interested in a particular subject, information on that subject is not information which "may influence" him. There was a not dissimilar declaration in *Doheny v New India* (above).
[13] [2010] EWHC 2578 (Comm).

applies if "the Assured" are privy to the relevant unseaworthiness or unfitness of the vessel at the time of loading and there is an unqualified waiver of the implied warranties. The new provisions, which are discussed at para.20–41 below in this Supplement, plainly cannot affect the usual scope of the duty of disclosure.

Other examples

The rule enacted in s.18(3)(d) of the 1906 Act only applies where there is an **16–253** express or implied warranty. Disclosure is only excused where the insurers have the full protection of a warranty and the sub-section does not excuse the non-disclosure of material facts that do not amount to a breach of warranty enabling the insurers to avoid liability.[14]

In *Garnat Trading & Shipping (Singapore) Pte Ltd v Baominh Insurance Corp*,[15] a warranty had been included in several successive drafts of the policy but was removed at the last minute from the final policy document. It was removed because the underwriters were content to proceed on the basis that the towage plan for the insured voyage had been approved by the Classification Society. The warranty was no longer needed. In those circumstances, s.18(3)(d) did not apply, but disclosure of the matters subsequently relied upon as grounds for avoidance was excused for a different reason. The draft warranty rendered disclosure superfluous because it indicated that the underwriters were not relying on the insured to make disclosure of the contents of the towage plan. An underwriter who, in effect, indicates that he does not require information from the insured about a towage plan because he wants the information vetted to the satisfaction of someone else, is not, when such satisfaction is expressed, then entitled to turn round and say that the insured now owes him a duty to provide the information. It is information as to which he has waived disclosure.[16]

Effect of proposed warranties

Although s.18(3)(d) of the Marine Insurance Act 1906 can only have effect where **16–255A** there is a warranty covering the fact which has not been disclosed, Christopher Clarke J. in *Garnat Trading & Shipping (Singapore) Pte Ltd v Baominh Insurance Corporation*[17] expressed the view that a fact could be regarded as immaterial if the parties had intended to incorporate a warranty relating to it but by oversight had failed to do so in the final policy document. Here, earlier drafts of the policy contained a towage plan warranty on the part of the assured, but the final version omitted the warranty. In the court's view, although s.18(3)(d) was by its terms inapplicable to this situation, the short period of time between the draft wording and the final wording showed that the underwriters had not sought disclosure of any matters referred to in the towage plan and were content to rely upon the warranty.[18]

---

[14] See *Synergy Health (UK) Ltd v CGU Insurance Plc* [2010] EWHC 2583 (Comm), paras 180-184. The relevant stipulations never became terms of the contract at all, let alone warranties, which was the short answer to the point on s.18(3)(d) in that case.

[15] [2010] EWHC 2578 (Comm).

[16] *Ibid*, para. 155.

[17] [2010] EWHC 2578 (Comm).

[18] But contrast *Synergy Health (UK) Ltd v CGU Insurance Plc* [2010] EWHC 2583 (Comm).

CHAPTER 17

MISREPRESENTATION

Proposals for reform

The English and Scottish Law Commissions have put forward proposals[1] to **17–01A**
reform the law on misrepresentation and non-disclosure in consumer insurance,
which are described at para.15–07 above in this Supplement. The Commissions'
proposals for commercial insurance, to be dealt with in a separate bill, have yet
to be published. Apart from yacht insurance, the existing proposals are unlikely
to have a significant impact in the field of marine insurance, but the entirety of
this chapter should be read in the light of the fact that, at least where the assured
is an individual, the existing law may soon be substantially replaced. There
will be no substantial change to the position where a misrepresentation is made
fraudulently or recklessly. Where the misrepresentation is made negligently,[2]
the insurer will be entitled to avoid only if he can show that, but for the misrepresentation, he would not have entered into the policy on any terms. The right to
avoid for a wholly innocent misrepresentation will be abolished, so far as
consumer insurances are concerned, if the draft Bill becomes law.

Distinction between a representation and a warranty

If the Consumer Insurance (Disclosure and Misrepresentations) Bill 2009,[3] is **17–06**
enacted in its present form it will no longer be open to insurers to convert pre-
contractual misrepresentations into warranties in contracts of consumer insurance
by means of a basis clause.

Difference in effect

Note 10: The reference in this footnote should be to the decision of the House of **17–07**
Lords in *The Good Luck* [1992] 1 A.C. 233. The principle, which was settled by
this decision, that there is an automatic discharge from liability from the time a
breach of warranty is committed is discussed at paras 19–09 and 19–10 in the
main work.
  Note 15: The reference in this footnote should be to the decision in the House **17–10**
of Lords, [1992] 1 A.C. 233.

---

[1] In the form of the Consumer Insurance (Disclosure and Misrepresentations) Bill; Law Commission
Report No. 319, published December 15, 2009.
[2] The extent to which the proposed legislation will affect the position as to representations of expectation or belief carrying an implied representation of reasonable grounds remains to be seen. Under
the existing law, this is an area of some difficulty. See especially the discussion in the main work
of *Economides v Commercial Union Ass Co Plc* [1998] Q.B. 587 (which was a case of consumer
insurance). The subject is dealt with in detail in this chapter of the main work at paras 17–46 *et seq.*
[3] See para.17–01A above.

Mere puffs

17–14   The suggestion that statements made on behalf of the reassured in *Limit No.2 Ltd v Axa Versicherung AG* were "mere puffs" was not pursued on appeal. The Court of Appeal held that the relevant statements were statements of intention, rather than statements of the reassured's policy with regard to deductibles. On either view, those would be statements of fact.

Representation inferred from silence

17–24   *Note 35*: The relevant part of the decision of Mr Hirst QC, sitting as a Deputy Judge, in *Limit No.2 Ltd v Axa Versicherung AG*[4] was reversed on appeal. The general propositions contained in the text of this paragraph of the main work are not affected, but *Limit No.2 Ltd v Axa* can no longer be regarded as an illustration. The Court of Appeal[5] held that the representation made prior to the placing of the treaty in 1996 had been a representation of the reassured's intention at that time with regard to deductibles, and that it could not be supposed that a statement of intention made 19 months earlier was still operative at the time of the 1998 renewal. No statement of the reassured's intentions in 1998 was made, or could be implied. A Court should not struggle to hold that everything said at inception is to be impliedly repeated on renewal.[6]

Difference between a promissory and an affirmative representation

Arnould's conclusion

17–28   *Note 44*: In *Synergy Health (UK) Ltd v CGU Insurance Plc* [2010] EWHC 2583 (Comm) Flaux J. held that *Dennistoun v Lillie* (1821) 3 Bli. 202 was no longer good law insofar as it held that a statement of future intention is a statement of fact.

Later authority

17–32   In *Limit No.2 Ltd v Axa Versicherung AG*,[7] Longmore treated it as axiomatic that for a representation to have legal effect it must be a representation of existing fact not of future fact or opinion. *Limit No.2 v Axa* was a case of marine reinsurance. Although the point was not in issue, the reasoning of the Court of Appeal affords another strong indication that the doctrine of promissory representation no longer has any place in the modern law of marine insurance. The same conclusion was reached by Flaux J. in a case invovling property insurance.[8] The only case which suggests that a promissory representation, as such, is actionable is the old case of

---

[4] *Limit No.2 Ltd v Axa Versicherung AG* [2009] Lloyd's Rep. IR 396.
[5] *Limit No.2 Ltd v Axa Versicherung AG* [2009] Lloyd's Rep. IR 396, at paras 22–27.
[6] *Ibid*, per Longmore L.J. at para.27.
[7] [2009] Lloyd's Rep. IR 395, at para.4.
[8] *Synergy Health (UK) Ltd v CGU Insurance Plc* [2010] EWHC 2583 (Comm), *Limit No.2 Axa* (above) does not appear to have been cited.

Dennistoun v Lillie[9] which, albeit a decision of the House of Lords, was either impliedly overruled by s.20 of the Marine Insurance Act or is on a proper analysis, a case where by the time the representation was actually communicated to underwriters it was a statement of past fact.[10]

Discussion

The views expressed in this paragraph of the main work are further reinforced by **17–39** the decision and reasoning of the Court of Appeal in *Limit No.2 Ltd v Axa Versicherung AG* (above) and by reasoning of Flaux J. in *Synergy Health (UK) Ltd v CGU Insurance Plc* (above).

Representations of intention

The representation in *Limit No.2 Ltd v Axa Versicherung AG* (above) was held **17–63** by the Court of Appeal to be one of intention, rather than a statement of the reassured's policy or practice in relation to deductibles. Both types of representation are representations of an existing fact.[11] The Court of Appeal reversed the decision of the Deputy Judge with regard to the 1998 renewal of the treaty,[12] holding that the representation of intention made in 1996 did not continue to be operative in 1998. A representation of intention, as Longmore L.J. observed, may be thought to be a somewhat artificial concept.[13] A person's intentions are always subject to change. A representation of intention cannot last forever, and there must come a time when it is spent.

It is submitted that a useful comparison can be made between the old case of *Traill v Baring*[14] and *Limit No.2 v Axa* (above). In *Traill v Baring*, the reinsured said he intended to retain one-third of the risk, but changed his mind before the risk incepted. Any statement of intention would (as Longmore L.J. said in *Limit No.2 v Axa*)[15] of course be intended to be operative when the risk began, and would continue up to that time. It does not follow that it would continue to be operative on renewal; in *Limit No.2 v Axa*, the reassured's statement of intention had become a spent force well before the 1998 renewal.

In *Synergy Health (UK) Ltd v CGU Insurance Plc* (above), a representation (made some months prior to renewal) that an imporved intruder alarm system was to be installed at one of the insured premises was held to be one of existing fact, not intention. By the time that the representation was actually communicated, the

---

[9] (1821) 3 Bli. 202.

[10] [2010] EWHC 2583 (Comm), para.156. The decision at paras 17–33 to 17–41 in the main work was cited in support of this analysis. The actual time of communication was an important consideration in *Synergy v CGU*; see para.17–63 below.

[11] In *Synergy v CGU* (above), where *Limit No.2 v Axa* does not appear to have been cited, Flaux J. suggested that a representation of intention is not one of existing fact but is to be equated rather with a representation of expectation or belief. A representation of intention must, however, on any view constitute a statement as to what in fact was intended when it was made.

[12] [2008] Lloyd's Rep. IR 330; reversed in part, [2009] Lloyd's Rep. IR 395.

[13] *Ibid*, at para.23.

[14] (1864) 4 De. G & S.318.

[15] [2009] Lloyd's Rep. IR 395, at para.23. It was not seriously arguable that the statement of intention prior to inception in 1996 did not justify the avoidance of that year's treaty (*ibid* para.17).

work should have been substantially complete if the system was to be installed by what had been said to be the intended date. Flaux J. held that, as the representation was one of fact, it was to be regarded as being impliedly repeated on the renewal. Had it been merely a representation of intention, Flaux J. would, it seems, have held that it could have no effect at renewal.

Ambiguous representation

17–69A Ambiguity in a representation made by or on behalf of the assured may sometimes be the result, or be said to be the result, of some ambiguous phrasing in a question asked by the prospective insurer. This is most likely to arise in relation to the questions and answers in a proposal form. The cases in point are non-marine. The authorities have recently been reviewed by Mr Nicholas Strauss QC, sitting as a Deputy Judge, in *R&R Developments Ltd v Axa Insurance UK Plc*[16] The better view appears to be that it is not necessary or relevant to determine what the assured's subjective understanding of the question may actually have been,[17] and that it is sufficient that the assured's answer was substantially true upon a reasonable interpretation of the question posed by the insurer.[18]

The approach adopted in *R & R Developments v Axa Insurance* is essentially that adopted in *Revell v London Gen Ins Co Ltd*[19] where MacKinnon J. said it was elementary:

> "that if there is an ambiguity in this question so that upon one view of the reasonable meaning which is conveyed to the reasonable reader of it the answer is not false, the company cannot say that on the other meaning of the words the answer was untrue so as to invalidate the policy."

There must of course be a genuine ambiguity in the question posed by the insurer before any suggestion can arise of the assured's answer being substantially true on the basis of the words used by the insurer being given one meaning rather than another.[20]

The Misrepresentation Act 1967

17–111 *Note 208*: See now, *Chitty*, 30th ed paras. 6–017 and 6–152.
17–112 *Note 209*: See now, *Chitty*, 30th ed para.6–098.

---

[16] [2009] EWHC 2429 (Ch). *Condogianis v Guardian Ass Co* [1921] 1 A.C. 125, 130 was cited as the leading authority in point. See also, *Revell v London General Ins Co Ltd* (1934) 50 Ll.L. Rep. 114; *Taylor v Eagle Star Ins Co Ltd* (1940) 67 Ll.L. Rep. 136.
[17] Different considerations would, of course, apply to any suggestion of fraud or dishonesty on the assured's part.
[18] While concluding that the authorities do not support the proposition that it is necessary to consider in what sense the insured actually understood the question, Mr Strauss QC expressed some doubt as to how satisfactory this is; it seems unreasonable for an insured to be able to rely on a meaning which (but for the *contra proferentem* principle) would not have been the meaning attributed to the question and which was not how he understood it. Nevertheless, in this context as in all others except for fraud "objective construction reigns supreme and subjective understanding is irrelevant" *ibid* para.27).
[19] (1934) 50 Ll.L. Rep. 114, 116.
[20] See *Doheny v New India Ass Co Ltd* [2005] Lloyd's Rep. IR 251; *R & R Developments v Axa* (above) at para.28.

CHAPTER 18

THE POST-CONTRACTUAL DUTY OF UTMOST GOOD FAITH

Note 39: The Third Parties (Rights against Insurers) Act 1930 is to be replaced, **18–24** from a date to be announced, by the Third Parties (Rights against Insurers) Act 2010. The point made in the text is unaffected by the new Act.

Other situations

In addition to the situations listed here, there may be other occasions when the **18–36** assured and the insurers have post-contractual dealings involving the supply of information by the assured. Thus the assured may be under a duty to inform insurers of any post-inception material alteration in the risk as presented to the insurers, although a failure to comply does not render the policy voidable ab initio but merely gives the insurers the contractual right to refuse a claim following a breach of the provision.[1] A renewal is a fresh contract so that there is a new duty of utmost good faith in respect of it. Similarly, an endorsement extending the duration of the risk pending renewal attracts the duty of utmost good faith.[2]

Follow the settlements and claims co-operation clauses

Note 77: There are also cases involving direct insurance which show that the **18–43** insurer is under some form of implied duty not to make unreasonable demands of the assured, although this duty is contractual rather than an aspect of the duty of utmost good faith. See, e.g., *Widefree Ltd v Brit Insurance Ltd* [2009] EWHC 3671 (QB) (insurer not entitled to demand irrelevant information in support of a claim). Cf also *Quinn Direct Insurance Ltd v The Law Society* [2010] EWCA Civ 805, where the Court of Appeal rejected a suggestion by liability insurers that a clause entitling them to information in respect of actual and potential claims against the assured also allowed them unlimited access to the assured's records and bank accounts to determine whether there had been fraudulent conduct by the assured unconnected with the claims in question.

The meaning of a fraudulent claim

Exaggeration of a genuine claim

Note 107: There remains an issue as to what constitutes a "claim" for this **18–57** purpose. In *Yeganeh v Zurich Insurance* [2010] EWHC 1185 (QB) the assured

---

[1] *Ansari v New India Assurance Ltd* [2009] Lloyd's Rep. IR 562.
[2] *Limit No.2 Ltd v Axa Versicherung AG* [2009] Lloyd's Rep. IR 396.

suffered a fire at his house, and made a claim for damage to both the house and its contents. The contents claim was found to have been exaggerated, and it was held that nothing was recoverable even in respect of the house itself. The result was not one that caused the court any dissatisfaction, as there were clear doubts as to the origins of the fire, but the case does illustrate the strictness of the principle.

Fraudulent devices

18–86 *Note 157*: See also *Direct Line Insurance Plc v Fox* [2010] Lloyd's Rep. IR 324.

Effect of settlement

18–93 Where the parties have settled the assured's claim, any subsequent fraud by the assured cannot affect the validity of the settlement agreement. This was so held in *Direct Line Insurance Plc v Fox*,[3] where the claim was settled for £46,524.50, consisting of an initial payment of £42,412.00 and a further payment of £4,112.50 on production by the assured of a VAT invoice for work performed by a contractor. The assured produced a forged invoice, and the insurers refused to pay the additional sum and also sought repayment of the sum paid earlier. It was held that the settlement itself had not been tainted by fraud, and the VAT invoice was simply a precondition to payment of a sum representing VAT: because the assured had not produced a valid invoice he was not entitled to that sum, but the earlier payment of £42,412.00 was unaffected.

Reform of the law

18–94 In July 2010 the English and Scottish Law Commissions published Issues Paper No.7 on fraudulent claims and the continuing duty of utmost good faith. The bulk of the Issues Paper is concerned with the former topic. The Issues Paper is for the most part a consultation document, setting out the law, posing various questions and on occasion suggesting the way forward. For the most part the Law Commissions do not contemplate any major changes in the law, other than clarification of the present complex position.

18–95 As to fraudulent claims, the Law Commissions recognise the need for a rule which precludes all recovery in the event of fraud in any part of the claim, to remove the incentive for fraud, although there is no attempt to ascertain exactly when a series of different losses can be treated as a single claim for this purpose. There is some discussion of the juridical basis of the prohibition on fraudulent claims, the Law Commissions recognising that it is not yet conclusively determined that fraudulent claims are distinct from the duty of utmost good faith[4] but nevertheless preferring a contractual approach to the problem. The model which is provisionally adopted by the Law Commissions is that the making of a fraudulent claim is a repudiatory breach of contract which entitles the insurers to refuse

---

[3] [2010] Lloyd's Rep. IR 324.
[4] See paras 18–46 to 18–52 of the main work.

to pay the claim and also to terminate the contract for breach. However, genuine claims post-dating the fraud but pre-dating termination are preserved. The Law Commissions are contemplating only one adjustment to the categories of fraudulent claim identified by *Axa v Gottlieb*,[5] namely that of fraudulent devices: it is seen to be unjust that a genuine loss can be lost entirely by a minor fraud, e.g., the submission of a forged invoice for work done when such work plainly has to be done anyway. One further recommendation is extension of the rule that the fraud of one composite assured does not affect the rights of innocent composite assureds to married couples and cohabitees, removing the English law principle (rejected in many other common law jurisdictions) that their interests are joint and not composite so that fraud by either defeats both. This change, if effected, would appear not to affect the ruling in *Direct Line Insurance Plc v Khan*,[6] which turned on the finding that the fraudulent husband had acted as the agent of his innocent wife in pressing an exaggerated claim, so that there was no need to decide whether the insurance was joint or composite, although it is difficult to see any facts which justified agency and it appears that the Court of Appeal simply chose to sidestep the joint/composite dichotomy.

As to other aspects of the continuing duty, the Law Commissions have rela- **18–96** tively little to say. The Issues Paper is uncertain as to whether there is any residual duty, and makes no recommendations on the point.

---

[5] [2005] Lloyd's Rep. IR 369.
[6] [2002] Lloyd's Rep. IR 364. See para.18–89 of the main work.

CHAPTER 19

EXPRESS WARRANTIES

What words amount to a warranty

In *A.C. Ward & Son Limited v Catlin (Five) Ltd*[1] (a non-marine case) the policy **19–03** contained an express definition of the term "warranties" in a definition clause, where the legal consequences of any breach were spelt out.[2] The presence of such a definition in a policy would appear to constitute the clearest possible indication of an "intention to warrant" under clauses where the word "warranty" or "warranted" is used.

Note 15: The decision of H.H. Judge Mackie QC in *Pratt v Aigaion Ins Co SA* **19–04** *(The Resolute)*[3] was reversed on appeal.[4] The Court of Appeal took this opportunity to restate the principles of construction applicable to express warranties.

It was common ground between the parties in *The Resolute* that the "warranty" under consideration was "what is sometimes called a delimiting warranty."[5] Despite the reservations expressed at this point in *Arnould* as to the use of the word "warranty" to describe such provisions, the trend appears to be irreversible.

After the decision in *The Resolute* (above) it is questionable whether it is of any advantage to underwriters (in cases where this makes no difference on the facts) to argue that a stipulation on which they rely containing warranty language is delimiting or suspensory in effect rather than a strict promissory warranty.[6] It seems clear from *The Resolute* that there is no essential difference in the approach to construction which should be adopted, once it has been determined, or is conceded, that the relevant stipulation is suspensory rather than promissory in kind or vice versa.[7]

---

[1] [2010] Lloyd's Rep. IR 30. For the subsequent trial, see *A.C. Ward & Son Limited v Catlin (Five) Ltd (No.2)* [2009] EWHC 3122 (Comm).

[2] The definition was as follows: "A warranty is a fundamental term or condition of the Insurance the breach of which voids the Contract from the time of breach." While this does not state the consequences of breach of a promissory warranty with complete accuracy (on which, see para.19–09 in the main work) the intention could not be clearer. The Defendant Underwriters in *Ward v Catlin* (above) initially sought to argue that the clauses on which they relied (prefaced by the words "It is warranted that . . .") were merely suspensive conditions and not promissory warranties, no doubt in the hope that those clauses would then be construed more favourably, but conceded the point in the Court of Appeal; see further at para.19–04 below.

[3] Now reported at [2008] Lloyd's Rep. IR 610.

[4] [2009] Lloyd's Rep. 225.

[5] [2009] Lloyd's Rep. 225, para.13. Sir Anthony Clarke M.R. expressed no view of his own on that point. The editors venture to doubt whether the relevant clause was in fact "delimiting" and not a promissory warranty.

[6] Underwriters have sought to gain forensic advantage by arguing that clauses on which they rely are merely suspensory in a number of recent cases; see *The Newfoundland Explorer* [2006] Lloyd's Rep. IR 704; *The Resolute* (above); and *Ward v Catlin* (above). In *Ward v Catlin*, the policy wording made that position completely untenable; see the discussion at para.19–03 above. See also *Sugar Hut Group Ltd v Great Lakes Reinsurance (UK) Plc* [2010] EWHC 2636 (Comm) (term described as "warranty" held to be such, and not merely a suspensory provision).

[7] See further, at paras 19–18 and 19–19 below.

Statements of fact normally to be construed as warranties

19–06 *Note 20*: The relevance of the well-known dicta cited in this footnote to the construction of warranties, or provisions relied upon as having warranty status or similar effects, is now firmly established; see *The Resolute* above; *Ward v Catlin*, above. The words "In other contexts" at this point in the text of para.19–06 should be ignored.

Note 21: The principle stated in *Hussain v Brown* was taken into account in *The Resolute*, above, and is not confined to non-marine cases. See also *A.C. Ward & Son v Catlin (Five) Limited* (above) at para.28, where Etherton L.J. stated that "It is trite law that if underwriters wish to have a warranty with draconian consequences they must stipulate for it in clear terms", citing *Pratt v Aigaion* for the proposition. In *The Resolute*, the dictum of Saville L.J. was treated as being of relevance to the construction of stipulations which are determined or are conceded to be of a suspensory character, as well as to the construction of promissory warranties.[8]

Note 25: See now, *MacGillivray*, 11th ed para.10–031.

Express warranty requires exact and literal fulfilment

19–08 *Note 45*: See also *Pratt v Aigaion Ins Co SA (The Resolute)* [2009] Lloyd's Rep. IR 149 where the words "Warranted Owner and/or Owner's experienced Skipper on board and in charge at all times and one experienced crew member" in a policy covering a fishing vessel could not sensibly be given their ordinary and natural (or literal) meaning; the words "at all times" had to be qualified in order to give the warranty a reasonable and businesslike meaning having regard to its context and purpose, and the natural qualification to adopt was that it applied to those times when both a skipper and experienced crew member could be expected to be needed.[9]

Breach and loss need not be connected

19–11 *Note 60*: See also *Thomas*, Vol.3 (2009), Ch.5 ("Warranties and utmost good faith in US marine insurance contracts", contributed by Professor Martin Davies).

Construction of warranties—further discussion

19–18 and 19–19 A comprehensive restatement of the principles to be applied to the construction of warranties in insurance contracts was provided by the Court of Appeal in *Pratt v Aigaion Insurance Co SA (The Resolute)*,[10] which has already come to be regarded as one of the leading cases on the subject.[11] It does not appear to the

---

[8] [2009] 1 Lloyd's Rep. 225, 229 (para.13).

[9] [2009] 1 Lloyd's Rep. 225, at paras 23–25, 27, 34. It was common ground that some qualification to the words "at all times" was required. The debate between the parties was as to the extent to which the literal meaning should be qualified. The Court of Appeal based its decision primarily on the *contra proferentem* principle of construction. See further at paras 19–18 and 19–19 below.

[10] [2009] 1 Lloyd's Rep. 225.

[11] See *A.C. Ward & Son Ltd v Catlin (Five) Ltd* [2010] Lloyd's Rep. IR 30; *AC Ward & Son Ltd v Catlin (Five) Ltd (No.2)* [2009] EWHC 3122 (Comm).

present editors that any of the propositions contained in these paragraphs of the main work are invalidated, but paras 19–18 and 19–19 should now be read in the light of and in conjunction with what was said in *The Resolute*.

Sir Anthony Clarke M.R. began his discussion of the relevant principles[12] by emphasising that a warranty, like any other clause in a contract, must be construed having regard to its context within the contract, which must in turn be set in its surrounding circumstances or factual matrix, and referring to the *Investors Compensation Scheme* guidelines[13] and other well known statements of general principle.[14] He then went on to refer to further considerations in the context of continuing warranties in insurance contracts, which, Sir Anthony Clarke M.R. accepted, were also relevant to warranties of the kind with which the Court was concerned in *The Resolute*,[15] citing the proposition of Saville L.J. in *Hussain v Brown*[16] that if underwriters want such protection, it is up to them to stipulate for it in clear terms[17] and approving the following passages in the 10th edition of *MacGillivray* on Insurance Law.[18]

"10.50 The first relevant rule of construction is that the apparently literal meaning of the words in a warranty must be restricted if they produce a result inconsistent with a reasonable and businesslike interpretation of such a warranty. A warranty in a contract must, like a clause in any other commercial contract, receive a reasonable interpretation and must, if necessary, be read with such limitations and qualifications as will render it reasonable. The words used ought to be given the interpretation which, having regard to the context and circumstances, would be placed upon them by ordinary men of normal intelligence conversant with the subject matter of the insurance."

"10.53 The second principle of construction[19] which assists the assured who contends that he complied with the warranty is that any ambiguity in the terms of a policy must be construed against the insurer . . ."

The Resolute was a fishing trawler based at Fleetwood, and was insured under a policy incorporating the insurers' standard Trawler Wording[20] and containing a series of typed Conditions one of which read: "Warranted Owner and/or Owner's

---

[12] [2009] 1 Lloyd's Rep. 225, paras 9 *et seq* in the judgment. Stanley Burnton L.J. delivered a separate judgment in which he agreed with the judgment and reasoning of the Master of the Rolls; Kay L.J. agreed with both judgments.

[13] [1998] 1 W.L.R. 896 at 912–3; see para.3–03 in the main work where the guidelines are quoted and discussed.

[14] Notably, those in *The Antaios* [1988] 1 A.C. at 201; *Sirius Intl Ins Co v FAI Gen Ins Ltd* [2005] Lloyd's Rep. IR 294 at para.19; and *L Schuler A.G. v Wickman Machine Tool Sales Ltd* [1974] A.C. 235 at 251.

[15] It was common ground between the parties that the relevant stipulation was "what is sometimes called a delimiting warranty"; see the commentary at paras 19–04, 19–06 above in this Supplement.

[16] [1996] 1 Lloyd's Rep. 627, 630. See para.19–06, fn. 21, in the main work and above in this Supplement.

[17] This proposition was said to be trite law in *Ward v Catlin* (above), per Etherton L.J. at para.28.

[18] See now, 11th ed. Paras 10–052 and 10–055.

[19] This second principle, as Sir Anthony Clarke M.R. observed, is simply a particular application of the *contra proferentem* principle.

[20] The standard Trawler Wording included a warranty that the vessel should not be navigated without at least two persons on board, one of whom should be competent to be in command. This was regarded by the Court of Appeal as casting light on the purpose and intended scope of the typed warranty.

experienced Skipper on board and in charge at all times and one experienced crew member." It was accepted by the defendant underwriters that the words "at all times" could not be given their ordinary and natural (or literal) meaning. The question was how far this expression should be qualified. H.H. Judge Mackie QC accepted the insurers' submission that the qualifications should only be those recognised by Gross J. in *The Newfoundland Explorer*,[21] namely limitations restricted to emergencies or other crewing duties requiring departure from the vessel. The Court of Appeal reached a different conclusion. The primary ground of decision was that the language of the warranty was ambiguous because it did not make clear or give any indication as to what the extent of the qualification on its literal meaning should be; if the insurers wanted the owner or skipper and an experienced crew member on board when the vessel was safely tied up alongside, they should have clearly so stipulated.[22] Applying the *contra proferentem* principle, a breach of warranty was not established.[23]

If there was no ambiguity, it being common ground that "at all times" must be qualified, the natural qualification to adopt in the context[24] was that the warranty required the owner or his experienced skipper and one experienced crew member to be on board at times when their presence could be expected to be needed. The parties could not have contemplated that a skipper might be required or that more than one crew member might be required in the circumstances in which *Resolute's* crew went ashore and the casualty occurred.

As can be seen, the Court of Appeal adopted a purposive approach to construction in *The Resolute*. The terms in which Sir Anthony Clarke M.R. expressed his preferred construction of the warranty (if contrary to his view there was no ambiguity) are substantially the same as those used by him to describe its purpose.[25]

Note 90: The decision of H.H. Judge Mackie QC in *Pratt v Aigaion Insurance Co SA (The Resolute)*, which is now reported at [2008] Lloyd's Rep. I.R. 610, was reversed on appeal, [2009] 1 Lloyd's Rep. 225. The two earlier cases on crewing warranties which are referred to in this footnote were distinguished by the Court of Appeal. See the discussion above in this Supplement. There were significant

---

[21] [2006] Lloyd's Rep. IR 704. Both at first instance and in the Court of Appeal, The Defendant underwriters in *The Resolute* relied on the two earlier decisions on crewing warranties in *The Milasan* and *The Newfoundland Explorer*, cited at para. 19–18 fn. 90 in the main work. The Court of Appeal did not consider that any real assistance was to be gained from either of these cases. The policy wording was significantly different in each case, and *The Milasan* involved the insurance of a very different type of vessel in very different circumstances. Sir Anthony Clarke did not therefore consider the principle that the Court should be consistent in its approach to policy wording to be of any assistance; [2009] 1 Lloyd's Rep. 225 para.23. Nothing that was said in *The Resolute* was intended to conflict with or cast doubt on the reasoning in the two earlier cases; *ibid*, paras 17–20, 28.

[22] [2009] 1 Lloyd's Rep. 225, paras 25, 26.

[23] The Court of Appeal left it open whether the qualifications suggested in the *Newfoundland Explorer* (above) should also be made; *ibid* para.28.

[24] The relevant background which would have been known to both parties in the context of the insurance of a fishing vessel such as *The Resolute* is described, *ibid*, at para.15. The incorporation of the standard Trawler Wording was also material; the warranty fell to be construed in the context of the policy as a whole, and the Trawler Wording cast light on the qualifications to the words "at all times" which must have been intended; see per Stanley Burnton L.J. at paras 32–34.

[25] *Ibid*, paras 24 and 27.

differences in the language of the warranties in each of these three cases, and the context was very different in *The Milasan*. It is clear from the decision in *The Resolute* that the principle of adopting a consistent approach to the construction of similarly-worded provisions can only be applied with caution, in relation to warranties.

Note 95: The *contra proferentem* principle was applied by the Court of Appeal in *The Resolute*, above.

The Classification Clause

The Classification Clause in the 1995 Institute Hull Clauses and the **19–32A** Classification and ISM Clause in the International Hull Clauses, which are discussed at para.19–32 in the main work, are warranties in the proper sense. A different technique is employed in cargo insurance. It is common practice[26] when cargoes are insured pursuant to open cover arrangements for the open cover contract to incorporate the Clause named the Institute Classification Clause[27] which imposes restrictions with regard to the classification and age of vessels. Under this clause, cover is only afforded in respect of cargo declared for shipment on a vessel which is not entered in a qualifying Classification Society[28] subject to prompt notice being given for rates and conditions to be agreed. The current version of the Clause specifies that:

"Cargoes and/or interests carried by vessels not classed as above must be notified promptly to underwriters for rates and conditions to be agreed. Should a loss occur prior to such agreement being obtained cover may be provided but only if cover would have been available at a reasonable commercial market rate and on reasonable commercial market terms."[29]

---

[26] The practice is described in Dunt, *Marine Cargo Insurance* (2009), at paras 8.73 to 8.81.

[27] The current version is the Institute Classification Clause 1/1/01. The previous (1997) version of this Clause was construed by the Singapore Court of Appeal in *Everbright Commercial Enterprises Pte Ltd v Axa Ins Singapore Pte Ltd* [2001] 2 S.L.R. 316 and by the Hong Kong High Court in *Nam Kwong Medicines & Health Products Ltd v China Ins Co Ltd (The Pacifica)* [2002] 2 Lloyd's Rep. 591. There are no English decisions on either version of this Clause.

[28] Under the previous version of the Clause, the leading Classification Societies that were acceptable were listed by name. The current (2001) version requires the carrying vessel to be classed with a Classification Society which is a member or associate member of the International Association of Classification Societies (IACS) or, in certain circumstances, a National Flag Society. With regard to the Age Limitations which are contained in the second part of the Clause, see Dunt, *op cit*, para.8.76.

[29] This wording is evidently intended to reflect the established approach to held covered clauses (discussed at paras 19–40 *et seq* in the main work) without resort to technical jargon. The previous version of the Clause used the held covered formula and did not state expressly that shipments which could not be insured on reasonable market terms could not be covered. *Everbright v Axa* (above) and *The Pacifica* (above) were "phantom ship" cases, and in both these cases it was held that the assured could not rely on the held covered proviso to the 1997 version of the Institute Classification Clause, as the risk was uninsurable. The principle that a held covered clause cannot be invoked to cover a risk that cannot be insured in the market at commercial rates was applied (see *Liberian Ins Agency v Mosse* [1977] 2 Lloyd's Rep. 560). The revisions to the Change of Voyage Clause (cl.10.2) in the Institute Cargo Clauses 1/1/09 which were designed to redress the perceived injustice of the assured being deprived of cover in "phantom ship" cases as a result of the decision in *The Prestrioka* [2003] 2 Lloyd's Rep. 327 are therefore unlikely to enable an assured who is the victim of a phantom ship fraud to recover if the Institute Classification Clause is incorporated (as will very often be the case). See the discussion at para.13–18 above.

The practical effect is similar to that of imposing a classification warranty in respect of the individual declaration subject to a "held covered" proviso, achieved by a different route.

The Reasonable Despatch Clause

19–35 The references to "the Reasonable Despatch Clause" in this paragraph, including the paragraph heading, require amendment. In the 1982 edition of the Institute Cargo Clauses, the title of each clause appeared in two places, above the clause and in the margin. The marginal heading for cl.18 was "Reasonable Despatch Clause". This has now disappeared in the 2009 Cargo Clauses, and only the title heading "Avoidance of Delay" above the Clause has been retained. In deference to what appears to be a change of usage, "the Avoidance of Delay Clause" should be substituted for references to "the Reasonable Despatch Clause" in this paragraph.

Apart from the deletion of the marginal title, cl.18 in the 2009 Clauses is in identical terms to its predecessor in the 1982 Clauses. It has been included in successive editions of the standard Clauses since 1952.[30] The statement in this paragraph of the main work that the Clause has yet to be judicially construed is incorrect. There are still no English decisions, but the Clause has been judicially construed in Australia. The important decision in *Verna Trading Pty Limited v New India Ass Co Limited*,[31] which had been overlooked, is discussed below.

The meaning of the Avoidance of Delay clause is uncertain and controversial. Fortunately, the matter appears to be of little more than academic interest.

Arnould's position on the interpretation of this Clause has changed. In the 16th edition, it was suggested[32] that the Clause was confined to failure to act with reasonable despatch following a casualty. In the 1997 Supplement, the editors concluded that the Clause probably applied both to delays during the transit and delay in responding to a casualty.[33] This view is still maintained in the current (17th) edition, but the analysis of the clause as a strict condition has been modified. The view now taken at para.19–35 of the main work is that the most satisfactory interpretation of the Clause is that it is an innominate term.

Arnould's views on the Avoidance of Delay Clause are forcefully criticised in *Dunt* on Marine Cargo Insurance. This author's view,[34] based in part on the analysis in *Verna Trading* (above) and the historical antecedents of the Clause, is that the Avoidance of Delay Clause operates as a promissory warranty, confined to delays in prosecuting the insured adventure or transit.

---

[30] See Dunt, *Marine Cargo Insurance* (2009), at para.11.38.

[31] [1991] 1 V.R. 129. The decision in *Verna Trading* is also discussed in this Supplement in the context of the Transit Clause (para.13–40, above) and in connection with the statutory provisions on Delay (para.14–53 above).

[32] At para.704. This was the current view expressed in *Arnould* at the time of the *Verna Trading* decision (which Ormiston J. found persuasive).

[33] In the commentary on the standard Clauses at para.304 (p.183).

[34] Dunt, *op cit* paras 6.26, 6.29, 11.38–9. The references to South African decisions in those earlier paragraphs should be to Australia. See also J. Dunt and W. Melbourne "Insuring cargoes in the New Millennium: The Institute Cargo Clauses 2009", in R. Thomas, *The Modern Law of Marine Insurance*, Vol. 3 (2009), Ch.6.

One point on which there is complete agreement is that insofar as the Clause is confined to or applies to delays in transit, it serves little if any purpose, since it is difficult to conceive of any circumstances where the insurers would not have a defence anyway under the terms of the Transit Clause or by virtue of s.48 in the 1906 Act[35] and would need the further protection of cl.18 to defend any claim.

Dunt's view that cl.18 operates as a warranty applying to delays in transit is supported by the majority decision in *Verna Trading* (above). However, in adopting that construction of the Clause, Kaye and McGarvie JJ. proceeded on the basis that s.54 of the Marine Insurance Act 1907 (Commonwealth) only applies to delays during the sea transit and not to transit delays on land. Ormiston J. took the view that s.54 applies to delay at any stage of the insured adventure. The equivalent section in the 1906 Act, s.48, ought clearly to be construed in that manner.[36]

Since the assured's claim in *Verna Trading* failed in any event, both under the terms of the Transit Clause and (on his analysis) by virtue of s.54 in the Australian Act, Ormiston J. did not find it necessary to reach a firm conclusion on "the difficult question as to the operation and effect of Clause 18 of the Institute Cargo Clauses."[37] He was inclined, however, to accept what was then the current view in *Arnould*,[38] that the Clause is to govern the assured's post-casualty obligations, leaving the regimes of s.54 and of the Transit Clause itself to govern delays during transit.

The present editors are not persuaded that cl.18 should be construed, in effect, as a warranty coexisting alongside s.48 of the Act and the terminating provisions contained in the Transit Clause. There is also no reason why the application of the Clause should be confined to transit delays and should not extend to post-casualty delays. The editors remain of the view that cl.18 is best construed as an innominate term, applying to delays at any stage. The recent decisions on the approach to the construction of warranties, discussed under earlier paragraphs at Chapter 19 in this Supplement, reinforce this view.[39] If cargo insurers wished to have the draconian protection of a promissory warranty, in addition to the protection already afforded under the terms of the Transit Clause and by s.48 of the 1906 Act, this has not been stipulated for in clear terms.[40]

---

[35] There would be more scope for the Clause to make a practical difference if the statutory provision (s.54 in the Australian Act; s.48 in the English Act of 1906) did not extend to delays on land during the transit, which was the majority view in *Verna Trading*; but we do not consider that s.48 is confined to the marine leg of any insured transit. It is also worth noting that the earlier case in New South Wales, *Wiggins Teape (Austr) Pty Ltd v Baltica Ins Co Ltd* [1920] 2 N.S.W.L.R. 77, which was followed in *Verna Trading*, was decided at a time when the words "continues during the ordinary course of transit" did not form part of the Transit Clause; while that was the position, the Avoidance of Delay Clause might also more plausibly have been seen as filling a gap in the protection afforded to cargo insurers against unreasonable delays.

[36] See at para.14–53 in the main work, and above in this Supplement. This view regarding the scope of s.48 is supported in Dunt, *op. cit.* Paras 11.5, 11.39.

[37] [1991] 1 V.R. 129, 171.

[38] 16th edn, para.704.

[39] See the discussion at paras 19–06, 19–18, 19–19 above; *Hussain v Brown* [1996] 1 Lloyd's Rep. 627; *The Resolute* [2009] 1 Lloyd's Rep. 225; *Ward v Catlin* [2009] EWCA Civ 1098; [2010] Lloyd's Rep. IR 30.

[40] The position was "considered sufficiently clear" when the decision was taken to retain cl.18 as it stood in the 2009 revision of the Cargo Clauses; see Dunt and Melbourne, *op. cit.* Para.6.123.

Whatever view ultimately prevails, if the Clause ever comes to be construed in the English Courts, cl.18 can add little if anything to the protection which underwriters already possess in cases involving unreasonable delay on the part of the assured.

Waiver by express provision

19–39 The Institute Cargo Clauses 1/1/09 also provide that the insurers waive any breach of the implied warranties, at cl.5.3. This waiver clause, unlike that in the 1982 Clauses, is unqualified.[41]

Held covered clauses

19–40 *Note 190*: The "held covered" formula has also been dispensed with in the Institute Classification Clause (2001)[42] and in the first part of the Change of Voyage Clause (cl.10.1) in the Institute Cargo Clauses 1/1/09.[43] The wording of these provisions is plainly intended to have the same effect as a "held covered" clause, without resorting to jargon which might be misunderstood. It seems likely that the hallowed phrase will gradually fall out of use.

19–41 *Note 200*: The "futility principle" is still sometimes invoked, but there appear to be no recent examples in an insurance context. The principle was discussed at first instance in *Mansel Oil Limited v Troon Storage Tankers SA (The Ailsa Craig)*.[44]

19–42 *Note 209*: See also *Everbright Commercial Enterprise Pte Ltd v Axa Insurance Singapore Pte Ltd*[45]; *Nam Kwong Medicines & Health Products Ltd v China Ins Co Ltd (The Pacifica)*.[46] These were "phantom ship"[47] cases, where the Institute Classification Clause was a term of the cover. The principle that a held covered clause cannot extend to the declaration of a risk which is uninsurable was applied in both cases, by the Singapore Court of Appeal and the Hong Kong High Court respectively. Under the current (2001) version of the Institute Classification Clause this principle is expressly spelt out.[48] The same approach has been adopted in the 2009 revision of the Institute Cargo Clauses, where the assured's entitlement to cover under the first part of the Change of Voyage Clause (cl.10.1) is also subject to the proviso "but only if cover would have been available at a reasonable commercial market rate on reasonable market terms."[49]

---

[41] Clause 5 in the 2009 Clauses is discussed at para.20–41 below in this Supplement.

[42] See the discussion at para.19–32A above.

[43] See para.14–93 above in this Supplement.

[44] [2008] 2 Lloyd's Rep. 384. Christopher Clarke J. would if necessary have applied the principle, had he taken a different view on construction of the charterparty. His decision on construction was affirmed on appeal, and the futility principle was not considered by the CA; [2009] 2 Lloyd's Rep. 371.

[45] [2001] 2 S.L.R. 316.

[46] [2002] 2 Lloyd's Rep. 591.

[47] The "phantom ship" phenomenon is described in *The Prestrioka* [2003] 2 Lloyd's Rep. 327.

[48] See at para.19–32A above.

[49] Para.14–93 above.

CHAPTER 20

IMPLIED WARRANTIES: SEAWORTHINESS

General doctrine of warranty of seaworthiness

Note 6: The Institute Cargo Clauses have been revised. Under the new **20–02** Clauses (1/1/09), which are already in widespread use, the wording of the Unseaworthiness and Unfitness Exclusion Clause (cl.5) has been amended so that there is now an unqualified waiver of the implied warranties of seaworthiness of the ship and fitness of the ship to carry the goods to their destination where these Clauses are used. The exclusion (cl.5 in the 2009 clauses) is discussed at para.20–41 below.

Note 7: The proposition that a ship will be deemed seaworthy pursuant to s.39(4) of the 1906 Act if she is in a reasonably fit state as to repairs, equipment, crew and all other respects to encounter the ordinary perils of the voyage insured at the time of sailing on it was accepted by Christopher Clarke J. in *Garnat Trading & Shipping (Singapore) Pte Ltd v Baominh Insurance Corp.*[1] The relevant passage contains a summary of relevant principles, in a series of numbered propositions. Several of these propositions are referred to at later points in this section of the supplement. While the principles themselves may be uncontroversial, the restatement of these principles in *Garnat Trading* is particularly welcome as there are hardly any modern decisions in the English Courts on the warranty of seaworthiness in marine policies.[2]

Note 8: Referring to this footnote in the main work, Christopher Clarke J. stated in *Garnat Trading* (above)[3] that the fact that a vessel was in Class at the time of sailing on the voyage is of significant weight (albeit not of course determinative) when considering whether she was seaworthy particularly where the vessel has been surveyed and approved by Class shortly before sailing.

Warranty of seaworthiness in policies on goods: "seaworthiness admitted"

The principle that there is no implied warranty in a cargo policy that the goods **20–04** are seaworthy for the voyage was relied upon in *The Cendor Mopu*[4] where it was argued that the insurers were, in effect, seeking to introduce such a warranty by the back door inconsistently with the scheme of the Act under the guise of the doctrine of inherent vice which is referred to in a different part of the 1906 Act,

---

[1] [2010] EWHC 2578 (Comm) at para.160.
[2] There appears only to have been one other decision in recent years, *Project Asia Line Inc v Shone (The Pride of Donegal)* [2002] 1 Lloyd's Rep 659.
[3] [2010] EWHC 2578 (Comm) at para.160.
[4] *Global Process Systems Inc v Syarikat Takaful Malaysia Berhad* [2009] 2 Lloyd's Rep. 72; [2010] 1 Lloyd's Rep. 243.

at s.55(2)(c). The meaning and effect of the doctrine of inherent vice is discussed under Chapter 22 below, in the light of *The Cendor Mopu*.

The Unseaworthiness and Unfitness Exclusion Clause (cl.5) has been revised under the Institute Cargo Clauses 1/1/09. The new wording contains an unqualified waiver of the implied warranties. The circumstances in which the exclusion is to apply, where the assured was privy to the unseaworthiness or unfitness giving rise to the loss, have also been made substantially narrower in scope; see the Appendix below for the text of the 2009 Clauses; para.20–41 below for discussion of the new wording of cl.5.

The doctrine of stages

20–08 to 20–11 The doctrine of stages and its application were considered by Christopher Clarke J. in *Garnat Trading* above.

The relevant principle was formulated by Christopher Clarke J. in these terms[5]:

> "By reason of the 'doctrine of stages' it is sufficient if the ship is seaworthy for some definite, well recognised and separate stage of the voyage, even though some work, or change, to the vessel, her equipment, supplies or crew is required before she is fit for a second or later stage of the voyage. Different parts of a sea voyage can be separated into distinct stages. Indeed, in many cases the circumstances of the voyage are such that it will be necessary to introduce an intermediate stage before the commencement of the open sea voyage."

The vessel in *Garnat Trading* (above) was a floating dock, insured for a voyage under tow from Vladivostok to a port in Vietnam. At the start of the voyage, the vessel's draft was increased on the advice of the Port Authority in order to reduce windage during the towage out of Vladivostok through Golden Horn Bay. The insured dock was then linked to two tugs for the ocean voyage proper, and her draft was reduced (as planned) for the ocean voyage. Christopher Clarke J. held[6] that it was legitimate to regard the voyage as having at least two stages. It did not matter that the Towcon contract did not divide the voyage into stages. It was sufficient that there were two definable stages that were distinct because they called for or justified different treatment of the vessel.

What constitutes seaworthiness

20–16 The relevant principles were summarised by Christopher Clarke J. in *Garnat Trading & Shipping (Singapore) Pte Ltd v Baominh Ins Corp*[7] in the following terms:

> "Seaworthiness is 'relative to the nature of the ship'.[8] The ship should be 'in a condition to encounter whatever perils of the sea a ship of that kind and laden

---

[5] *Ibid*, para.160. Paras 20–09 to 20–11 in the main work were cited in the footnotes to this passage in the judgment.

[6] *Ibid* para.249. The reasoning on this point was obiter. The application of the doctrine of stages did not have to be determined, having regard to the learned Judge's conclusions as to the vessel's seaworthiness on sailing.

[7] [2010] EWHC 2578 (Comm), at para.160.

[8] Citing *Scrutton* on Chartparties, 21st edn (2008), Art. 51.

in that way may be fairly expected to encounter.'[9] When it is known that a particular ship is not capable of being made as fit to encounter the perils of a voyage as an ordinary vessel, the most that the warranty of seaworthiness requires is that the particular ship, given its limitations, is made as fit for the voyage as is practicable.[10] Thus, seaworthiness is to be judged flexibly and by reference to the adventure insured, and the assured does not warrant the prudence of the adventure, which is for the insurers to judge when deciding whether to accept the risk and the level of premium."

The Collision Liability Clause

Note 116: The Third Parties (Rights against Insurers) Act 1930 is to be replaced, **20–21** from a date to be announced, by the Third Parties (Rights against Insurers) Act 2010. The effect of the decision in *The Fanti* and *The Padre Island (No.2)* [1991] 2 A.C. 1, upholding pay to be paid clauses, is preserved in relation to marine policies by s.9(6) of the 2010 Act, unless the claim is one for death or personal injury. This qualification will have no practical effect in relation to claims against hull insurers under the standard Collision Liability Clause, which expressly excludes liabilities for loss of life or personal injury, see para.23–25 in the main work and below.

Christopher Clarke J. summarised the relevant principles in the following terms **20–24** in *Garnat Trading v Baominh* (above), at para.160:

"One, often applied, test of seaworthiness is to ask whether a reasonably prudent owner would have required that a particular defect, if he had known of it, must be made good before sending the ship to sea.[11] In that context, the reasonably prudent owner should take into account the probable circumstances of the voyage and the weather and sea conditions likely to be encountered on it . . .

Temporary matters, which can be quickly remedied, do not render a vessel unseaworthy. Thus, a defect which can be easily remedied at sea does not render the ship unseaworthy".[12]

The draft of the insured vessel in *Garnat Trading* was increased in order to reduce windage during her towage out of Vladivostok prior to commencing the ocean voyage proper, when her draft was reduced. Reduction of the vessel's draft could

---

[9] *Steel v State Line SS* Co (1877) 3 App. Cas. 72.

[10] *Haracopos v Mountain* (1934) 49 Ll.L. Rep. 287. The insured vessel in *Garnat Trading* was a floating dock. The observations of Fletcher Moulton L.J. in relation to the insured vessel (also a floating dock) in *Cantiere Meccanico Brindisiano v Janson* [1912] 3 K.B. 452, 466, were in point: "nobody supposes that a structure of this kind could sustain the perils of the seas which a ship ought to be able to sustain; and I should think that nobody imagines that such a vessel on being sent to sea is safe and seaworthy in the same sense as a tramp steamer or an Atlantic liner."

[11] Citing, Scrutton, op. cit., at p.92. This test, although frequently applied in shipping cases, does not replace the statutory definition in s.39(4) of the 1906 Act; see the editors' comments at para.20–24 fn 133 in the main work.

[12] *Scrutton, op. cit.*, p.92; *Leonard v Leyland* [1902] 18 T.L.R. 727; *The Diamond* [1906] P. 282; *Virginia Carolina Chemical Co v Norfolk, etc, SS Co* (1912) 17 Com. Cas. 277.

be and was easily achieved. If the doctrine of stages was to be applied, the vessel was seaworthy at each stage.[13] If that doctrine was not applied, the fact of the vessel's sailing with an increased draft that was inappropriate for the ocean voyage did not render her unseaworthy, as this was a temporary condition easily capable of being remedied.

Proof of unseaworthiness

20–28 The behaviour of the vessel on the voyage is evidence, albeit not conclusive, of its seaworthiness or unseaworthiness. In *Garnat Trading v Baominh* (above) the insured vessel had withstood a typhoon a few days before its loss when hit directly by a tropical storm. Christopher Clarke J. considered that the fact that the vessel survived the typhoon was at least some evidence that it was seaworthy; the fact that it failed to survive the tropical storm, on the other hand, was at least some evidence of unseaworthiness. In the event, Christopher Clarke J. held that none of the alleged breaches of the warranty of seaworthiness was made out.

The Seaworthiness Admitted Clause

20–38 *Note 207*: The revised Institute Cargo Clauses (the 2009 Clauses) have been adopted in some overseas markets, such as the Japanese cargo insurance market, where the 1982 edition of the Cargo Clauses had been relatively little used; see Thomas (ed) *The Modern Law of Marine Insurance*, Vol. 3 (2009), Chapter 6 "Insuring Cargoes in the New Millennium" (Dunt and Melbourne) at para.6.128. As a result, the subject of the Seaworthiness Admitted Clause has become of less practical importance, but it is not, or at least is not yet, one of merely historical interest.

The Unseaworthiness and Unfitness Exclusion Clause

20–41 The wording of this important exclusion in the standard Institute Cargo Clauses has been substantially revised under the 2009 Clauses.

The discussion in this paragraph of the main work remains apposite where the 1982 Clauses are used. The commentary which follows deals with the background to the revised 2009 wording, the differences between these two versions of the standard cl.5 exclusion, and the interpretation of cl.5 in the 2009 Clauses, which are increasingly likely to be used.

The full text of the revised cl.5 is reproduced in the Appendix to this Supplement and need not be quoted here.

The previous version of this exclusion in the standard 1982 Clauses met with considerable resistance in the market, and as a result wording which was much more favourable to assureds and their assignees was adopted for cl.5 in the Institute Commodity Trades Clauses and in some of the other Institute Clauses for Special Trades, when these were revised following the introduction of the main (A), (B) and (C) Clauses.[14] The new wording adopted in 2009 substantially

---

[13] See the discussion at paras 20–08 to 20–11 above in this Supplement.
[14] See fn.7 at this point in the main work; George, *op. cit*; Dunt and Melbourne, *op. cit.* para.6:48; Dunt, *Marine Cargo Insurance* (2009), paras 8.67 to 8.71.

reflects the position under cl.5 of the Institute Commodity Trades Clauses 5/9/83 (ICTC), but in one respect is even more favourable to the assured than either the standard exclusion in the main Cargo Clauses or the modified version in the current ICTC. (The Trade Clauses have been revised or will no doubt be revised in due course, in line with the amendments to the main Clauses).

Under the 1982 version of cl.5, the exclusion applied to cases of loss arising from unseaworthiness of vessel or craft or unfitness of vessel or craft conveyance container or liftvan for the safe carriage of the subject matter insured where (and only where) "the Assured *or their servants*[15] are privy to such unseaworthiness or unfitness, at the time the subject-matter insured is loaded therein." As was noted at this point in the main work, the draftsman of the 1982 Clauses must plainly have intended the word "privy" to be given a similar meaning to the word "privity" in s.39(5) of the 1906 Act, but with the obvious difference that the use of the words "or their servants" meant that the *alter ego* test and rules regarding the attribution of knowledge would not apply.

Under cl.5 in the ICTC, the exclusion in respect of unseaworthiness or unfitness of vessel or craft applied only where "the assured" was privy to such unseaworthiness or unfitness at the time of loading. The words "or their servants" were omitted, and the *alter ego* test therefore applied to this part of the Clause. However, cl.5 in ICTC then went on to deal with the unfitness of container liftvan or conveyance in terms which were distinctly less favourable to assureds. Loss arising from such unfitness was excluded where the subject-matter insured was loaded therein prior to attachment of the insurance or by the assured or their employees, irrespective of whether they were privy to the unfitness giving rise to the loss.

The revised wording at cl.5 in the 2009 Clauses deals with the unseaworthiness and unfitness of vessel or craft and with the unfitness of container or conveyance[16] in separate sub-clauses. The exclusion at cl.5.1.1 relating to unseaworthiness of vessel or craft applies only where "the Assured" are privy to such unseaworthiness or unfitness at the time of loading. In this respect, the new wording of cl.5 follows the scheme of the ICTC[17]; the exclusion is no longer triggered by privity of the assured's employees, as had been the case under cl.5 in the 1982 Clauses. Moreover, this exclusion at 5.1.1 does *not* apply where the contract of insurance has been assigned to a claimant who has bought or agreed to buy the subject-matter insured in good faith.[18]

The exclusion at cl.5.1.2 with regard to unfitness of container or conveyance, by contrast, can be invoked against bona fide purchasers.[19] The saving provision at cl.5.2 which disapplies the exclusion in cl.5.1.1 relating to unseaworthiness or unfitness of vessel or craft in favour of bona fide purchasers does not extend to unfitness of container or conveyance, to which cl.5.1.2 applies.

---

[15] Emphasis added here for purposes of discussion.

[16] The word "liftvan" has been omitted from the 2009 Clauses. It had no generally accepted meaning; see *Dunt & Melbourne, op. cit.* para.6.15.

[17] In broad terms, the scheme is similar to that under s.39(5) of the 1906 Act.

[18] See cl.5.2, Appendix 1 below. The ICTC contained similar wording to protect bona fide purchasers. The standard exclusion in the 1982 Clauses did not. This was one of the main reasons for market resistance to using the 1982 Clauses without amendment. See fn.219 at this point in the main work.

[19] The position under the ICTC was similar.

The exclusion concerning unfitness of container or conveyance, at cl.5.1.2 in the 2009 Clauses, is more favourable to assureds than either the wording in the 1982 Clauses or that in the ICTC, but is still wider in scope than cl.5.1.1 in one important respect.[20] The new wording applies where two requirements are met.

The scheme of the 1982 Clauses is followed insofar as the exclusion applies where the assured *or their employees* are privy to the unfitness at the time of loading. This is more generous to assureds than the equivalent part of cl.5 in the ICTC where privity did not have to be shown, but the wording is still less generous to assureds than that now adopted with regard to unseaworthiness or unfitness of vessel or craft in cl.5.1.1.

At the same time, the new wording limits the scope of this exclusion by imposing a requirement that the loading into or onto the container or conveyance shall have been carried out before attachment of the insurance or by the assured or their employees, in addition to the requirement of their being privy to such unfitness at the time of loading. Under the 1982 Clauses, only the latter require-ment (privity of the assured or its employees at the time of loading) applied. Under ICTC cl.5 only the former requirement (of the loading having been carried out before attachment or by the Assured or their servants) applied, and there was no requirement for privity to be shown under this limb of the exclusion.

In parallel with the revisions to the exclusion concerning unfitness of container or conveyance, the wording of exclusion 4.3 (insufficiency or unsuitability of packing or preparation) has also been revised under the 2009 Clauses. This exclu-sion is discussed elsewhere.[21]

As already noted, the revised wording at cl.5.2 disapplies the first but not the second part of cl.5.1 as against bona fide purchasers of the insured property.

Finally, the new Clause differs from cl.5 in the 1982 Clauses in that it contains an unqualified waiver of the implied warranties of seaworthiness of the ship and fitness of the ship to carry the subject matter to its destination. The ICTC and Clauses for Special Trades and many brokers' wordings already contained provi-sions to similar effect. The amendment removes any question as to whether cl.5 might affect the scope of an assured's duty of disclosure.[22]

Doctrine of seaworthiness in the United States

20–42 *Note 225*: This subject has again been visited in the latest volume of *Thomas*, the Modern Law of Marine Insurance, Vol. 3 (2009), at ch.5, "Warranties and utmost good faith in U.S. marine insurance contracts" contributed by Professor Martin Davies.

Note 226: There is Supreme Court authority supporting the proposition that there is an implied absolute warranty of seaworthiness in a voyage hull policy

---

[20] The important difference in relation to the position of bona fide purchasers has already been discussed.
[21] See para.22–28 below. See also, Dunt, *op. cit.*, at paras 8.31 to 8.34 and 8.67 to 8.68 where the complex interaction between the revised cl.4.3, revised cl.5.1.2 and revised duration of the transit under cl.8 is more fully considered.
[22] By virtue of s.18(3)(d) in the 1906 Act. This question is discussed briefly in the main work at (p.868), in the context of the 1982 Clauses which contained a qualified waiver of the implied warranties. The previous wording in the 1982 Clauses also left room for uncertainty as to when the assured would have to have been privy to the unseaworthiness or unfitness so as to keep the implied warranties in place. That difficulty is, of course, removed under the 2009 Clauses.

under Federal maritime law: Davies *op. cit.* para.5.9, citing *The Caledonia* 157 U.S. 134 (1895).

Note 229: See also Davies, *op. cit.*, for a yet more recent discussion of the problems resulting from the *Wilburn Boat* case.

The analysis contained in these paragraphs of the main work appears (to the **20–43 to** editors, at least) to be consistent with Professor Davies' more up-to-date treat- **20–45** ment of the subject, *op. cit.* at paras 5.9 to 5.11. Recent cases have continued the judicial trend in favour of applying a "knowledge standard" similar to that of privity under s.39(5) of the 1906 Act to the implied negative warranty adumbrated in the seminal case of *The Spot Pack*.[23] According to Professor Davies "the implied modified negative warranty is almost exactly equivalent in effect" to the latter part of s.39(5). Most courts in the United States now apply this more stringent standard, and some academic writers consider that the relevant standard is no longer open to controversy.[24]

---

[23] See *Continental Ins Co v Lone Eagle Shipping Ltd* 952 F. Supp. 1046; (1997) A.M.C. 1099; *Federal Ins Co v PGG Realty* 538 F. Supp. 2d. 680 (2008); Davies, *op. cit.*, para.5.10.

[24] See Davies, *op. cit.*, para.5.10.

CHAPTER 21

ILLEGALITY OF THE RISK

Contracts tainted by illegality

Note 16: This footnote should be deleted. The matter is discussed in para.21–19. **21–03**

Unlawfulness in the course of performance

As a matter of the general law of contract, where neither party intends, at the time **21–16** of contracting, to perform the contract illegally, the mere fact of an unlawful act being committed in the course of performance does not render the contract illegal *in its formation* and thus unenforceable by the party committing the unlawful act.[1] As is discussed in para.21–19, illegality in the course of performance may, however, as a matter of common law, in exceptional circumstances prevent recovery by the guilty party on the basis of his illegal performance. Illegality in the course of performance may, independently of the common law, amount to a breach of the warranty of legality set out in s.41 of the Marine Insurance Act 1906, also discussed in para.21–19 below.

Unlawful act in the course of performance

The majority of cases are concerned with the position where the contract or adventure **21–19** can lawfully be performed, but some illegality is committed in the course of it which was not intended at the time when the policy was effected: that is to say, the case which is provided for by the second part of s.41 of the Marine Insurance Act 1906.

Turning first to the warranty of legality, it is necessary to consider whether the illegal act was one over which the parties had any control or to which they were privy.[2] If it was not, their rights are unimpaired. If the assured could have controlled and did not control the unlawful performance, then he will be in breach of the warranty under s.41 and the underwriter will be discharged from the date of the breach. In exceptional cases, a party who is implicated in the unlawful performance may still be able to recover moneys paid under the contract; the principles are similar to those which apply in the case of an adventure that is illegal

---

[1] *Wetherell v Jones* (1832) 3 B. & Ad. 221; *St John Shipping Corporation v Joseph Rank Ltd* [1957] 1 Q.B. 267.
[2] The Marine Insurance Act 1906, s.41, refers only to illegality over which the assured has "control", but it is submitted that the principle is somewhat wider. Mere knowledge that an illegality is to be or is being committed is plainly insufficient to preclude recovery: see, e.g., *Cunard v Hyde (No.1)* (1858) E.B. & E. 670. But it is submitted that if the assured or, for that matter, the underwriter, as well as knowing of the intended illegality consents to it or acquiesces in it in such manner as to suggest that it has his consent, this must preclude the party concerned from enforcing the policy. *Cunard v Hyde (No.1)* (1858) E.B. & E. 670 supports this view of the law.

129

at the outset.[3] The implied warranty that the adventure shall be carried out in a lawful manner is of equal relevance to time and to voyage policies. It is not every unlawful act that arises in the course of performance which will amount to a breach of the implied warranty. It is necessary to consider what the "insured adventure" is in any one case, and an unlawful act which is incidental to that adventure and falls outside its scope does not infringe the s.41 warranty.[4]

The implied warranty in s.41 is quite distinct from the common law principle that an assured may be precluded by public policy from enforcing a claim under his policy. An assured who deliberately destroys the insured subject matter, or allows it to be destroyed with reckless disregard for its safety, is unable to recover whether or not his conduct is criminal.[5] The conduct must, however, be that of the assured, and not simply a person for whom the assured is vicariously liable[6] unless the assured has in some way participated in their acts.[7] Although uncertainly still remains, it would see that the courts will not deprive the assured of a claim on public policy grounds unless two conditions are satisfied: there is causal connection between the illegality and the loss; and the illegality is of a sufficiently serious nature to justify the court refusing to lend its assistance to the claimant. The causation test reflects the principle that an assured who is driven to relying upon his own illegal act cannot recover from his insurers.[8] It follows that if the assured does not need to rely upon illegality, then he is entitled to recover, as where the assured has purchased the cargo with the proceeds of an illegal cargo.[9] The second requirement, that of culpable behaviour, is more complex. In *Tinsley v Milligan*[10] the House of Lords overruled a series of cases which held that the court would permit recovery despite illegality if the conduct of the claimant did not offend the "public conscience".[11] *Tinsley* was a case involving a contract illegal in its formation, not in its performance, and for some time there was a dispute as to whether *Tinsley* extended to the latter situation.[12] However, the

---

[3] See para.21–26 of the main work.

[4] *Royal Boskalis Ltd v Mountain* [1998] 2 Q.B. 647, per Phillips L.J. at 736. The view was expressed that the s.41 warranty is concerned only with English law.

[5] Marine Insurance Act 1906, s.55(2)(a) (wilful misconduct). See: *Samuel v Dumas* [1924] A.C. 431; *Beresford v Royal Insurance Co* [1938] A.C. 586; *Gray v Barr* [1971] 2 Q.B. 554; *National Oilwell (UK) Ltd v Davy Offshore Ltd* [1993] 2 Lloyd's Rep. 582; *Ronson International Ltd v Patrick* [2006] Lloyd's Rep. IR 194; *Porter v Zurich Insurance Co* [2010] Lloyd's Rep. IR 373.

[6] *Lancashire County Council v Municipal Mutual Insurance Ltd* [1995] L.R.L.R. 393; *London Borough of Redbridge v Municipal Mutual Insurance Ltd* [2001] Lloyd's Rep. IR 545; *Hawley v Lurninar Leisure Plc* [2006] Lloyd's Rep. IR 307. On this basis an assured may recover under a liability policy for an award of punitive damages against him based on the conduct of his employees, provided that the policy is consistent with such recovery.

[7] *Midland Insurance v Smith* (1881) 6 Q.B.D. 561; *Samuel v Dumas* [1924] A.C. 431.

[8] Or, for that matter, bring an action in contract or tort against an alleged wrongdoer: *Vellino v Chief Constable of the Greater Manchester Police* [2002] 1 W.L.R. 218; *Gray v Thames Trains Ltd* [2009] UKHL 33; *Moore Stephens v Stone & Rolls Ltd* [2009] UKHL 39.

[9] *Bird v Appleton* (1800) 8 T.R. 562. See para.562.

[10] [1993] 3 All E.R. 65.

[11] *St John Shipping Corporation v Joseph Rank Ltd* [1957] 1 Q.B. 267; *Euro-Diam Ltd v Bathurst* [1987] 1 Lloyds Rep. 178, affirmed [1988] 2 All E.R. 23. See also: *21st Century Logistics Solutions Ltd v Madysen* [2004] EWHC 231 (QB); *K/S Lincoln v CB Richard Ellis Hotels Ltd* [2009] EWHC 2344 (TCC).

[12] Indeed, the editors of Arnould have vacillated on the point. See para.21–03, fn.16, of the 17th edition of the main work.

weight of authority now supports the proposition that the degree of culpability remains a part of the test if the assured is to be denied recovery for an illegal act committed in the course of his performance of the contract or the conduct of the adventure, recent cases having decided that the assured's conduct must be "reprehensible or grossly immoral"[13] in that "there must be an element of moral turpitude or moral reprehensibility involved in the relevant conduct."[14]

Fines and sanctions

A fine, whether administrative or criminal in nature, is in principle irrecoverable **21–20A** under an insurance policy, in particular under P&I Club rules which indemnify the assured for defence and other costs.[15] However, if the offence is based on negligence or does not entail personal culpable criminality, it is arguable that the insurers may have to respond to any claim.[16]

Effect of counter-terrorism legislation

The Counter-Terrorism Act 2008 authorises the Treasury to issue a prohibition on **21–27** transactions and business relationships involving foreign terrorist organisations. The issue of such a prohibition would have the effects of: (a) rendering illegal any future contract of insurance taken out with a proscribed organisation; and (b) discharging by frustration any existing contract of insurance with such an organisation. In *Islamic Republic of Iran Shipping Lines v Steamship Mutual Underwriting Association (Bermuda) Ltd*[17] 28 vessels belonging to IRISL were entered into the defendant P&I Club, IRISL being insured against liability for, inter alia, bunker oil pollution as required by the Bunkers Convention. An order prohibiting transactions with IRISL made under the 2008 Act came into force on October 12, 2009. On October 30, 2009 the Club terminated IRISL's membership, but less than twenty-four hours later IRISL suffered a casualty. The Club denied liability, arguing that the Order operated to discharge the insurance by reason of frustration or supervening illegality. Beatson J. held that the validity of the cover had been preserved by a temporary licence issued by the UK Government on October 30, 2009 so that the policy was unaffected.

---

[13] *United Project Consultants Pte Ltd v Leong Kwok Onn* [2005] 4 S.L.R. 214; *Moore Stephens v Stone & Rolls Ltd* [2009] UKHL 39, the formulation of Lord Phillips at paras 24–27.
[14] *Safeway Stores Ltd v Twigger* [2010] EWHC 11 (Comm), per Flaux J. at para.26.
[15] *Gray v Thames Trains Ltd* [2009] UKHL 33.
[16] *Safeway Stores Ltd and Others v Twigger* [2010] EWHC 11 (Comm); *Griffin v UHY Hacker Young & Partners* [2010] EWHC 146 (Ch).
[17] [2010] EWHC 2661 (Comm).

CHAPTER 22

LOSSES COVERED BY THE POLICY: GENERAL PRINCIPLES

Included and excluded losses

Note 2: The editors' suggestion that these exclusions might result in a substantial **22–01** reduction in the scope of the cover under the Institute Cargo Clauses was prompted by the decision in *Mayban General Insurance Bhd v Alstom Power Plants Ltd*.[1] The reasoning in that case has since been disapproved by the Court of Appeal, in *Global Process Systems Inc v Syarikat Takaful Malaysia Berhad (The Cendor Mopu)*.[2] If this decision is upheld the impact of these exclusions is unlikely to be as far-reaching as was suggested in this footnote, in any future cases; see the discussion at paras 22–25 to 22–28 below in this Supplement.

Time when the proximate cause must operate

The importance of the temporal limitations in a time policy was emphasised **22–02** by the House of Lords in *Wasa International Insurance v Lexington Insurance*.[3] In the opinion of the present editors, *Wasa v Lexington* does not affect the proposition at the end of this paragraph in the main work that, depending on the language used in the policy, loss proximately caused by a peril operating during its currency which may not have eventuated or developed to its full extent until after the policy had run off can still be recovered. *Knight v Faith*,[4] which is commonly regarded as the source of the "death blow principle", was treated by both Lord Mance and Lord Collins as a leading authority, and Lord Mance noted expressly[5] that the emphasis in *Knight v Faith* was on the need for the peril insured against to occur during the continuance of the risk: "damage materialising or developing from it after the policy period would still be covered."

Remote causes

The "but for" test, which is referred to in the course of this paragraph, was **22–05** discussed in an insurance context in *Orient-Express Hotels Ltd v Assicurazioni Generali SpA*,[6] where, unusually, the policy contained an express stipulation referring to this test for causation.

---

[1] [2004] 2 Lloyd's Rep. 609.
[2] [2010] 1 Lloyd's Rep. 243. At the time of going to press, the judgment of the Supreme Court is awaited.
[3] [2009] Lloyd's Rep IR 675; see also *Loyaltrend Ltd v Creechurch Dedicated Ltd* [2010] Lloyd's Rep IR 466.
[4] (1850) 15 Q.B. 649.
[5] [2009] Lloyd's Rep IR 675, para.39.
[6] [2010] EWHC 1186 (Comm).

Effect of misconduct of the assured or his employees or agents

22–07 The regime that was introduced under the Institute Cargo Clauses (1/1/82) and is discussed in this paragraph of the main work has been continued under the 2009 Clauses. Before the new Clauses were introduced in 2009, the 1963 Clauses (which contained the Seaworthiness Admitted Clause) were still used in some overseas markets, notably in Japan. It appears that the 2009 Clauses (unlike the 1982 Clauses) are gaining acceptance worldwide.

Loss by combination of causes

22–18 The propositions that there may be more than one cause which can properly be regarded as a proximate cause of loss and that the assured can recover where one of those causes of approximately equal efficiency is an insured peril and the other cause, though falling outside the scope of the policy, is not the subject of an express exclusion were not in issue in *Global Process Systems Inc v Syarikat Takaful Malaysia Berhad (The Cendor Mopu).*[7] However, the illustration given in this paragraph of the main work, of cases where an unseaworthy vessel is damaged or lost as a result of adverse but not exceptional weather or sea conditions which she would have been able to withstand if she had been in seaworthy condition, now merits further discussion.

First, it appeared to be clearly established that the loss in such cases is still to be regarded as a loss by perils of the seas.[8] This was called into question by the insurers' arguments in *The Cendor Mopu*; the principle as just stated was confirmed in the Court of Appeal. It remains to be seen whether this view is upheld by the Supreme Court.

Second, this illustration given in the main work, supported by reference to the important decision in *The Miss Jay Jay*,[9] was put forward as an example of a situation of a kind which may lend itself to being analysed as one where there are two proximate causes.

It is this aspect which now requires discussion. It will be appreciated that the practice in hull insurance is that unseaworthiness is not an excepted peril. In hull cases, therefore, it will generally make no difference whether a peril of the seas is the sole proximate cause of loss or whether the peril of the seas and the unseaworthy condition of the vessel are both to be classed as proximate causes. The modern practice in cargo insurance, on the other hand, is that inherent vice is the subject of an express exclusion, under the Institute Cargo Clauses.[10] In this context, it would matter whether the peril of the seas or external fortuity is the sole proximate cause, or whether inherent vice can be regarded as also being a proximate cause of loss.[11]

---

[7] [2009] 2 Lloyd's Rep. 71 (Blair J.); [2010] 1 Lloyd's Rep 243 (CA). It was suggested in the assured's printed case in the Supreme Court that the proposition that there can be more than one proximate cause of a loss may merit re-examination in some future case, but the issue was not raised on this appeal.
[8] See the cases cited at note 181 in this paragraph of the main work; and paras 22–30, 23–15 in the main work and below.
[9] [1987] 1 Lloyd's Rep. 32.
[10] Clause 4.3 in both the 1982 and the 2009 Clauses (the wording is the same).
[11] The principle discussed at para.22–19 in the main work would apply if there were two proximate causes, one of which was inherent vice.

The *Cendor Mopu* was a case of cargo insurance. The Court of Appeal held that the sole proximate cause of the loss was a peril of the seas, an external fortuity covered under the policy, and that the concept of inherent vice does not extend to inability of an insured cargo to withstand the external operation of an insured peril.[12] Inherent vice is not the same as unseaworthiness.[13] In the Supreme Court, the insurers argued strenuously that the case should be regarded as one where there were two proximate causes (if inherent vice was not the sole cause). At the time of going to press, the Supreme Court has still to deliver its judgment in *The Cendor Mopu*.[14] In short, while the conclusion reached in *The Miss Jay Jay* (that there were two proximate causes) may sometimes be appropriate in situations of the kind postulated by the example given at this point in the main work, it is unlikely (unless the decision the Court of Appeal in *The Cendor Mopu* is reversed) that a similar conclusion could properly be reached in relation to cargo insurance claims, so as to treat perils of the seas and inherent vice as both being proximate causes. The subject is more fully discussed under later paragraph headings in this Supplement.[15]

Loss by combination of causes–one excepted

The proposition discussed in this paragraph of the main work was not in issue in **22–19** *The Cendor Mopu* (above). While continuing to maintain that Blair J. had rightly decided that inherent vice was *the* proximate cause of the loss, the insurers presented their case before the Supreme Court on the basis that inherent vice was at least *a* proximate cause which, being the subject of express exclusion, would be a bar to any recovery by the assured (in accordance with the principle established by the *Wayne Tank*[16] case discussed in this paragraph). It remains to be seen whether the Supreme Court upholds the view of the Court of Appeal that *The Cendor Mopu* was not a case where there were two proximate causes. The point is further discussed at paras 22–25G *et seq*, below.

Inevitable damage

Inevitability of loss was one of the defences raised at trial by the insurers in *The* **22–24** *Cendor Mopu*.[17] It was not disputed that the principle discussed in this paragraph exists, but as in every other case (so far as we aware) where this defence has been attempted, insurers were unable to prove that the loss was inevitable. It was common ground that the question of inevitability has to be judged as at the time when the policy incepted, and that "inevitability" in this context means that the

---

[12] [2010] 1 Lloyd's Rep. 243.
[13] Unseaworthiness amounting to general debility of a vessel can no doubt be equated with inherent vice; but unseaworthiness in the broader sense of an inbility to withstand adverse but not exceptional weather and sea conditions cannot be, under the Court of Appeal's reasoning. It remains to be seen whether the Supreme Court holds the same view. The general debility cases were discussed in *The Miss Jay Jay* [1985]. 1 Lloyd's Rep. 264; [1987] 1 Lloyd's Rep. 32. And see paras 22–30 and 23–15 in the main work.
[14] The hearing of the appeal took place on 29 and 30 July 2010.
[15] See at paras 22–25 to 22–28 below.
[16] [1974] Q.B. 57.
[17] [2009] 7 Lloyd's Rep. 71, paras 85–89. This issue was not pursued on appeal.

loss in question is certain to happen. Probability, however high, does not bring a case within the ambit of inevitability.[18] There was a strong probability of failure of the legs as the rig was being towed round the Cape, but this was not inevitable.

In these circumstances, Blair J. did not need to decide the question discussed in the main work, as to whether, in addition to the loss being inevitable, it must be shown that there was a known certainty of loss, but was content to accept the analysis in this paragraph of *Arnould* without deciding that point.[19]

Inherent vice or nature of the subject matter insured

22–25   The paragraphs in the main work dealing with this subject have now all to be read in the light of the decision in *The Cendor Mopu*.[20] The principle that loss caused by the inherent vice or nature of the subject-matter insured is not covered by a marine policy has been an established principle of English law for at least two centuries.[21] Inherent vice is not defined in s.55 (2)(c) of the Marine Insurance Act 1906, where this principle is enacted, and there have been remarkably few cases in which the meaning of inherent vice has been considered by the Courts.[22] Indeed, prior to *The Cendor Mopu*, there appears only to have been one case where the concept was considered at the highest appellate level (*Soya v White*[23] in 1982), and only a handful of cases at Court of Appeal level. In *The Cendor Mopu*, the meaning of inherent vice and the proper causation analysis in cases where this defence is asserted had to be explored in more depth than had been found necessary in any previous case on the subject.[24]

22–25A   The definition of inherent vice contained in the second edition of this work is repeated verbatim at the outset of para.22–25. After quoting *Arnould*'s definition, the definitions given by Lord Diplock and Donaldson L.J. respectively in *Soya v White* were then quoted and the relationship between these definitions was discussed. *The Cendor Mopu* puts a fresh perspective on these formulations of the test for inherent vice.

22–25B   Taking first Sir Joseph Arnould's formulation, this places the emphasis firmly on inherent vice as referring to something which is internal to the goods themselves. In the view of the Court of Appeal, *Arnould*'s emphasis was clearly sound; all the cases in which a defence of inherent vice has prevailed have been cases

---

[18] *Ibid*, para.87.

[19] *Ibid*, para.89.

[20] [2010] 1 Lloyds' Rep. 243. The facts are outlined at para.23–15A below. The decision of the Supreme Court is awaited, at the time of going to press.

[21] Since at least *Boyd v Dubois* (1811) 3 Cowp. 133.

[22] Perhaps reflecting that there has never been much controversy about its meaning (at least until the *Mayban* case, [2004] 2 Lloyd's Rep. 609). Thus for example in *Noten v Harding* [1990] 2 Lloyd's Rep. 283, at 287, Bingham L.J. said there was "not much doubt" as to the meaning of inherent vice, before going on to cite the definition given by Lord Diplock in *Soya v White* and the definition in *Arnould* with approval.

[23] [1983] 1 Lloyd's Rep. 122 (HL).

[24] The facts in *The Cendor Mopu* are outlined at para.23–15A below. Because the case involved the operation of an external fortuitous cause, the arguments covered a wide range of issues, including the ambit of the fortuity requirement inherent in the concept of perils of the seas. *The Cendor Mopu* is therefore an important decision on the meaning of perils of the seas, as well as now being the leading case on inherent vice. The case is also discussed at paras 23–15 *et seq* below in the context of the sections of this work dealing with perils of the seas.

where the inherent vice was something internal to the goods themselves,[25] and where there was no operation of an external insured peril causing the damage.[26] However, Waller and Carnworth L.JJ. both considered that *Arnould*'s definition, referring to "loss or deterioration which arises *solely*[27] from a principle of decay or corruption inherent in the subject insured" is not to be taken literally. Waller L.J. said[28] that:

"I do not think that Arnould's original suggested definition of inherent vice can be taken literally ... inherent vice can be a cause even though some outside agency such as the motion of the waves has contributed causally to the loss ... Arnould almost certainly intended his definition to be understood as meaning that inherent vice would be the sole cause where any other outside causative factor did not amount to a peril insured against."

Carnworth L.J. said[29]:

"This wording with its emphasis on something inherent in the subject insured, as opposed to the impact of external factors, has proved remarkably resilient over the ensuing 150 years. It is true that the cases (both before and since) show that this emphasis cannot be taken too far, and that external factors may be relevant"

(giving the example of weather conditions hastening the deterioration of the gloves in *Noten v Harding*).

It was common ground in the Court of Appeal in *The Cendor Mopu* that the **22–25C** definition of inherent vice given by Lord Diplock in *Soya v White*[30] was to be accepted and applied, although there was of course considerable debate as to what he meant. The suggestion at para.22–25 in the main work that there is no reason to suppose that Lord Diplock disagreed with Donaldson L.J.'s approach in the Court of Appeal in *Soya v White* can no longer be maintained[31] in the light of what was said by Waller and Carnworth L.JJ. in *The Cendor Mopu*. Waller L.J. said[32] that it was not clear to him that Lord Diplock was supporting Donaldson L.J.'s view; if anything, by implication he was saying he did not need to go into the question. Carnworth L.J. took a similar view, stating[33] that he understood the

---

[25] As Phillips J. observed in *Noten v Harding* [1989] 2 Lloyd's Rep. 527, 530.

[26] The only exception is the *Mayban* case, which has now been disapproved. Every other case where the loss has been held to have been caused by inherent vice, so far as the editors are aware, fell squarely within the scope of *Arnould*'s definition.

[27] Emphasis added for purposes of discussion.

[28] [2010] 1 Lloyd's Rep. 243, para 56.

[29] *Ibid*, para.70.

[30] [1983] 1 Lloyd's Rep. 122, 125. The relevant passage is quoted at para.22–25 in the main work. In summarising the facts, Lord Diplock had noted that "no incident was shown to have occurred upon the voyage whereby the moisture content present in the bulk on shipment had been increased from any external source."

[31] The suggestion at footnote 250 in the main work that Lord Diplock's test was treated in *Noten v Harding* as not differing from Donaldson L.J.'s test is incorrect. Only the Diplock test was referred to by the CA in *Noten v Harding*.

[32] [2010] 1 Lloyd's Rep. 243, para.53. Waller L.J. also doubted whether Donaldson L.J.'s view was supported by the other members of the Court, in the CA in *Soya v White* (see para.52).

[33] [2010] 1 Lloyd's Rep. 243, para.69.

relevant passage in Lord Diplock's speech "not as an endorsement of the much fuller and more controversial analysis by Donaldson LJ . . . but rather as a concise summary of the conventional understanding, in a context where the issue did not arise directly for decision." Carnworth L.J. then went on to suggest that the views expressed by Donaldson L.J. (which were obiter dicta) should be treated with some care, and to question whether these dicta required the substantial reinterpretation of the concept of inherent vice in the current (17th) edition of *Arnould*, compared with previous editions.[34] Subject to what the Supreme Court may decide in *The Cendor Mopu*, that criticism is accepted as fair, but it would not be appropriate now simply to reinstate the 16th edition.[35]

22–25D   In the light of the Court of Appeal judgments in *The Cendor Mopu*, it would seem that Donaldson L.J.'s view of the meaning of inherent vice ought not to be given weight, if and to the extent that it could be interpreted as meaning something different from what Lord Diplock had intended by his definition in *Soya v White* (above). It would also seem that the editors' acceptance in the first sentence of para.22–26 of the main work that, after *Soya v White*, inability to withstand the ordinary incidents of the voyage is clearly an appropriate test of inherent vice, which was prompted by Donaldson L.J.'s remarks in *Soya v White* and the *Mayban* case, can no longer stand, at least in that form. The crux of the matter is what meaning is to be given to Lord Diplock's reference to "the ordinary course of the contemplated voyage" and (if relevant) to the ordinary incidents of the voyage, in Donaldson L.J.'s analysis.

22–25E   The Court of Appeal's analysis in *The Cendor Mopu*, substantially accepting the arguments advanced by the assured, was that what Lord Diplock had in mind was the distinction between fortuitous events and the ordinary action of the winds and waves.[36] It is by that standard that the "ordinary" is to be judged.[37] The fact that the weather and sea conditions encountered on the voyage are within the range of those that might reasonably be expected to be encountered, and are not exceptional, does not mean that they are "ordinary." Adverse weather which is not exceptional is still a peril of the seas.[38] Approaching the matter from the other end, the Court of Appeal appear to have interpreted Lord Diplock's formulation as meaning that inherent vice cannot be the proximate cause of the loss where the damage is occasioned by some outside causative factor that amounts to the operation of an insured peril. In effect, the Court of Appeal married the concepts of inherent vice and the fortuity requirement in relation to perils of the seas and "all risks" coverage so as to produce a coherent position.[39] Both parts of Lord Diplock's test have their part to play here. If there is no adverse weather or other external operation of an insured peril, the conclusion is likely to be that the

---

[34] *Ibid*, para.20.

[35] For example, earlier editions sought to distinguish between inherent frailty and inherent vice; see note 251 at para.22–26 in the main work. There would seem to be no particular advantage to be gained by revisiting such material, however interesting in itself. The law with regard to inherent vice has now to be viewed through the prism of *The Cendor Mopu*. The treatment of the subject in recent editions of *Arnould* is by the by.

[36] Rule 7 of the Rules for Construction scheduled to the 1906 Act; see para. 23–13 in the main work.

[37] [2010] 1 Lloyd's Rep.243, paras 59–62, 68–9.

[38] *Ibid*, para. 59, citing *N. E. Neter & Co v Licenses & Gen Ins Co* (1943) 77 LL.L. Rep. 202; and see para.23–15 in the main work.

[39] See the discussion at paras 23–15A *et seq* below.

damage occurred in "the ordinary course of the contemplated voyage", the source of the damage therefore being internal to the goods themselves; where there has been an operation of an external cause which is an insured peril ("the intervention of any fortuitous external accident or casualty") the resulting loss will not be a loss by inherent vice. There would appear, in truth, to be no real difference between Arnould's original definition and that provided by Lord Diplock, as these were interpreted by the Court of Appeal in *The Cendor Mopu*.

The Court of Appeal held that the casualty in *The Cendor Mopu* was caused by **22–25F** an external fortuity covered under the policy, the impact of a "leg-breaking wave" hitting the tow in just the right way to cause one of the legs to break off,[40] and that the susceptibility of the rig to fatigue cracking induced by the motion of the barge as it was towed through the seas and its inability to withstand conditions within the range of those that might reasonably be expected to be encountered on the voyage was not to be treated as amounting to inherent vice.

Waller L.J. expressed his conclusion in the following terms in two paragraphs of his judgment which were strongly criticised by the insurers on the subsequent appeal to the Supreme Court as laying down a new test. In the first passage,[41] Waller L.J. stated that even if the question to be considered was whether the cause was an inability to withstand ordinary incidents of the voyage, "the answer cannot be found by reference to what might be reasonably foreseeable as the ordinary incidents of that voyage, but by reference to wind or wave which, it would be the common understanding, would be bound to occur as the ordinary incidents on any normal voyage of the kind being undertaken." The second passage[42] was also phrased in similar terms, referring to "a leg-breaking wave, not bound to occur in the way that it did on any normal voyage round the Cape of Good Hope" as the cause of the loss, and a risk covered by the policy.

Whether these passages in fact contain any new test, and whether they are consistent with the general principles comprised in Lord Diplock's formulation[43] of what is meant by inherent vice, fell to the Supreme Court to determine. At the time of going to press, the judgment of the Supreme Court has still to be delivered.

Both at first instance and in the Court of Appeal in *The Cendor Mopu* the case **22–25G** was approached as one where there was a straight choice to be made, between finding that the loss was solely caused by inherent vice and that it was solely caused by perils of the seas. Waller L.J. stated that the possibility of there being two proximate causes was not canvassed in the Court of Appeal[44] and expressed some scepticism as to whether it is possible to analyse a situation where an external insured peril has operated as one where there are two proximate causes, one of which is inherent vice: "Lord Diplock does not say whether one may have concurrent proximate causes but, taking Arnould's definition, it would appear

---

[40] See para.23–15A below.
[41] [2010] 1 Lloyd's Rep. 243, para.62.
[42] *Ibid*, para.64.
[43] The Court of Appeal's interpretation of Lord Diplock's test and of Arnould's original definition of inherent vice is discussed in the preceding paragraphs of this Supplement. Waller L.J.'s use of the phrase "bound to occur" appears to reflect the Court's interpretation of the Diplock and Arnould tests.
[44] [2010] 1 Lloyd's Rep. 243, para.16.

difficult to have concurrent causes where one candidate is inherent vice."[45] However, it was only when *The Cendor Mopu* reached the Supreme Court that the possibility that the case should be analysed as one where there were two proximate causes was debated. The outcome of that debate is presently unknown.

22–25H   If the decision of the Court of Appeal in *The Cendor Mopu* is upheld, the likelihood of a "two causes" analysis being adopted where the possible candidates are an insured peril and inherent vice now seems remote, and the concerns expressed in the main work, at paras 22–26 and 22–28, as to the potential impact of the express exclusion of inherent vice in the Institute Cargo Clauses will have been overstated. Under the Court of Appeal's reasoning, it is difficult to envisage circumstances in which a two causes analysis is likely to be applied so as to defeat a claim for loss of or damage to insured cargo caused by an external fortuity covered under the policy on the ground that inherent vice, excluded under cl. 4.3 in the Cargo Clauses, was a concurrent proximate cause.

22–26   This paragraph in the main work may now be disregarded. It is substantially replaced by the discussion at paras 22–25A *et seq* above, and may in any event be overtaken by the Supreme Court decision in *The Cendor Mopu*. The proposition that inherent vice will afford a defence when it is the sole cause of loss is of course unaffected. It may be that the discussion of inherent frailty in recent editions of *Arnould*, referred to at note 251 under this paragraph is validated by *The Cendor Mopu*, but the editors do not think that anything is to be gained by seeking to revisit that interesting question. The controversial decision in *Mayban v Alstom*, referred to at footnote 253, was overruled by the Court of Appeal in *The Cendor Mopu* as already noted in preceding paragraphs in this Supplement. The likelihood of a two causes analysis being applied where one of the possible candidates is inherent vice may now have become rather remote, at any rate where the other potential candidate is a peril of the seas.

22–27   *Noten v Harding*[46] was followed by the British Columbia Court of Appeal in *Nelson Marketing International Inc v Royal & Sun Alliance Co of Canada*.[47] The facts of the two cases were very similar, and in both cases the assured was unable to establish an external cause; there was no evidence of any external fortuity having operated.[48] The insured goods in *Nelson Marketing* were three consignments of laminated wood flooring. This product was susceptible to absorbing and releasing moisture upon changes in temperature and humidity. All three shipments were found upon discharge to have been damaged by moisture. The case was decided upon the ground that there was no fortuitous event covered by the Institute Cargo Clauses, rather than on the ground of inherent vice, but it seems clear from the description of the facts that *Nelson Marketing* is a textbook example of loss resulting from moisture emanating from the goods themselves present before shipment, which is inherent vice. As the Court stated, the case seems to be indistinguishable from *Noten v Harding*.

---

[45] *Ibid*, para.57. The argument that inability to withstand a peril and the operation of that peril are concurrent causes does seem rather circular. It could be said of any case where property is damaged by a peril that it was unable to withstand that peril.

[46] [1990] 2 Lloyd's Rep. 283.

[47] [2006] BCCA 327.

[48] Changes in ambient temperature and humidity in the course of a voyage cannot generally be regarded as fortuitous events or as an operation of insured perils.

The wording of the inherent vice exclusion (cl.4.4) was left unaltered when the **22–28** Institute Cargo Clauses were revised in 2009. See the Appendix below. The likelihood of this exclusion being applied in future cases, after the decision in *The Cendor Mopu*, has been sufficiently discussed in preceding paragraphs in this Supplement. The exclusion with regard to Insufficiency of Packing or Preparation (cl.4.3), on the other hand, has been substantially revised in the 2009 Clauses. The potential impact of this exclusion, and the relationship between cl.4.3 and cl.4.4 merit some further discussion.

The wording of cl.4.3, in its revised form in the 2009 Clauses, reads as follows:

"4 In no case shall this insurance cover . . .

4.3 Loss damage or expense caused by insufficiency or unsuitability of packing or preparation of the subject-matter insured to withstand the ordinary incidents of the insured transit where such packing or preparation is carried out by the Assured or their employees or prior to the attachment of this insurance (for the purpose of these Clauses 'packing' shall be deemed to include stowage in a container and 'employees' shall not include independent contractors)."

The revisions to this Clause, which are linked to changes in the wording at other places in the 2009 Clauses, are explained in Dunt, Marine Cargo Insurance, para. 8.31 onwards, and need not be discussed in detail here. The insertion of the words "to withstand the ordinary incidents of the voyage," which did not appear in cl. 4.3 of the 1982 Clauses, appears to have been inspired by *Mayban v Alstom*,[49] but even without that addition it seems to the present editors that this exclusion may well be of greater practical significance than the ensuing exclusion of inherent vice, at cl. 4.4. As already discussed, the likelihood of a two causes analysis being applied, where one of the candidates is inherent vice, may now be remote in the light of *The Cendor Mopu* (subject to what the Supreme Court may decide). The same cannot so easily be said with regard to the insufficiency of packing exclusion. Indeed, it would seem from the description of the facts in *Mayban v Alstom* that this exclusion (which was not invoked by the insurers) could well have been applied, using a two causes analysis, to defeat the claim in that case.[50]

The previous version of cl.4.3, in the 1982 Clauses, has been construed in one case in Australia.[51] There are no English decisions on cl.4.3.

Note 268: On further consideration, the editors regard it as an open question whether bad packing can generally be said to fall within the scope of the concept of inherent vice. The cases referred to do not really establish that proposition. But whatever the general position may be, it is clear that as a matter of construction the inherent vice exclusion (cl.4.4) cannot extend to bad packing; it is only where the carefully circumscribed exclusion at cl.4.3 can be applied that insufficiency

---

[49] [2004] 2 Lloyd's Rep. 609 (since disapproved by the Court of Appeal in *The Cendor Mopu*, see above).
[50] The insufficiency of packing or preparation exclusion would not have been relevant in *The Cendor Mopu*.
[51] *Helicopter Resources Pty Ltd v Sun Alliance Australia Ltd*; see [1991] L.M.L.N. 312, Dunt, *op. cit.* para. 8.35.

of packing or preparation can afford a defence. This view, stated in relation to the 1982 Clauses at footnote 268, applies equally to the 2009 Clauses. The same view is expressed in Dunt, *op. cit.*, at para.8.30.

Mortality among animals

22–29 Mortality is a form of inherent vice ("the inherent vice or nature of the subject matter insured"). *Lawrence v Aberdein*[52] and *Gabay v Lloyd*[53] were cited to the Supreme Court in *The Cendor Mopu* as being cases directly in point in the assured's favour.

Loss arising from unseaworthiness

22–30 The threshold for the fortuity requirement for perils of the seas was extensively discussed in the Court of Appeal in *The Cendor Mopu*[54] where most of the cases referred to in this paragraph were cited. The editors do not consider that the treatment of this topic at this point in the main work needs to be qualified at present, but *The Cendor Mopu* can be seen as an important addition to the authorities in which the principles to be applied when distinguishing between a fortuitous loss and one caused by unseaworthiness have been considered. The subject may call for further discussion when the decision of the Supreme Court becomes available.

Loss proximately caused by delay

22–32 The wording of this exclusion in the Institute Cargo Clauses (1/1/09) no longer contains the word "proximately", but is otherwise unchanged from that in previous editions of the Institute Cargo Clauses. The change in wording of cl.4.5 is said[55] to have been intended by the Joint Cargo Committee to enable it more easily to be argued in appropriate cases that delay was a concurrent proximate cause, thus widening the scope for the exclusion to be applied. The present editors doubt whether the omission of the word "proximately" can be regarded as a change of substance. The word "caused" in an insurance context is usually construed as referring to proximate cause and the exclusion is likely to be construed as having the same meaning as before. That said, as will be apparent from the discussion in the main work, the effect of the delay exclusion is in some respects controversial. The revised wording does not appear to do anything to help resolve that controversy.

---

[52] (1821) 5 B. & Ald. 107.
[53] (1825) 2 B. & C. 793.
[54] [2010] 1 Lloyd's Rep. 243; see also, *Bennett* "Fortuity in the law of Marine insurance", (2007) L.M.C.L.Q. 315, discussed at para. 23–15D below in this Supplement.
[55] See *Dunt*, Marine Cargo Insurance (2009) at para.7.27.

CHAPTER 23

MARINE RISKS

Perils of the Seas

Note 26: That the meaning of perils of the seas is still capable of giving rise to **23–10**
controversy is apparent from the decision in *The Cendor Mopu*.[1]

Perils of the seas must be fortuitous

The principle that it is sufficient that the event was in some way fortuitous and that it **23–13**
does not have to be shown that it was brought about by extreme weather or any violent
action of winds or waves was confirmed in the Court of Appeal *The Cendor Mopu*,[2]
in which it was argued that the proper causation analysis where the insured cargo was
damaged in weather and sea conditions within the range of those reasonably to be
expected to be encountered on the voyage which it was unable to withstand was that
the loss was proximately caused by inherent vice. *The Cendor Mopu* is an important
decision both on the meaning of inherent vice and on the meaning of perils of the
seas.[3] The latter aspect is discussed in more detail at paras 23–15A *et seq* below in
this Supplement. The decision of the Court of Appeal with regard to the meaning of
inherent vice and the causation issues arising from the insurers' reliance on inherent
vice have been discussed under the previous Chapter heading (Chapter 22 above).

    Note 51: The amendments to the Unseaworthiness and Unfitness Exclusion **23–14**
Clause under the Institute Cargo Clauses 1/1/09 do not affect the point made in
this footnote. The interpretation of the 2009 wording and the differences between
the 1982 and 2009 versions of this exclusion are discussed at para.20–41 above
in this Supplement.

Loss by incursion of sea water, or by foundering at sea.

The principle[4] that where a vessel encounters adverse weather or some unusual **23–15**
conditions of the seas, which she is unable to withstand due to her unseaworthy

---

[1] *Global Process Systems Inc v Syarikat Takaful Malaysia Berhad* [2009] 2 Lloyd's Rep. 71; [2010]
1 Lloyd's Rep. 243.
[2] [2010] 1 Lloyd's Rep. 243 (CA). At the time of going to press, the judgment of the Supreme Court
is pending.
[3] The policy was one of cargo insurance under the Institute Cargo Clauses (A) 1/1/82. In the factual
context, it made no difference that the insurance was against "all risks" rather than perils of the seas
as a named peril. If the assured had been unable to establish that the loss was caused by a peril of the
seas, it would not have been covered.
[4] The main authorities supporting this principle are those cited at fn.62 at this point in the main work.
See also the decisions in Singapore in *Kin Yuen Co Pte Ltd v Lombard Ins Co Ltd* [1994] 2 S.L.R. 887;
[1995] 1 S.L.R. 643; *Marina Offshore v China Ins Co* [2007] 1 Lloyd's Rep. 66. And see the citations
at fn.60, for the proposition that adverse, but unusual, weather conditions will suffice. Particular
reliance was placed on *N.E. Neter & Co v Licenses & General Insurances*, in *The Cendor Mopu*.

condition upon sailing, the resulting loss is still to be attributed to perils of the seas, came under scrutiny in *The Cendor Mopu*, above.

Perils of the seas, Inherent vice and unseaworthiness: *The Cendor Mopu*

23–15A The oil rig *Cendor Mopu* was the subject of a cargo policy incorporating the Institute Cargo Clauses (A) 1/1/09. In the course of the insured voyage from Texas to Malaysia, in which the rig was being towed on a barge with its legs in place and elevated in the air above the deck, the legs fell off in quick succession because of fatigue cracking caused by the repeated bending of the legs under the influence of the motions of the barge as it was being towed through the sea. The weather and sea conditions were within the range that could reasonably have been expected to be encountered, and with hindsight the failure of the legs was very probable, but it was not inevitable.[5] The legs would not have fractured if the tow had not encountered a "leg-breaking wave" catching the legs in just the right way to cause one of them to break off.[6] The encounter with the leg-breaking wave was plainly an external fortuitous event of the kind insured under an all risks policy or a policy containing a list of named perils including perils of the seas unless (as the insurers argued) the inability of the insured cargo to withstand it was a bar to recovery.

The trial judge (Blair J.) held that the insurers had a valid defence on the ground that the proximate cause of the loss was inherent vice.[7] His decision was reversed on appeal. Waller L.J. who delivered the leading judgment in the Court of Appeal expressed his conclusion in these terms:

"It is not that the legs simply suffered severe metal fatigue and cracking, i.e. normal wear and tear. Metal fatigue was not the sole cause of the loss of the legs. A leg-breaking wave, not bound to occur in the way it did on any normal voyage round the Cape of Good Hope caused the starboard leg to break off. This led to the others being at greater risk and then breaking off. It was not certain that that would happen and although with the benefit of hindsight we know that it was highly probable, that probability was unknown to the insured and that was a risk against which the appellants insured".[8]

The insurers then appealed to the Supreme Court which has reserved judgment (at the time of going to press).

23–15B At first instance in *The Cendor Mopu* Blair J. followed the decision of Moore-Bick J. in *Mayban General Assurance Bhd v Alstom Plants Ltd*,[9] where the insured cargo (an electrical transformer) was damaged in periods of heavy

---

[5] The insurers' contention that the loss was inevitable was rejected by Blair J, and the point was not pursued on appeal.

[6] [2009] 2 Lloyd's Rep. 71 at paras 48, 87.

[7] *Ibid* para.112.

[8] [2010] 1 Lloyd's Rep. 243 at para.64. Carnwath L.J. expressed similar sentiments in a short concurring judgment. Patten L.J. agreed with both judgments.

[9] [2004] 2 Lloyd's Rep. 609. This decision was treated with reserve in the main work, at paras 22–26 and 23–69, and is criticised in H. Bennett, *Law of Marine Insurance*, 2nd edn (2006), para.15–54. See also, the article by Professor Bennett, "Fortuity in the law of marine insurance", (2007) L.M.C.L.Q. 315, which was referred to extensively by Waller L.J. in *The Cendor Mopu*.

weather, which were held not to have been outside the range of conditions reasonably to be expected, and the proximate cause of the loss was held to be inherent vice. None of the cases on perils of the seas appears to have been cited. Moore-Bick J. put forward the following test,[10] in the course of his judgment:

> "If the conditions encountered by the vessel were more severe than could reasonably have been expected, it is likely that the loss will have been caused by perils of the seas. . . . . If, however, the conditions encountered by the vessel were no more than could reasonably have been expected, the conclusion must be that the real cause of the loss was the inherent inability of the goods to withstand the ordinary incidents of the voyage".

The Court of Appeal rejected the *Mayban* test, in *The Cendor Mopu*,[11] and held **23–15C** that the reasoning in that case, which would lead to the conclusion that an all risks cargo policy only covers loss or damage caused by wholly unusual perils or wholly unusual examples of known perils,[12] was erroneous. In reaching that conclusion, the Court of Appeal relied on Professor Bennett's analysis[13] and on the classification of different points in the spectrum of weather and sea conditions which may or may not amount to perils of the sea in the judgment of Mustill J. in *The Miss Jay Jay*.[14]

Professor Bennett observed in the course of his article, in a passage referred to **23–15D** by Waller L.J. in *Cendor Mopu*,[15] that it is clear that weather and sea conditions are not disqualified from giving rise to fortuitous losses in the context of perils of the sea merely because they were such as might reasonably be expected,[16] but that: "The precise threshold posed by fortuity is, however, uncertain". The intention behind the fortuity requirement is to exclude ordinary wear and tear and accordingly:

> "It may be that circumstances will not quality as fortuitous so as to give rise to a loss by perils of the seas if they are so characteristic of the relevant waters at the relevant time of year that an informed seaman would consider it highly unusual not to encounter such circumstances, even if they are occasionally not encountered . . ."[17]

---

[10] [2004] 2 Lloyd's Rep. 609, at para.21. This passage was in answer to the question that Moore-Bick J. posed to himself. The immediate cause of the damage was the violent movement of the vessel due to the actions of the wind and sea: "These in themselves were certainly events of a fortuitous nature and were external to the cargo but were they the real cause of the loss?"

[11] [2010] 1 Lloyd's Rep. 243.

[12] *Ibid* paras 55, 71; (2007) L.M.C.L.Q. 315, 348.

[13] (2007) L.M.C.L.Q. 315. See para.23–15D below.

[14] [1985] 1 Lloyd's Rep. 264, 271. Mustill J. suggested that weather conditions might be divided into the following categories: "abnormally bad weather", outside the range of conditions which could reasonably be foreseen on the voyage in question; "adverse weather", which lies within the range of what could be foreseen, but at the unfavourable end of that range; "favourable weather" which lies within that range, but is not bad enough to be classed as "adverse"; and "perfect weather".

[15] [2010] 1 Lloyd's Rep. 243 at para.39.

[16] The editors agree with that analysis. See paras 23–13 to 23–15 in the main work, and the authorities there cited.

[17] (2007) L.M.C.L.Q. 315, 331.

In later passages[18] discussing the meaning of inherent vice, Professor Bennett made a similar distinction, proposing that inherent vice might be regarded as the operative cause where the insured goods are not reasonably fit to withstand those perils which it would be unusual not to encounter, but that if they are fit to encounter perils that might reasonably be foreseen, but equally might not be encountered, this would not be inherent vice.

23–15E   The proposition that "adverse weather" (under Mustill J.'s classification, see above) is a peril of the seas was not in dispute in *The Cendor Mopu*. What was in dispute was whether a loss taking place in "adverse weather" is still to be regarded as having been proximately caused by it, where the insured vessel or cargo was unable to withstand those conditions due to its unseaworthy condition upon sailing.[19] On the insurers' case, the proper causation analysis in such circumstances is that the proximate cause is the inherent vice of the subject-matter insured.[20] On the assured's case, inherent vice could not be regarded as the proximate cause where a loss is occasioned by the operation of an external fortuity insured under the policy.

23–15F   Both Blair J. and the Court of Appeal addressed the matter on the basis of a straight choice[21] between an external fortuity (a peril of the seas) and inherent vice being regarded as the sole proximate cause. In the Supreme Court, while the insurers continued to maintain that Blair J. had correctly found inherent vice to have been *the* proximate cause, it became the main thrust of their case that inherent vice was at least *a* proximate cause, relying on the principle that where there are two causes of approximately equal efficiency, one of which is excluded under the policy, the assured cannot recover.[22] The "two causes" analysis is dealt with separately in this Supplement, under Chapter 22 above[23]; at this point we are concerned with the closely-related questions of the threshold for the fortuity requirement in connection with perils of the seas and all-risks policies and the ceiling below which inherent vice could not sensibly or properly be regarded as the cause of loss.

23–15G   The proposition that a loss taking place in "adverse weather" is still to be regarded as proximately caused by peril of the seas where the insured vessel or cargo was unable to withstand those conditions due to unseaworthiness on sailing,[24] which

---

[18] *Ibid* at 345, 360.

[19] The authorities for this proposition, which had appeared to be clearly established in relation to hull policies, are cited at para.23–15, fn.62 in the main work. See also, at para.23–15 above in this Supplement

[20] In response to the development of this argument in the insurers' printed Case on the appeal to the Supreme Court, the assured submitted (at para.61 of the Respondents' Statement of Case) that on that analysis, all the hull insurance cases, starting with *Dudgeon v Pembroke* and *The Xantho*, at the latest, and continuing unbroken for the next 150 years, up to and including the decision of Mustill J. and the Court of Appeal in *The Miss Jay Jay* would have been wrongly decided.

[21] [2010] 1 Lloyd's Rep. 243, at para.16. Waller L.J. was sceptical as to whether it is possible for there to be two proximate causes, one of which is an insured peril and the other of which is inherent vice, *ibid* para.57.

[22] See e.g. *The Miss Jay Jay* [1985] 1 Lloyd's Rep. 264, [1987] Lloyd's Rep. 32; paras 22–18, 22–19 in the main work, and above.

[23] On the assured's case, to suggest that inability to withstand an external peril is the cause of damage and that the external peril is not causative is circular. By definition, if property is damaged by a peril, it was unable to withstand that peril.

[24] See para.23–15 in the main work and above.

Mustill J. had described in *The Miss Jay Jay*[25] as "clearly established", was accepted by the Court of Appeal in *The Cendor Mopu*. On Waller L.J.'s analysis, what Mustill J. described as "favourable weather" conditions may not meet the required test for a fortuity,[26] and if an insured cargo is damaged by the motion of the vessel in "favourable weather" or "perfect weather" the obvious inference in most cases would be that the damage was caused by the inherent vice or nature of the cargo.[27] Waller L.J. did not accept what had been *Arnould's* view[28] that the concept of inherent vice only applies where something internal to the insured property is the *sole* cause of damage: "Inherent vice can be a cause even though some outside agency such as the motion of the waves has contributed causally to the loss".[29]

It was common ground in the Court of Appeal in *The Cendor Mopu* that Lord **23–15H** Diplock's summary of what is meant by inherent vice in *Soya v White* was to be applied. Both Waller and Carnworth L.JJ. considered that what Lord Diplock must have had in mind when referring to the "ordinary course of the voyage" was the contrast drawn in Rule 7 of the Rules for Construction between perils of the seas and the ordinary action of the winds and waves.[30] Insofar as unseaworthiness or inability to withstand the ordinary incidents of the voyage can constitute inherent vice the crucial question was therefore what the word "ordinary" means in this context. It does not mean, as Moore-Bick J. had thought in the *Mayban* case and as Blair J. had accepted in *The Cendor Mopu*, inability to withstand any conditions that might reasonably be expected to be encountered, including "adverse weather". Under the analysis adopted by the Court of Appeal in *The Cendor Mopu*, even if the question to be asked is whether the cause of loss was an inability to withstand the ordinary incidents of the voyage:

> "the answer cannot be found by reference to what might be reasonably foreseeable as the ordinary incidents of that voyage, but by reference to wind or wave which, it would be the common understanding, would be bound to occur as the ordinary incidents of any normal voyage of the kind being undertaken. This is not equating inherent vice with certainty, but it is recognising that an insurer would not cover damage to cargo flowing from the motion of the vessel in such seas, even if it was not certain to occur".[31]

This passage followed immediately from Waller L.J.'s conclusions that **23–15I** "favourable weather" may not amount to a peril of the seas and that damage caused by the motion of the vessel in such weather would be likely in most cases to be regarded as caused by inherent vice or the nature of the cargo. The "bound to occur" test would appear to confine the ordinary course of the voyage or ordinary incidents of the voyage, for the purposes of the doctrine of the inherent vice, substantially to weather and sea conditions falling below the fortuity threshold required for a peril of the seas ("the ordinary action of the winds and waves"),

---

[25] [1985] 1 Lloyd's Rep. 264, 271.
[26] [2010] 1 Lloyd's Rep. 243, para.60.
[27] *Ibid* para.61. See also the discussion of the debility cases at para.23–15 in the main work.
[28] See para.22–25 in the main work, and above.
[29] [2010] 1 Lloyd's Rep. 243, para.56.
[30] [1983] 1 Lloyd's Rep 122; see para.22–25 in the main work and above.
[31] *Ibid* para.62.

and to be similar to, but not identical with, the test proposed by Professor Bennett.[32]

23–15J   At the time of going to press, the Supreme Court has reserved judgment on the appeal in *The Cendor Mopu*. It remains to be seen whether the "found to occur" test proposed by Waller L.J., which was strongly criticised by the appellant insurers, has been upheld and what will take its place if some other test is laid down by the Supreme Court.

Stranding

23–17 The relevant provisions in the Institute Cargo Clauses 1/1/09 are the same as those in the 1982 Clauses referred to in this paragraph of the main work.

Perils of the seas contrasted with natural causes, or wear and tear

23–19 The distinctions between a loss by perils of the seas and a loss caused by inherent vice or wear and tear were considered in *The Cendor Mopu* (above). It is unnecessary at this point to repeat the discussion of *The Cendor Mopu* in earlier paragraphs of this Supplement.

The Collision Liability Clause

23–21 *Note 136*: The efficacy of the pay to be paid wording in the Collision Liability Clause will not be affected by the Third Parties (Rights against Insurers) Act 2010. Under the 2010 Act, which has yet to be implemented, marine insurers will continue to be able to rely on pay to be paid clauses (insofar as they could do so under the existing law) except in relation to loss of life and personal injury claims; see the discussion of the 2010 Act at Chapter 8 above in this Supplement. The Collision Liability Clause expressly excludes liabilities in respect of loss of life and personal injury. Those risks are in practice borne by the P&I Clubs; see para.23–25 in the main work and below.

Meaning of "damages" in the Collision Liability Clause

23–22 The view which is expressed in this paragraph of the main work, departing from that taken in earlier editions and from the view taken in *O'May on Marine Insurance*, is that the Collision Liability Clause is not confined to liabilities in tort and that the essential requirement conveyed by the words "legally liable by way of damages" is only that the collision was in some measure attributable to a breach of duty on the part of the assured. The editors' interpretation is confirmed by the decision of the Court of Appeal in *Bedfordshire Police Authority v Constable*.[33] The expression "legally liable to pay as damages" (in that case, contained in a public liability policy) is a term of art having a settled meaning. *Hall Brothers v Young (The Trident)*[34] (which is discussed at this point in the main

---

[32] See para.23–15D above.
[33] [2009] Lloyd's Rep. IR 607; the first instance decision which is referred to at this point in the main work (fn.126) is now reported at [2009] Lloyd's Rep. IR 39.
[34] [1939] 1 K.B. 748.

work) was treated as the leading case on the meaning of this expression, and as a decision of general application, not confined to collision liabilities under marine policies. In the light of the reasoning in *The Trident*, Longmore L.J. concluded that the relevant question is simply whether the liability falls to be paid "by reason of some breach of duty or obligation".[35] The liability of a police authority to pay compensation under the Riot (Damages) Act 1886 arises from the fact that it is responsible for the preservation of law and order within its area. The owners of *Trident* were not in any sense responsible for the safety of the pilot boat; they just had to pay the cost of repair, if the boat suffered damage during pilotage. It is this concept of responsibility which affords the distinction between sums for which an insured is liable in damages and sums for which he is not so liable.[36]

Limited protection afforded by Collision clause

Note 151: As these liabilities are excluded from the collision liability cover under hull and machinery policies the provisions in the Third Parties (Rights against Insurers) Act 2010 which will preclude reliance on pay to be paid clauses under marine policies in relation to loss of life and injury claims are only likely to affect P&I insurers. **23–25**

Scope of "fire" as an insured peril

Since it is of no consequence how a fire was caused, unless the insurer can prove wilful misconduct of the assured or the operation of some excepted peril, the fact that the cause of a fire damaging the insured property is unexplained plainly does not constitute any bar to recovery by the assured: see e.g. *Yeganeh v Zurich Plc*.[37] **23–28**

Piracy

Since the current edition of *Arnould* was published, there have been numerous cases, well over 200, involving the seizure or attempted seizure of vessels in the Gulf of Aden and in the Indian Ocean by armed gangs operating out of Somalia with the objective of extracting ransom payments for the release of the vessel, any cargo, and the crew. This phenomenon is described in *Masefield AG v Amlin Corporate Member Ltd*.[38] It is generally thought that these hi-jacking episodes are purely for private gain and are not politically motivated. There is plainly no intention, on the part of those involved, to retain the vessels or cargoes and to assert dominion over the property. **23–21 and 23–22**

Since "piracy" has been discussed, in the few reported cases and in the textbooks including *Arnould*, in terms which might be taken to suggest that it is an essential ingredient in this peril that the objective of "pirates" is to steal the property and to keep it for themselves, the question now has to be asked: Does the forcible seizure of a vessel and/or cargo at sea for the purpose of extracting a

---

[35] The language used by Sir Wilfrid Greene M.R. in *The Trident*, above.
[36] [2009] Lloyd's Rep. IR 607, para.25.
[37] [2010] EWHC 1185 (QB).
[38] [2010] Lloyd's Rep. IR 345.

ransom, for private gain, constitute piracy under a marine policy? The answer to that question, in the opinion of the present editors, is plainly yes. It makes no difference that the objective is ransom, rather than to steal the property. So far as we are aware, this is the generally accepted view.[39]

Distinctions between violent theft and piracy

23–33 The fact that piracy may be committed for ransom, not in order to steal the property, has now to be added to the list of distinctions between the two perils discussed in this paragraph. See above, where the recent spate of piracy cases is discussed.

It is understood that the Violent Theft Piracy and Barratry Exclusion Clauses and corresponding Endorsement, referred to at the end of this paragraph in the main work, are now much more widely used—as a result, evidently, of the activities of Somali pirates.

Incidence of loss: latent defect and breakage of shafts

23–57 *Note 352*: See also *IRB Brasil Resseguros SA v CX Reinsurance Co Ltd*[40] upholding an arbitration award in which a similar approach, to the allocation of product liability claims to successive insurance and reinsurance policy years, appears to have been adopted.

The Additional Perils Clauses

23–58 The effect of the provision that the insurance is extended to cover loss of or damage to the vessel caused by any accident is that these Clauses afford what is essentially an all risks cover. This comparison, which the editors support, was drawn by the Nova Scotia Court of Appeal in *Secunda Marine Services Ltd v Liberty Mutual Ins Co*.[41]

The due diligence proviso

23–62 *Note 417*: *The Brentwood* seems to be an isolated case. In *Secunda v Liberty Mutual*, above, the Court refused to follow the approach which had been adopted at first instance in *The Brentwood*, and held that the due diligence proviso is an exclusion, on which the insurer has the burden of proof. Numerous decisions of American Courts to the same effect, in the context of claims under the Inchmaree Clause or Liner Negligence Clauses, were cited to the Nova Scotia Court of Appeal.

---

[39] Staughton J. gave the term piracy a popular or business meaning in *The Andreas Lemos* [1983] Q.B. 647, in holding that a vessel need only be "at sea" for piracy to be committed. On that approach, hi-jacking for ransom can plainly be piracy. Although this is not determinative, it is also to be noted that the International Law definition in UNCLOS art.101 includes "any illegal acts of detention."

[40] [2010] EWHC 974 (Comm).

[41] [2006] NSCA 82 at para.37. The policy incorporated the 1995 Institute Time Clauses with the American Hull Institute Liner Negligence Clause added. The latter clause is very similar to the Additional Perils Clauses.

Cargo perils: outline of the current practice

The practice described in this paragraph of the main work, by reference to the **23–67** Institute Cargo Clauses 1/1/82, has been continued without substantial alteration under the new Clauses introduced in 2009, the Institute Cargo Clauses 1/1/09. The 2009 Clauses are reproduced in the Appendix to this Supplement. There have been no changes of substance to the wording of the Risks Clauses in the (A) (B) and (C) Clauses. Revisions of substance have been made in respect of the Transit Clause, the Change of Voyage Clause and some of the exclusions, which are discussed elsewhere at appropriate points in this Supplement.

The (A) Clause cover; meaning of "all risks"

The principles discussed in this paragraph of the main work are of continuing **23–68** application in the context of the Institute Cargo Clauses (A) 1/1/09 which have largely but probably not yet entirely replaced the 1982 Clauses in current use. The Risks Clause has not been changed in any material respect.

   The analysis of all risks cargo insurance in *British & Foreign Marine Insurance Co v Gaunt*[42] has stood the test of time. There was no dispute as to the nature of all risks insurance in *The Cendor Mopu*[43] to which extensive references have already been made in this Supplement. It was common ground that all risks policies cover losses caused by external fortuities including perils of the seas subject to any relevant exclusions and that all risks policies do not cover inherent vice and wear and tear; those are not risks.

   Given the nature of the casualty in *The Cendor Mopu*, there was no call for the Courts to distinguish between "all risks" and a policy covering perils of the seas as a named peril, when considering the appropriate test to meet the requirement for the event to be fortuitous. There was considerable debate in *The Cendor Mopu* concerning the threshold required for a fortuity, the meaning of inherent vice, and the proper causation analysis where unseaworthiness and an external fortuity are both causative factors. The reasoning of the Court of Appeal on these questions in *The Cendor Mopu* has been sufficiently discussed at earlier points in this Supplement. It is unnecessary to repeat that discussion, beyond stressing the obvious point that *The Cendor Mopu* is of prime importance as illustrating the meaning and scope of all risks cargo insurance cover.

All risks and inherent vice

The decision and reasoning in *Mayban v Alstom*[44] were disapproved by the Court **23–69** of Appeal in *The Cendor Mopu*.[45] In the circumstances, the conclusion reached by Moore-Bick J. in *Mayban*, that the sole proximate cause of the loss was inherent vice, was erroneous. As noted in this paragraph of the main work, the test proposed

---

[42] [1921] 2 A.C. 41.
[43] [2009] 2 Lloyd's Rep. 71; [2010] 1 Lloyd's Rep. 243. The decision of the Supreme Court is pending, at the time of going to press.
[44] [2004] 2 Lloyd's Rep. 609 45.
[45] [2010] 1 Lloyd's Rep. 243. There is no need at this point to repeat the discussion of *The Cendor Mopu* under earlier paragraphs in this Supplement.

by Moore-Bick J. at para.21 in his judgment, which is quoted at para.23–15B above in this Supplement, would have undermined the efficacy of the standard all risks cover.[46] It is now clear, subject to what the Supreme Court may decide in *The Cendor Mopu*, that damage to cargo resulting from the motion of the vessel under adverse weather conditions which could reasonably be expected to be encountered on the voyage is to be regarded as having been caused by an external fortuity within the scope of the (A) Clauses, notwithstanding the inability of the cargo upon shipment to withstand such conditions were they to be encountered on the voyage. It is also clear from *The Cendor Mopu* (unless the decision is reversed by the Supreme Court) that in such circumstances the exclusion of inherent vice at cl.4.4 in the (A) Clauses would not afford a defence to insurers.

The suggestion in this paragraph of the main work that the decision in *Mayban v Alstom* might have been justified if it had been based (which it was not) on inherent vice excluded under the policy[47] and the external fortuity of adverse weather being concurrent causes of approximately equal efficiency can no longer stand, in the light of the Court of Appeal decision in *The Cendor Mopu*. It may well be, however, that the decision in *Mayban* would have been justified had it been based on insufficiency or unsuitability of packing or preparation of the subject-matter insured) (which is excluded under cl.4.3)[48] as a concurrent cause of the loss.

The (B) Clause cover

23–70   The wording of the Risks Clause in the Institute Cargo Clauses (B) 1/1/09, which are reproduced in the Appendix, is in materially the same terms as the equivalent Clause in the 1982 Clauses. The discussion at this point in the main work is of continuing relevance, in relation to the new Clauses.

The (C) Clause cover

23–71   The wording of the Risks Clause in the 2009 Clauses (reproduced in the Appendix below) is also materially unchanged from that in the 1982 Clauses. The discussion at this point in the main work is of continuing relevance.

The Both to Blame Collision Clause

23–72   The wording of this Clause has been revised, under the Institute Cargo Clauses 1/1/09. The revisions do not appear to affect the substantive meaning of the Clause. In the Consultation Paper issued in May 2008, containing the Joint Cargo Committee's proposals for revision of the Cargo Clauses, the JCC rightly observed that the then current wording of the Both to Blame Collision Clause (in the 1982 Clauses) was "convoluted and hard to follow." The revised Clause (to quote from

---

[46] Professor Bennett made the same criticism of *Mayban*, in stronger terms; see para.23–15B above.
[47] Under cl.4.4 whatever the position may be in other contexts, in the context of the Institute Cargo Clauses the inherent vice exclusion cannot, as a matter of construction, extend to bad packing, which is the subject of the separate carefully circumscribed exclusion at cl.4.3.
[48] The wording of cl.4.3 in the 1982 Clauses and in the 2009 Clauses differs in some respects, but this observation would hold good under both wordings. The interpretation of cl.4.3 is discussed briefly at para.22–28 in the main work and above.

the JCC's paper) "uses more readily understandable and updated cover. It neither widens nor narrows the cover." The effect of this Clause, nevertheless, requires some explanation in order for it to be understood. The lengthy discussion in this paragraph of the main work remains in point, in the context of the 2009 Clauses as well as the 1982 Clauses.

The Institute Malicious Damage Clause

The description of cargo insurance practice in this paragraph of the main work **23–73B** is of continuing relevance, following the introduction of the revised Clauses in 2009.

Cargo Exclusions

The exclusion clauses in the Institute Cargo Clauses (A), (B) and (C) 1/1/09 are **23–74** laid out in the same manner as their equivalents in the 1982 Clauses referred to in this paragraph of the main work, in the sequence of Clauses numbered 4, 5, 6 and 7. Most of the exclusions are unchanged, and none of them is entirely new. The same areas are addressed under the same clause-numbers as before. However, within this framework which is basically unchanged, there have been some significant revisions. The amendments to cl.4.3 (insufficiency or unsuitability of packing or preparation of the subject-matter insured), cl.4.5 (delay), cl.5 (unseaworthiness and unfitness of vessel or craft) and cl.7 (terrorism) are discussed elsewhere in this Supplement. Only cl.4.6 (the insolvency exclusion) calls for any discussion at this point.

The insolvency exclusion at cl.4.6 in the 1982 Clauses was a new provision, which had not appeared in previous editions of the Institute Cargo Clauses. As was noted in this paragraph of the main work, this exclusion met with resistance in the market and narrower exclusions were adopted, under the Institute Commodity Trades Clauses and many of the Special Trades Clauses.[49] Under the Institute Cargo Clauses 1/1/09, the wording of cl.4.6 in the Institute Commodity Trades Clauses (A) 5/9/83 has duly been adopted without alteration into the text of the main (A) (B) and (C) Clauses. The meaning of the revised cl.4.6 and the differences between the revised wording and the previous wording in the 1982 Clauses do not require any further explanation. The 2009 Clauses are reproduced in the Appendix to this Supplement.

Note 519: The reasoning in *Mayban v Alstom* was disapproved by the Court of Appeal in *The Cendor Mopu*.[50] The effect of the exclusions with regard to inherent vice and bad packing is discussed, in the light of *The Cendor Mopu*, at paras 22–25 *et seq* above in this Supplement. Subject to what the Supreme Court may decide, the effect of the exclusions is not as far-reaching as might have been supposed, if the *Mayban* test had to be applied.

---

[49] The market reaction to cl.4.6 when this was first introduced and the background to the adoption of the ICTCA version of this exclusion in the 2009 Clauses are described in *Thomas*, Modern Law of Marine Insurance, Vol. 3 (2009), Ch. 6, para. 6.40 ("Insuring cargoes in the new millennium", Dunt & Melbourne) and in J. Dunt, *Marine Cargo Insurance* (2009) at paras 8.56 to 8.59.

[50] [2010] 1 Lloyd's Rep. 243.

CHAPTER 24

WAR RISKS

The new clauses: Cargo Insurance

The description of cargo insurance practice in this paragraph of the main work **24–06** remains valid in the context of the 2009 revision of the Institute Cargo Clauses. The Risks Clause (cl.1) in the Institute War Clauses (Cargo) 1/1/09 is in the same terms as cl.1 of the equivalent 1982 Clauses, quoted in the text of para.24–06 of the main work. The Risks Clause in the 2009 Institute Strike Clauses has been revised principally so as to include a definition of "terrorism", which appears to the editors to be a change in presentation rather than a change of substance.[1] The new wording reads as follows:

"1.   This insurance covers, except as excluded by the provisions of Clauses 3 and 4 below, loss of or damage to the subject-matter insured caused by

1.1.   strikers, locked-out workmen, or person taking part in labour disturbances, riots or civil commotions.

1.2   any act of terrorism being an act of any person acting on behalf of, or in connection with, any organisation which carries out activities directed towards the overthrowing or influencing, by force or violence, of any government whether or not legally constituted.

1.3   any person acting from a political, ideological or religious motive."

Principal differences between the f.c.&s. Clause and the current war exclusions

Note 68: The editors are informed that the new clauses referred to in this footnote **24–07** are now much more widely used, as a direct result of the recent upsurge in piracy incidents. The risks of violent theft, piracy and barratry are covered by the vessel's war risk underwriters when these clauses are used.

Meaning of capture and seizure

Note 177: The proposition that capture is prima facie a case of constructive **24–17** total loss, and cannot generally amount to an actual total loss straightaway, was confirmed by David Steel J. in *Masefield AG v Amlin Corporate Member Ltd*.[2]

---

[1] See the discussion at paras 24–29 and 24–30 below in this Supplement.
[2] [2010] Lloyd's Rep. IR 345. See also the passage from the judgment of Porter J. in *Marstrand Shipping Co v Beer* [1937] 1 All E.R. 158, cited in *Masefield v Amlin* at para.50.

Referring to the dictum of Rix J. in *Kuwait Airways Corp v Kuwait Insurance Co SAK*,[3] David Steel J. said that this passage, which is but a side observation in a non-marine case, is rightly described in *Arnould*[4] as a "doubtful" suggestion.[5]

The frustration clause

24–23 *Note 222*: The wording of the frustration clause in the 2009 revision of the Institute War Clauses (Cargo) is unchanged from that in the 1982 Clauses. The word "proximately" has been removed from the delay exclusions in the 2009 Clauses.[6] That change of wording does not affect the suggestion in this footnote that the frustration clause may often overlap with other exclusions, including the delay exclusion at cl.3.5 in the Institute War Clauses.

Strikes, riots and civil commotions

24–26 Cargo insurance practice with regard to this group of perils remains unaltered by the 2009 revision of the Institute Cargo Clauses. The Clauses are reproduced in the Appendix below.

Riots and civil commotions

24–28 The recent upsurge in the number of incidents of piracy[7] has made the proposition that the term "riot" is to be given its technical meaning in the criminal law of some considerable practical importance. The analysis of the overlap between "piracy" and "riot" in the main work,[8] leading to the conclusion that an attack by 12 or more pirates is likely to fall within the war risks cover (as a case of "riot") whereas an attack by 11 or less pirates will typically fall within the marine risk cover, is not universally accepted in the market, but so far as the editors are aware has yet to be challenged in litigation. The editors remain of the opinion stated in the main work, at para 23–33 and at para.24–28.[9]

---

[3] [1996] 1 Lloyd's Rep. 664, 687.

[4] 17th ed para.28–03.

[5] *Masefield v Amlin* (above) at para.49(iii). At the time of going to press, the judgment of the Court of Appeal in *Masefield* is still pending.

[6] The editors do not consider that the omission of the word "proximately" materially alters the scope of the delay exclusions in the Institute Cargo Clauses; see the discussion at para.22–32 above in this Supplement.

[7] See *Masefield AG v Amlin Corporate Member Ltd* [2010] Lloyd's Rep. IR 345. There have been many more incidents since those described in *Masefield*.

[8] At paras 23–33 and 24–28.

[9] Other commentators concur in the view that "riot" is to be given its technical meaning, and as regards the effect of that approach on the cover afforded for piracy risks under the standard Clauses. See *MacGillivray on Insurance Law* edited by N. Legh-Jones et al, 11th edn (2008) paras 11–013 and 26–029; Bennett, *Marine Insurance*, 2nd edn (2006) paras 14–12 to 14–14; Clarke, *Law of Insurance Contracts* (Looseleaf) para.19.3E; D. O'May and J. Hill, *O'May on Marine Insurance* (1993) pp 306–309. Professor Bennett considers that s.10(2) of the 1986 Act places it "beyond question" that the criminal law meaning is to be applied. The editors of *MacGillivray* consider it unlikely that the approach adopted by United States and Canadian Courts will ever commend itself to the English Courts.

Terrorists and persons acting from a political motive

The practice with regard to malicious acts cover is unaltered, in the context of the **24–29**
Institute Cargo Clauses 1/1/09. The wording used to describe the insured perils of
acts of terrorism and politically-motivated acts under the 2009 revision of the
Institute Strike Clauses (Cargo) and to describe the matching excluded perils
under the (A), (B) and (C) Clauses differs from that used at equivalent points in
the 1982 Cargo Clauses, and in the Hull Clauses and Freight Clauses. The text of
cll.1.2 and 1.3 in the 2009 Strike Clauses is set out at para.24–06 above. The
interpretation of this new wording, so far as it requires discussion, is commented
on at para.24–30, below.

What is meant by terrorism and "political motive"

The peril of "acts of terrorism" is now defined in the exclusions under the **24–30**
(A), (B) and (C) Clauses 1/1/09 and in the Risks Clause in the 2009 Institute
Strike Clauses (Cargo). The wording is set out at para.24–06 above and in the
Appendix to this Supplement. The definition used in these Clauses is taken from
s.2(2) in the Reinsurance (Acts of Terrorism) Act 1993[10] and differs from some
other statutory definitions and (arguably) the market understanding of what
constitutes terrorism.[11]

As can be seen, the definition of "act of terrorism" is such that the actions of a
lone terrorist, who is not acting on behalf of or in connection with an organisation which carries out activities aimed at overthrowing or influencing any government by force or violence, will not be covered under cl.1.2. The actions of a lone
terrorist would, however, plainly fall within the scope of cl.1.3, as actions taken
from a "political, ideological or religious motive."

These two sub-clauses are not mutually exclusive. As appears from para.24–08
in the main work, the editors do not consider a "steps on the ladder" approach to
be appropriate in relation to the standard clauses used in marine war risks and
strikes risks insurance. The insured perils frequently overlap. Thus, the cover
afforded by cl.1.3 is on the face of it wide enough to include acts of terrorism as
defined in cl.1.2, where the perpetrator is part of an organisation, as well as the
actions of an individual acting on his own initiative.

The cover in cl.1.3 is also wider than that in cl.1.2 in that there need have been
no threat or use of force of violence either by the individual or any organisation,
and the cover extends to actions which are not directed towards overthrowing any
government or influencing some government policy but are aimed, for example, at
forcing a cargo-owner to desist from engaging in some trade or business to which

---

[10] See J. Dunt, *Marine Cargo Insurance* (2009) at para.10.43.
[11] See e.g. the definition in s.1 of the Terrorism Act 2000, discussed in this paragraph of the main
work. The definition in the 2009 Cargo Clauses does not require any use or threat of force or violence
at the time where the "act of terrorism" is committed, does not extend to actions which are designed
to intimidate the public but are not designed to overthrow or influence any government, and does not
contain any express limitation referring to political, religious or ideological motives (although the
editors doubt whether the motives for terrorism, in the popular sense of the term, would ever fall
outside those categories).

the perpetrator objects on ideological grounds.[12] In the opinion of the present editors, the addition of the words "ideological or religious" does not, however, materially alter the scope of the previous wording referring to "any person acting from a political motive". Nor is the cover afforded by cll.1.2 and 1.3, taken in combination, materially different from that previously afforded by cl.1.2 in the 1982 Cargo Clauses ("Any terrorist or any person acting from a political motive"). This new wording in the Cargo Clauses amounts to a change in presentation, not a change of real substance.

What is meant by "acting maliciously"

24–31 The editors have reconsidered the comments at the end of this paragraph, where it is suggested that there is a real possibility that piracy losses might not be insured at all, where the number of pirates is less than is needed for a "riot" and where weapons of war[13] were used or displayed at the time of seizure. On reflection these comments are overstated. The Malicious Acts Exclusion has yet to be judicially construed, but it seems unlikely that it would be construed in such a way as to deprive the piracy cover in the Hull Clauses of any real scope (in practice, a piratical attack will almost always involve a display of weaponry).

The comments on the potential affect of the Malicious Acts Exclusion in this paragraph were speculative and are withdrawn. Further comment on its meaning is best left until such time as it is judicially construed.[14]

---

[12] For example, the actions of an "animal rights" activist would presumably fall within cl.1.3, whether or not also covered by cl.1.2.

[13] Shortened to "any weapon" in the International Hull Clauses.

[14] The editors are not aware of any instances in the current wave of piracy cases where the Malicious Acts Exclusion has been relied upon.

CHAPTER 25

SUE AND LABOUR EXPENSES

Introduction

Note 3: For the sake of completeness, it should be noted that the Clause headed **25–01** "General Average and Salvage" in the standard Hull Clauses in current use partly duplicates the cover afforded by the Clause headed "Duty of Assured (Sue and Labour)" discussed at paras 25–03 *et seq* in this Supplement and the main work.[1] The duplication occurs in relation to the cost of salvage services performed under special contract which in appropriate circumstances may be recovered under the General Average and Salvage Clause.[2] However, that possibility does not call for separate discussion, as there would appear to be no advantage to a shipowner in presenting his claim under that heading rather than on the usual basis as a claim under the sue and labour clause.[3]

The Duty of Assured Clause in the Institute Time Clauses (Hulls)

Note 23: The situation where a vessel is seized by pirates who then demand a **25–04** ransom for its release (recently, a frequent occurrence) may be one where the assured cannot be said to have owed a duty to bargain with criminals for the return of his property, although such expenses will have been reasonably incurred if the ransom is paid and loss of the vessel is thereby averted.[4]

The Duty of Assured Clause in the Institute Cargo Clauses

The wording of this Clause has not been altered materially in the Institute Cargo **25–06** Clauses 1/1/09. The discussion at this point in the main work is of continuing relevance in connection with the new Clauses, which are reproduced in the Appendix below.

Salvage Charges

Note 113: The effect of these exclusions and the position under the 1983 Clauses **25–16** (which do not contain similar exclusions) with regard to salvage expenses

---

[1] See cll.11 and 13 in the Institute Time Clauses—Hulls (1/10/83); App.2 in the main work. The numbering differs in the 1995 Clauses and in the International Hull Clauses.
[2] *Seashore Marine SA v Phoenix Assurance Plc (The Vergina)* [2002] Lloyd's Rep. IR 51, 57.
[3] The assured's argument that underwriters have the burden of proof on whether salvage expenses were incurred to avert or minimise loss by an insured peril if the claim is advanced under the General Average and Salvage Clause instead of being advanced under the Sue and Labour Clause was rejected in *The Vergina* (above), at paras [32] to [35].
[4] David Steel J. appears to have been of this opinion in *Masefield AG v Amlin Corporate Member Ltd* [2010] Lloyd's Rep. IR 345 at para.64. At the time of going to press, the Court of Appeal judgment in *Masefield* is awaited.

incurred or enhanced by reason of damage to the environment or pollution or the threat of such damage is discussed in this Supplement at para.25–18A.

What types of payments are recoverable

25–18 *Note 136*: If the reasoning of David Steel J. in *Masefield v Amlin* (above) is upheld, there would seem to be little doubt that ransom payments made to pirates of the order of magnitude typically demanded in recent incidents of this kind would be "reasonably and properly incurred." At the time of going to press, the Court of Appeal has reserved judgment in *Masefield*. In the majority of cases, any ransom will have been paid for the release of both ship and cargo (as well as the release of the crew) so that the situation is likely to be one of general average rather than one involving a claim for sue and labour expenses, but that does not affect the proposition in this footnote.

Notes 148 to 150: Under the reasoning of David Steel J. in *Masefield v Amlin* (above), the payment of ransom to pirates for the release of a ship, cargo (if any) and crew is not contrary to public policy. It was conceded in *Masefield* that the ransom payment was not illegal. If *Masefield* is upheld, it is submitted that there would be no proper basis for reducing the amount recoverable from underwriters (either as sue and labour expenditure or as a general average loss, depending on the circumstances) on the ground that the amount which had had to be paid in ransom had been inflated by the pirates' use of the threat to the crew as a bargaining counter. This point is discussed more fully at para.26–54B below in this Supplement. Subject to what the Court of Appeal may decide in *Masefield v Amlin*, the approach taken by Phillips L.J. in *Royal Boskalis Westminster NV v Mountain*[5] to the question whether the amount recoverable as sue and labour should be apportioned to reflect the fact that the assured was concerned to protect lives at risk, as well being concerned to regain his property, ought plainly to be followed in relation to ransom payments in piracy cases.

It is doubtful if there is any basis upon which the vessel's P&I insurers can be compelled to contribute to the cost of ransom payments which have been inflated as a result of the threat to the safety of the crew being used as a bargaining counter, at least unless the crew's ransom is separately negotiated or quantified (which is unlikely to happen), even though it can fairly be said that as insurers of the shipowner's liabilities in respect of the crew the Club has an interest in the safe and speedy release of the crew in cases of this kind. The editors are aware of attempts having been made to persuade Clubs to contribute to ransom costs on an *ex gratia* basis under the Omnibus Rule, but the general position appears to be that the owners and insurers of ship and cargo are left to bear the full cost. Apart from any considerations of public policy (which are expected to be resolved, one way or the other, by the Court of Appeal in *Masefield v Amlin*), the fact that the crew's ransom is not a separate quantified amount,[6] the fact that P&I Club Rules invariably contain "other insurance" exclusions,[7] and the fact that the Sue and Labour Rule under the Rules of many P&I Clubs is confined to expenses incurred

---

[5] [1997] L.R.L.R. 523, 647.
[6] See *Royal Boskalis*, above, at p.647.
[7] See *The Bosworth (No.3)* [1962] 1 Lloyd's Rep. 483.

"solely" to avert or minimise liabilities insured under those Rules would present formidable obstacles to any claim.

The insurance position where expenditure is incurred in salvage operations for a dual purpose of saving the maritime property and preventing environmental damage or pollution, which is touched on at this point in the main work at footnote 150 is now dealt with in somewhat more detail at para.25–18A below.

Prevention of damage to the environment

Salvage operations may be seen, in many cases, as involving expenditure for a **25–18A** dual purpose,[8] of saving the property at risk and of preventing or minimising the threat of environmental damage, presented by the casualty. This class of "dual purpose expenditure" merits separate discussion.

As we have already seen, "salvage charges" in the strict sense are outside the scope of a sue and labour clause. Salvage performed under special contract may, according to the circumstances, be treated as general average or as a sue and labour expense.[9]

There is also more than one way in which salvors may be remunerated, under the modern law and practice of salvage. This subject is more fully discussed at para.26–55A below in this Supplement. For the purposes of the present discussion, it is sufficient to note that:

(1) The salvage award under art.13 of the International Convention on Salvage 1989 may have been enhanced to take account of the salvors' skill and efforts in preventing or attempting to prevent damage to the environment; the art.13 award is to be paid by all of the vessel and other property interests in proportion to their respective salved values.

(2) The salvor may additionally be entitled to "special compensation", payable by the shipowner alone, under art.14.1 of the Salvage Convention, where there was a threat of environmental damage during the salvage operation and the art.13 award is insufficient to cover his expenses as defined.

(3) A further discretionary amount of "special compensation" may become payable under art.14.3, again by the shipowner alone, if the salvor's efforts have succeeded in preventing environmental damage.

---

[8] As salvors are under a legal obligation to attempt to minimise pollution or environmental damage when conducting salvage operations, and shipowners are legally bound to cooperate (under the Salvage Convention, 1989), to describe the expense as being for a dual purpose, or in part for an extraneous purpose, may not be wholly apposite. Indeed, in many cases, the salvage operation would not be allowed to proceed without complying with requirements of the authorities to prevent pollution, see J. Reeder, *Brice, on Maritime Law of Salvage*, 4th edn, (2008), para.6–51. Situations do of course arise from time to time where salvors perform environmental services which do not properly form part of the salvage operation but are more in the nature of clean-up operations to deal with the aftermath of the casualty. This is not, properly speaking, a situation of expenditure for a dual purpose, but of expenditure incurred in separate activities for a separate purpose. Any remuneration paid to salvors for extraneous services such as clean-up operations is outside the scope of policies on hull and machinery and on cargo, but in practice it may not always be easy to distinguish between activities which are extraneous and those which are not.

[9] The General Average and Salvage Clause in the Institute Hull Clauses and International Hull Clauses applies to all these permutations, see the comments at para.25–01 above in this Supplement.

(4) It has become increasingly common for salvage agreements to incorporate the SCOPIC Clause, as a safety-net to cover salvors' expenses in excess of the art.13 award. SCOPIC does not depend on there being any threat to the environment. SCOPIC remuneration is again payable by the shipowner alone.

There is also more than one way in which salvage is treated under successive editions of the York-Antwerp Rules still in current use. The development of the wording of Rule VI is discussed in Chap. 26 of the main work and at para.26–55A below. Special compensation under art.14 of the Salvage Convention "or under any provision similar in substance"[10] will be excluded from general average when any of the versions of the York-Antwerp Rules that are in current use are incorporated in the contract of affreightment. The 1974 Rules (as amended) and 1994 Rules expressly provide for salvage remuneration in which the skill and efforts of the salvors in preventing or minimising damage to the environment such as is referred to in art.13 of the Convention has been taken into account to be allowed in general average.

With all these different permutations in mind, the insurance position with regard to enhanced salvage awards, special compensation and SCOPIC can now be discussed. The 1995 Institute Hull Clauses and the International Hull Clauses contain express provisions dealing in a convoluted fashion with these matters, which are in the same terms apart from the numbering of the relevant clauses.[11] There are no similar provisions in the Institute Time Clauses (Hulls) 1/10/83 which are still the most widely-used Clauses in hull insurance, or in the Institute Cargo Clauses.

The General Average and Salvage Clause (cl.10) in the Institute Time Clauses (Hulls) (1/11/95) excludes special compensation under art.14 of the Convention "or under any other provision in any statute, rule, law or contract which is similar in substance".[12] This exclusion (at cl.10.5.1) is followed by another exclusion (at cl.10.5.2) in respect of expenses or liabilities incurred in respect of damage to the environment or the threat of such damage, or as a consequence of the escape or threat of escape of pollution from the vessel. But cl.10.6 then goes on to provide that cl.10.5 shall not exclude any sum paid to salvors in respect of salvage remuneration in which the skill and efforts of the salvors in preventing or minimising damage to the environment as is referred to in art.13 of the Convention have been taken into account. The Duty of Assured (Sue and Labour) Clause in the 1995 Clauses, cl.11, expressly excludes "special compensation and expenses as is referred to in Clause 10.5" from the sue and labour clause coverage (cl.11.2, cl.11.5). The cross-reference to cl.10.5 is plainly to be construed as referring to cl.10.5 as qualified by cl.10.6.

The scheme of the 1995 Clauses (and similarly the International Hull Clauses) is thus that the hull underwriters will meet an art.13 award which has been enhanced to reflect skill and efforts in protecting the environment and that special

---

[10] It is submitted that SCOPIC should be regarded as "similar". In the York-Antwerp Rules 2004, the words "such as SCOPIC" have been added under Rule VI.
[11] The relevant provisions in the 1995 Clauses are described below.
[12] See fn.10, above.

compensation under art.14 is excluded. The exclusion at cl.10.5.2, referred to above, appears to be aimed mainly at ensuring that the cost of environmental services performed by salvors which do not properly form part of the salvage operation, such as clean-up expenses, are kept out of the hull policy cover.

As already stated, there are no equivalent exclusions in the General Average and Salvage Clause[13] and Duty of Assured (Sue and Labour) Clause (cll.11 and 13) in the 1983 Clauses.[14] In practice, however, the position under the 1983 Clauses is still that hull underwriters will meet the cost of an enhanced art.13 award, and that special compensation payments will be treated as falling outside the scope of the hull cover even though such payments might, on the face of it, appear capable of being classed as sue and labour expenditure. So far as the editors are aware the practice which has invariably been followed, both in the context of the 1983 Clauses and the 1995 Clauses and 1HC, is that enhanced awards under art.13 are met by underwriters and that the cost of special compensation payments and SCOPIC remuneration[15] is borne by the vessel's P&I Club.[16] It would not appear to be in the interests of any of the parties concerned to disturb this division of responsibility, which has its origins in the Funding Agreement referred to in footnote 14 above.

Illegal payments

It was argued in *Masefield AG v Amlin Corporate Member Ltd*[17] that the payment **25–21** of ransom to pirates or other criminals for the release of a vessel and its cargo, in circumstances where the payment is not illegal under any relevant law, is nonetheless to be regarded as being contrary to public policy. David Steel J. was "wholly

---

[13] Similar exclusions may still apply where the situation is to be treated as one of general average, since under cl.11.2 where the contract of affreightment so provides the adjustment shall be according to the York-Antwerp Rules, and the Rules in current use exclude special compensation from G.A.

[14] A safety-net provision similar to the concept of special compensation but of more limited scope already existed, applying to salvage operations involving laden tankers, which had recently been added to Lloyd's Open Form (LOF 1980). The principle of enhancement of salvage awards to reflect skill and efforts to avert damage to the environment was also made explicit, for the first time, in LOF 1980. These provisions were the precursors of the regime in the Salvage Convention 1989, arts 13 and 14. The amendments to Lloyd's Open Form had been preceded by an agreement between the International Group of P&I Clubs and underwriters in the London market known as the Funding Agreement, whereby it was resolved that underwriters would "continue" to meet enhanced awards and that the Clubs would bear the cost of awards under the safety net provisions soon to be embodied in LOF 1980. For whatever reason, the draftsmen of the 1983 Institute Clauses did not reflect these developments in the wording of the new Clauses.

[15] It is arguable that hull underwriters would be entitled to resist any claim for them to cover SCOPIC remuneration, in the unlikely event of such a claim being made, as a third-party beneficiary of the SCOPIC clause, which provides at cl.14 that "no claim whether direct, indirect, by way of indemnity of recourse or otherwise relating to SCOPIC remuneration in excess of the Article 13 Award shall be made in General Average or under the vessel's Hull and Machinery Policy by the Owners of the Vessel." Although hull underwriters would not ordinarily be parties to the salvage contract of which the SCOPIC clause formed part, it might well be argued that they could rely on this provision by virtue of the Contracts (Rights of Third Parties) Act 1999 which is not excluded under the standard terms of LOF 2000.

[16] The Rules of the P&I Clubs include liabilities and expenses in respect of special compensation to salvors and SCOPIC remuneration in the classes of risks covered

[17] [2010] Lloyd's Rep. IR 345.

unpersuaded"[18] that the doctrine should be applied in situations of this kind, but gave the claimants permission to appeal. At the time of going to press, the decision of the Court of Appeal in *Masefield* is awaited. If the first-instance judgment were to be reversed, it would seem to follow that ransom payments in piracy cases would cease to be recoverable under the sue and labour clause in hull policies governed by English law, or in proceedings in the English Courts. The present position (unless *Masefield* is reversed) is that the payment of ransom to pirates, if not itself illegal, would ordinarily be recoverable from insurers where piracy is one of the insured perils as a sue and labour expense[19] or in general average,[20] depending on the circumstances.

The forwarding charges clause

25–23   The wording of this clause is unchanged, under the Institute Cargo Clauses (1/1/09). The discussion in this paragraph of the main work is of equal application to the 1982 and the 2009 Clauses.

Can particular charges be recovered where there is no suing and labouring clause in the policy?

25–24   The Forwarding Charges Clause and the Duty of Assured Clause in the Institute Cargo Clauses (1/1/82) to which reference is made in this paragraph are unaltered in the 2009 Clauses; see the Appendix below.

---

[18] *Ibid* at para.60.

[19] David Steel J. regarded the majority's view *in Royal Boskalis Westminster NV v Mountain* as a strong indication that the Claimants' position was misconceived; *ibid*, para.63. In the passage referred to in *Royal Boskalis*, Phillips L.J. approved *Arnould's* treatment of the subject and said that in his judgment "the assumption of the editors of *Arnould* that payment of a ransom, if not itself illegal, is recoverable as an expense of suing and labouring is well founded". It remains to be seen whether the Court of Appeal in *Masefield* takes the same view.

[20] See the discussion at paras 26–54A and 26–54B below in this Supplement.

CHAPTER 26

GENERAL AVERAGE

Ransom payments: further discussion

There has been a large number of incidents involving the seizure or attempted **26–54A**
seizure of vessels by pirates based in Somalia since the current edition of *Arnould*
was published. The objective in all these cases has been to obtain a ransom for
the release of the ship, cargo (if any) and crew, and in most if not all cases where
the property was seized ransoms have been paid. It was argued in *Masefield AG
v Amlin Corporate Member Ltd*[1] that the payment of ransom to pirates or other
criminals is contrary to public policy (although it was conceded that the payment
was not illegal under any relevant law). David Steel J. was wholly unpersuaded
that it would be right to categorise the payment of a ransom to pirates as being
contrary to public policy. Had that been the position, it would no doubt have
followed that such payments could not be brought into general average, or form
the subject of a claim against the insurers of the vessel or cargo.[2]

The decision of the Court of Appeal in *Masefield v Amlin* is expected to
provide a definitive answer on this question of public policy. Subject to the possibility that ransom payments to pirates may be open to objection on such grounds
(if *Masefield* is reversed) and to the possibility of ransom payments being illegal
in some cases,[3] it is generally accepted that money paid by way of ransom for the
release of a ship and cargo may be recovered in general average, as is submitted
at para.26–54 of the main work.[4]

The amounts which have had to be paid to the Somali pirates to obtain the **26–54B**
release of ship, cargo and crew in this recent wave of incidents have undoubtedly
been inflated by their use of the threat to the lives and well-being of the crew as
a bargaining counter. It is submitted that such an enhancement of the amount paid
will not affect the principles upon which general average is to be adjusted, by
reference to contributory values in the usual way.[5]

---

[1] [2010] Lloyd's Rep. IR 345. At the time of going to press, judgment has been reserved by the Court
of Appeal in this case.
[2] The point at issue in *Masefield v Amlin* was whether there was an actual total loss or constructive
total loss of the insured cargo, despite the strong probability that the cargo would be recovered on
payment of the pirates' demands for ransom (as in fact happened, soon after the deemed date of
commencement of proceedings). It was suggested that on grounds of public policy the prospect of a
recovery by such means was to be disregarded.
[3] As is likely to be the position where the property was seized or hi-jacked by terrorists. See further
at para.25–21 in the main work and above in this Supplement.
[4] See also, *Lowndes & Rudolf, The Law of General Average and the York-Antwerp Rules*, edited by
J. Cooke and R. Cornah, 13th edn (2008) para.A.68.
[5] It is suggested in *Lowndes & Rudolf, op. cit.* at para.A.69, that it might be argued that the expenses
in cases of this kind should be divided pro rata in some way, but the editors then go on to point out
that a similar argument was rejected by Phillips L.J. in *Royal Boskalis Westminster NV v Mountain*

The position is analogous to that where the amount of a salvage award is enhanced to reflect the skill and efforts of the salvors in saving the crew. For at least a century before this became enshrined in art.13 of the 1989 Salvage Convention, it had been common practice for such enhanced awards to be made. The service of saving life in the context of salvage operations has traditionally been regarded as one rendered to both ship and cargo benefiting both interests equally, and it also appears never to have been the practice for salvage arbitrators to quantify this element of enhancement; the full amount of the award will be borne rateably by the salved property interests in the usual way,[6] and in those cases where the salvage expenditure is to be treated as general average, the full amount of the award will be included in the adjustment and apportioned between the contributing interests in the usual way.[7] No reduction is made to reflect the fact that the award may be said to include an element of remuneration for operations undertaken for a purpose other than that of preserving from peril the property involved in the common maritime adventure[8] or for the dual purpose of saving lives and property.

The discussion at this point in Chapter 26 is concerned with the law and practice of general average as between the co-adventurers. The position as between the contributing parties and their insurers in ransom cases is discussed in the Sue and Labour Chapter 25.[9]

Salvage and prevention of damage to the environment

26–55A Under Rule VI of the York-Antwerp Rules, 1970 as amended in 1990 and Rule VI of the 1994 Rules, expenditure allowed in general average includes any salvage remuneration in which the skill and efforts of the salvors in preventing or minimising damage to the environment such as is referred to in art.13 para.1(b) of the International Convention on Salvage, 1989, have been taken into account (Rule VI(a)). Special compensation payable to a salvor by the shipowner under art.14 of the Convention "or under any other provision similar in substance"[10] is

---

[1997] L.R.L.R. 523, 647, citing the example of *The Bosworth (No3)* [1962] 1 Lloyd's Rep. 483. Except in the unlikely event of a ransom for the release of the crew being separately negotiated, it does not appear to the present editors that there can be any justification in principle, or that it would be practicable or desirable to depart from the usual basis of adjustment. See *Royal Boskalis*, above, and cf. *Brice on Maritime Law of Salvage*, 4th edn at 411; *Lowndes & Rudolf*, at para.6.25; *The M Vatan* [1990] 1 Lloyd's Rep. 336–344 (discussing the practical objections to departing from the general *pro rata* rule in cases of salvage).

[6] See *The Bosworth (No.3)* above; *The Fusilier* (1865) Brown & Lush. 341, 344. And see art.13.1(e), 13.2 in the International Convention on Salvage, 1989.

[7] *Lowndes & Rudolf, op. cit.*, para.6.27.

[8] The doubts as to whether the enhancement of a salvage award to reflect measures taken to minimise pollution was covered by the wording of Rule VI in the York-Antwerp Rules 1974 do not seem to have extended to salvage awards that were enhanced to reflect salvors' efforts in saving the crew. In any event, the subsequent changes to the wording of Rule VI, by amendment in 1990 and then in the 1994 and 2004 York-Antwerp Rules dealt with that problem; see *Lowndes & Rudolf* paras 6.07 *et seq* for the historical development of Rule VI.

[9] See paras 25–18, 25–21 in this Supplement and in the main work. Depending on the circumstances, the claim on insurers may either be advanced under the sue and labour clause or as a claim for general average loss. To avoid repetition, these can be dealt with together.

[10] It is submitted that SCOPIC would be regarded as similar. For a brief explanation of SCOPIC see below.

expressly excluded from general average under Rule VI(b) in the 1974 Rules as amended and the 1994 Rules. This exclusion also appears in Rule VI(c) of the 2004 Rules where the words "such as SCOPIC" appear after "any other provision similar in substance."

The Salvage Convention now has the force of law in the United Kingdom (Merchant Shipping Act 1995, s.224 and Sch.11). Its provisions were incorporated into the 1990 and 1995 editions of Lloyd's Open Form and apply by force of law to LOF 2000. Article 13.1 of the Convention lists various criteria which are to be taken into account when fixing the salvors' reward, including[11] the skill and efforts of the salvors in preventing or minimising damage to the environment. Under art.13.2, payment of a reward fixed in accordance with art.13.1 is to be made by all of the vessel and other property interests in proportion to their respective salved values. Article 14.1 of the Convention provided what is, in effect, a safety net, whereby a salvor who carried out salvage operations in respect of a vessel which by itself or by its cargo threatened damage to the environment is entitled to "special compensation" *from the owner of that vessel* if the art.13 reward is insufficient to cover his expenses (as defined by art.14.3). There is also provision in art.14.2 for a discretionary uplift to be awarded, in addition to the special compensation under art.14.1, where the salvage operations have succeeded in preventing or minimising damage to the environment.

The SCOPIC Clause[12] was introduced in 1999 largely because of concerns[13] about the adequacy of the "fair rate" provisions in art.14.2 of the Convention. When this Clause is incorporated in the salvage agreement[14] and has been invoked by the salvors, it provides a safety net in specified circumstances entitling the salvor to payments at fixed tariff rates in excess of the art.13 reward, in place of any special compensation under art.14, which is disapplied from the time when SCOPIC is invoked until withdrawal or termination under its terms.

A reward under art.13.1(b) may contain an element of enhancement for efforts to prevent environmental damage. The fact that it does so will not prevent the full amount from being brought into general average under the York Antwerp Rules 1974 or 1994. Special compensation under art.14 is payable only by the owner of the vessel, and as already mentioned is excluded from general average under the 1974, 1994 and 2004 Rules. For special compensation to be payable at all, there must have been a threat of damage to the environment, and the uplift is only payable where those efforts achieved some success. The SCOPIC Clause is commonly perceived as relating to environmental protection, but this is a misconception.[15] The

---

[11] Enhancement to reflect skill and efforts in saving lives, in conjunction with the property at risk, is also recognised in art.13. See the discussion at para.26–54B above in this Supplement.

[12] SCOPIC is an acronym standing for Special Compensation P&I Club Clause. Although referred to as if it were a single Clause, the SCOPIC Clause is a lengthy document consisting of 15 clauses, without counting its appendices.

[13] After the decision in *The Nagasaki Spirit* [1995] 2 Lloyd's Rep. 44 (Clarke J.); [1997] 1 Lloyd's Rep. 323 (HL).

[14] Which may be done simply by ticking the appropriate box on LOF 2000.

[15] See Kennedy and Rose, *The Law of Salvage*, 7th edn (2009) at para.10.189, where it is pointed out that it is unfortunate that the SCOPIC acronym used the initials "SC", which stand for a term used in art.14.2 of the Salvage Convention to describe payment for environmental services, "for the main function of SCOPIC is to provide salvors with a guaranteed form of payment to a specified scale, whether or not there is the threat of damage to the environment upon which Article 14 depends."

SCOPIC safety net can apply whether or not there is any risk of environmental damage, and does not depend on success in averting such damage. SCOPIC remuneration, like art.14 compensation, is payable by the shipowner alone. Clause 14 in the SCOPIC Clause provides:

> *"General Average*
> SCOPIC remuneration shall not be a General Average expense to the extent that it exceeds the Article 13 Award; any liability to pay such SCOPIC remuneration shall be that of the Shipowner alone and no claim whether direct, indirect, by way of indemnity or recourse or otherwise relating to SCOPIC remuneration in excess of the Article 13 Award shall be made in General Average or under the vessel's Hull and Machinery Policy by the owners of the Vessel."

For a fuller discussion on the subject discussed in this paragraph, the reader should refer to *Lowndes & Rudolf, op. cit.* at paras 6.07 *et seq* and to the specialist textbooks on the Law of Salvage. The insurance position where a salvage award has been enhanced to reflect efforts to avert environmental damage and where payments are made under the "special compensation" regime or under SCOPIC is discussed in this Supplement at para.25–18A.

The peril which occasioned the general average must be insured under the policy

26–93   *Note 407*: The wording of cl.2 in the Institute Cargo Clauses (A)(B) and (C), which is headed "General Average", is unchanged in the 2009 Clauses. It has been suggested that this extension of cover in respect of general average to the avoidance of loss from "any cause" except those which are expressly excluded might enable assureds whose cargo is insured under the (B) or (C) Clauses to recover in some piracy situations; see *Dunt*, Marine Cargo Insurance (2009) at para.9.37 The present editors venture to doubt whether this is likely to be the case in practice, since both "seizure" and "the consequences thereof or any attempt there at" are expressly excluded perils which will almost certainly be causative in relation to any sacrifice or expenditure of a general average nature. From a practical perspective, it is only those cargo owners who have purchased (A) Clause cover who are insured against general average loss occasioned by piracy.[16]

Effect of modern clauses

Cargo Clauses

26–108   The relevant provisions in the Institute Cargo Clauses 1/1/09 are the same as those referred to in the main work, contained in the 1982 Clauses.

---

[16] But where the cargo was insured under the (B) or (C) Clauses, it is still possible to envisage general average situations where it might be said that the sacrifice or expenditure was occasioned by a "riot", so that the cargo owner would be protected if insurance under the Strike Clauses had been purchased.

CHAPTER 27

PARTICULAR AVERAGE

Definition of a particular average loss and of particular charges

The proposition, in the text and at footnote 7 at this point in the main work, that **27–01**
the cause of action accrues at the date of the casualty should more accurately be
expressed in terms of the cause of action accruing at the date of loss. This will
normally but not necessarily be the same as the date when the casualty takes
place.

The English and Scottish Law Commissions have put forward proposals to
reform the law with regard to damages for late payment by insurers, in Issues
Paper No.6 published in March 2010. It is not clear whether these proposals, if
implemented, would affect the time of accrual of the cause of action and the
period for which interest can be awarded; see paras 12–04, 12–04A above in this
Supplement. The present position with regard to awards of interest, referred to in
passing at footnote 7 under this paragraph (27–01), is now discussed in more
detail at para.12–04A above.

Measure of indemnity

Notes 17 and 18: The English and Scottish Law Commissions have put forward **27–02**
proposals to reform the law so as to enable damages for late payment to be recovered, in Issues Paper No.6. See para.12–04 above in this Supplement. Although
The Italia Express (No.2) is discussed in Issues Paper No.6, the Law
Commissions did not refer to that part of Hirst J.'s reasoning based on the statutory scheme of the measure of indemnity sections in the 1906 Act being "conclusively definitive." It is not clear whether the Commissions' proposals would entail
amendments to s.16 and to s.67 and the sections which follow.

CHAPTER 28

ACTUAL TOTAL LOSS

What amounts to actual total loss

Note 9: The dictum of Rix J. in *Kuwait Airways v Kuwait Insurance*[1] which is **28–03** referred to in this footnote was relied on by the claimant assured in *Masefield AG v Amlin Corporate Member Ltd.*[2] The argument that capture by pirates constitutes an actual total loss, based on *Dean v Hornby* (above) and on this dictum in *Kuwait Airways*, was rejected by David Steel J. who observed [at para.49] that the intentions of pirates vary in different cases, and that the relevant passage in *Kuwait Airways* is rightly described by the editors as "doubtful" at this point in *Arnould*. In this regard, David Steel J. considered the judgment of Porter J. in *Marstrand v Beer*[3] to be particularly instructive (*Masefield v Amlin*, at para.50).

Partial or constructive total loss may develop into actual total loss after the policy expires

The decision in *Stringer v English and Scottish Marine Ins Co*, where the claim **28–06** for total loss succeeded despite the ability to post bail to prevent it, is consistent with the requirement for an actual total loss that it be legally and physically impossible to recover the goods; the crucial ingredient was that the condemnation had removed the goods from the owners' dominion and control: see per David Steel J. in *Masefield v Amlin* (above) at para.[44].

Deprivation

The question of actual total loss by deprivation was fully considered at first **28–07** instance in *Masefield v Amlin*,[4] where the relevant authorities are reviewed. This was a case of seizure by pirates operating from Somalia with a view to extracting

---

[1] [1996] 1 Lloyd's Rep. 664, 682. *Dean v Hornby* (1854) 3 EL-& BL. 180 (a case of piratical seizure) was cited by Rix J. in support of this proposition.
[2] [2010] Lloyd's Rep. IR 345. At the time of going to press, the decision of the Court of Appeal in *Masefield* is pending.
[3] In *Marstrand v Beer*, Porter J. said: "I think it was always a question of fact whether capture was an actual total loss or merely a possible constructive total loss. Capture followed by condemnation no doubt was actual total loss, but that was because the vessel had in fact been condemned. The capture alone I do not think was ever necessarily an actual total loss . . . Normally I think capture is a constructive total loss, and the confusion which has arisen, with regard to whether it is an actual or a constructive total loss, arose merely because, in the earlier cases, the distinction between those two classes of loss was not kept clear. . . . However that may be, whether under the old law capture was or was not actual total loss, the case is now governed by the Marine Insurance Act, 1906, ss.56 to 60. That Act provides in s.57 amongst its definitions of "actual total loss", "if the vessel be irretrievably lost".
[4] [2010] EWHC 280 (Comm).

a ransom for the release of ship, cargo and crew.[5] The cargo owners sought to argue that their property became an actual total loss at the moment of seizure, despite the strong likelihood that a ransom would be paid and that it would be released, as in fact happened, within a few weeks.

The claimant's principal submission was that capture by pirates constitutes an actual total loss without more.[6] Independently (it would seem) from that proposition, the claimant in *Masefield v Amlin* argued that the facility for recovering property by payment of a ransom should be disregarded when considering whether a vessel and her cargo are in practice irretrievable as the payment of a ransom to pirates (although admittedly not illegal) was contrary to public policy.[7] In addition, the claimant argued that it could not be regarded as being under any duty to pay the ransom,[8] and that for this reason also the ability to do so should be disregarded.

On the general question of what constitutes an actual total loss by deprivation, David Steel J. summarised the position in the following terms:

> "[29] The issue is whether on 18 September 2008 [the date when proceedings were deemed to have commenced] the Claimant was 'irretrievably deprived' of the cargo. The test is objective and is to be assessed on the true facts as at that date whether or not known or apparent to the assured: *Marstrand Fishing Co Ltd v Beer* . . .[9] Although the actual fact of recovery within a short period is not directly material let alone decisive the Court is entitled to consider what in fact happened after the relevant date as this 'may assist in showing what the probabilities really were, if they had been reasonably forecasted'; see *Bank Line, Limited v Arthur Capel and Company*[10] . . . per Lord Sumner at p.454 . . .

---

[5] It is understood that there have been over 200 similar incidents of seizure or attempted seizure by Somali pirates within the last two years. The judgment of David Steel J. contains a detailed description of this phenomenon, and of the Somali pirates' methods of operation. The objective, in all these cases, has been to secure payment of a ransom and generally, if not invariably, the outcome has been the release of the property and crew against payment within a short time-frame. In none of these cases have the pirates shown any desire whatever to assert dominion over the ship and/or cargo, as opposed to using their possession as a bargaining counter.

[6] The Claimant's argument appears, in effect, to have treated cases of capture as *sui generis*, and to have treated *Dean v Hornby* (above) as establishing a rule of law in a context which, by its nature, is very fact sensitive. Whatever the position may have been in earlier cases, the statutory test now is whether the assured has been "irretrievably deprived" of his property, which is a question of fact; see the passage from *Marstrand v Beer* cited at para.28–03, Note 7 above, and see the passage from the Award of Michael Kerr QC in the *Dawsons Field* arbitration which is quoted by David Steel J. at para.[51] in his judgment. *Dean v Hornby*, where the claim appears to have been for a constructive total loss and where the intention of the pirates was to steal the property, was plainly a very different case from *Masefield v Amlin* where the pirates were intending to ransom the property. In a ransom situation, "wait and see" is the order of the day; *Kuwait Airways v Kuwait Insurance* [1996] 1 Lloyd's Rep. 664, 685. It remains to be seen whether this analysis is upheld by the Court of Appeal.

[7] The issue on public policy is dealt with at paras [58] to [63] in the judgment.

[8] *Masefield v Amlin*, above, at para.[64].

[9] (1936) 56 Ll.L. Rep. 163.

[10] [1919] A.C. 435. A similar approach has been held to be applicable to questions of constructive total loss under s.60(2)(i)(a) of the 1906 Act (unlikelihood of recovery); *Bank Line v Capel* has been cited in a number of cases to support such an approach. See para.29–18, fn.129 in the main work.

[31] What degree of probability is sufficient for these purposes? The short answer, in my judgment, is that an assured is not irretrievably deprived of property if it is legally and physically possible to recover it (and even if such recovery can only be achieved by disproportionate effort and expense). ."

There were a number of insuperable difficulties with what appears to have been the claimant's main submission in *Masefield v Amlin*, that capture by pirates as such constitutes an actual total loss, as David Steel J. noted in the course of his judgment.[11] Seizure by pirates merely results in a transfer of possession and has no effect on proprietary interests. The question which thus arises is whether recovery of possession is legally or physically possible. A situation where a ransom is expected to be and is in fact demanded is very different from one where the intention of the captors is to assert title and dominion over the property from the outset. Subject to considerations of public policy and legality of payment, in a ransom situation deprivation cannot generally be said to be irretrievable at the moment of seizure, and "wait and see" is an essential ingredient in such cases.[12]

Thus, the key question for determination in *Masefield v Amlin* was whether the payment of ransom was contrary to public policy and therefore to be disregarded as a factor in deciding whether the claimant was "irretrievably deprived" of its cargo. David Steel J. was wholly unpersuaded that it would be right to categorise such payments, which were not illegal as a matter of English law, as being contrary to public policy.[13] The wider significance of this aspect of the decision, for other piracy cases involving payments of ransom, will be self-evident.[14] The decision of the Court of Appeal in *Masefield* is expected to provide a definitive answer to this important question.

David Steel J. also held[15] that the existence or otherwise of a duty to pay ransom is irrelevant to the question of actual total loss; the only issue is whether the required expenditure would or might lead to recovery.

Notes 39, 40: The established principle that considerations of cost are irrele- **28–08**
vant to the question of deprivation under s.57 was reaffirmed by David Steel J. in *Masefield v Amlin* (above).

---

[11] At paras [39] to [52]. It remains to be seen whether the Court of Appeal (which has reserved judgment in *Masefield* at the time of going to press) regards those difficulties as insuperable.

[12] *Ibid*, paras [49] to [52]. Even in a case where a vessel has been seized by pirates and made to disappear, an immediate conclusion that she has become an actual total loss is unlikely to be justified, see the decision of the Singapore Court in *Bayswater Carriers Pte Ltd v QBE Ins (Intl) Pte Ltd* [2006] 1 S.L.R. 69.

[13] [2010] EWHC 280 (Comm), paras [59] to [63]. It was common ground in *Masefield v Amlin* that the payment of ransom was not illegal under English law (the law governing the policy), and it was assumed that the payment was not illegal under any other conceivably relevant law.

[14] The issue of public policy would potentially affect any claim to recover ransom expenses from insurers as a sue and labour expenditure or as a general average loss, as well as affecting any rights to contribution in general average; the subject is discussed more fully at para.25–21 (in the context of sue and labour) and at para.26–54 (general average).

[15] *Masefield v Amlin* (above) at para.[64]. Since considerations of what it would cost to recover the property are irrelevant to the question of actual total loss, it must necessarily follow that the existence or otherwise of a duty to sue and labour is irrelevant. It remains to be seen whether the Court of Appeal decision in *Masefield* adopts this analysis.

CHAPTER 29

CONSTRUCTIVE TOTAL LOSS

General observations

The subject of abandonment, and the different senses in which the term is used, **29–03** is discussed in Chapter 30 of the main work. There has been a further important decision since the 17th edition was published, in which the statutory scheme with regard to abandonment and its effects was discussed; *The WD Fairway (No.2)* [2009] 2 Lloyd's Rep. 191; *(No.3)* [2009] 2 Lloyd's Rep. 420. The case is discussed extensively under the next chapter heading (30) below.

What is required under s.60(1)is not a notice of abandonment but the abandonment of any hope of recovery. In *Masefield AG v Amlin Corporate Member Ltd*,[1] the assured cargo-owners sought to rely on this sub-section, having given notice of abandonment at a time when negotiations for the release of the vessel and cargo from their detention by Somali pirates were nearing fruition.[2] It is submitted that *Masefield v Amlin* affords an obvious example of a situation where s.60(1) could not apply. The property had not been abandoned in the sense discussed in *Court Line Ltd v The King* (above); on the contrary, the shipowners and cargo owners had every intention of recovering their property, the shipowners were actively seeking to negotiate for its release, and there was every reason to expect those negotiations to succeed; there was no reasonable basis for regarding an actual total loss as unavoidable.[3]

Constructive total loss of goods; loss of possession

Note 230: The Constructive Total Loss Clause (cl.13) is unchanged in the **29–43** Institute Cargo Clauses 1/1/09; see Appendix below. The view expressed by the editors of this work, that cl.13 does not have the effect of excluding claims for constructive total loss of goods under s.60(2)(i) or by loss of voyage, is supported in Dunt, *Marine Cargo Insurance* (2009) at para.13.42, where the historical antecedents of this Clause are described and the contrary view expressed in Bennett, 2nd ed. at para.21.76 is criticised. It appears, however, to have been accepted by the assured in *Masefield v Amlin*[4] that cl.13 does have the effect of excluding the category of constructive total provided for in s.60(2)(i) relating to deprivation of possession in circumstances where recovery of the goods is

---

[1] [2010] Lloyd's Rep. IR 345, paras [54] to [57]. At the time of going to press, the Court of Appeal has reserved judgment in *Masefield*. The editors' comments are to be read subject to the Court of Appeal taking a different view.
[2] The ship, cargo and crew were released 11 days after the notice of abandonment had been given. The cargo-owners had been kept informed of the ongoing negotiations on a regular basis.
[3] *Ibid*, paras [56], [57].
[4] [2010] Lloyd's Rep. IR 345 at para. [8].

unlikely; but as the point was common ground, and the contrary view was not argued, it is submitted that this case cannot be seen as providing guidance on the matter in controversy.[5] The editors remain firmly of the view stated at this point in the main work and in *Dunt, op. cit.*, para.13.42.

Loss of Voyage may effect constructive total loss of goods

29–45 *Notes 251 and 252*: The relevant clauses are unchanged in the 2009 Cargo Clauses; see the Appendix below. The editors remain of the view, as stated, that cl.13 does not affect the application of the principle that loss of voyage may be treated as a constructive total loss of cargo. See the discussion at para.29–43, note 230 in the main work and in this Supplement (above).

29–47 *Note 258*: The wording of cl.13 is unchanged in the 2009 Cargo Clauses. The editors remain of the view that this Clause does not exclude the class of constructive total loss under discussion. See further, para.29–43 note 230 in the main work and above.

Effect of the Marine Insurance Act 1906 s.60(2)(iii)

29–59 *Note 295*: The terms of cl.13 are unchanged, in the 2009 Clauses. The wording does not precisely mirror that in s.60(2)(iii) of the Act. It would seem that the use of the words "recovering" and "reconditioning" instead of the words "cost of repairing the damage" was intended to clarify and extend the scope of this category of constructive total loss; see *Dunt, op. cit.* para.13–42. But this slight difference between the wording of cl.13 and of the relevant sub-section does nothing to resolve the controversy discussed at this point in *Arnould*.

---

[5] The concession (we consider) was wrongly made; but it would not have assisted the assured, in any event, to rely on s.60 (2)(i), since recovery of the goods within a reasonable time was likely from the moment the vessel was seized by pirates with a view to extracting a ransom for release of the property and crew, and was imminent when notice of abandonment was given.

CHAPTER 30

ABANDONMENT

"Abandonment" a term used in different senses

A detailed analysis of the "statutory scheme" was recently carried out by **30–02** Tomlinson J. in *The WD Fairway (No.2)*.[1] The case raised "a series of challenging questions"[2] which are referred to in the paragraphs that follow.

The election to abandon

The passages from Rix L.J.'s judgment in *The Kastor Too* cited in this paragraph **30–03** of the main work were discussed in *The WD Fairway (No.2)* (above).[3] Referring to the analysis of notice of abandonment as an offer to cede the property to the insurers which, until accepted, may be withdrawn, Tomlinson J. noted that the paradigm case of the offer being withdrawn by conduct inconsistent with a continued preparedness to abandon would be where the assured sells the wreck without reference to underwriters. Had the sale of *WD Fairway* taken place before payment had been made, the assured would undoubtedly have lost the right to claim for a total loss.[4] Tomlinson J. then went on to note that in the ordinary case an assured whose notice of abandonment is declined will be treated as continuing to make the offer constituted by his notice unless and until he does some act

---

[1] *Dornoch Ltd v Westminster International BV* [2009] 2 Lloyd's Rep. 191. See also *The WD Fairway (No.3)* [2009] 2 Lloyd's Rep. 420. The facts are outlined at para.30–11A below.

[2] *Ibid*, at para.1.

[3] *Ibid*, paras 32, 38. In support of this analysis of notice of abandonment as constituting an offer to cede the property which the insurer is *entitled* but not bound to accept Tomlinson J. referred, in addition to *The Kastor Too*, to the judgment of Scrutton L.J. in *Allgemeine Versicherungs-Gesellschaft Helvetia v Administrator of German Property* [1931] 1 K.B. 672 and to the drafting history of ss.63(1) and 79(1) of the 1906 Act; see *WD Fairway*, above, at paras 26-29. Under s.63(1), where there is a valid abandonment the insurer is *entitled* to take over the interest of the assured in whatever may remain of the subject-matter insured. Section 79(1) uses similar language with the same effect, referring to the insurer's becoming *entitled* to take over the subject-matter upon payment for a total loss. A clear distinction is drawn in s.79(1) between taking over the subject-matter, which is an entitlement of which the insurer may choose not to avail himself and the insurer's rights of subrogation which arise automatically on payment for a total loss ("he is *thereby* subrogated").

[4] *Ibid*, para.32. The unusual facts in *The WD Fairway* are described at para.30–11A below in this Supplement. Payment for the claimed CTL was made several months before any of the underwriters accepted the notice of abandonment, which had initially been declined in the usual non-committal fashion. The sale of the vessel by the assured to an associated company took place soon after the majority of the underwriters had expressly elected to take over the interest of the assured in the vessel under s.79(1) of the Act. In a case where the sale of the vessel had taken place after acceptance of notice of abandonment but before payment, then, in the opinion of Tomlinson J., this would not disentitle the assured from recovering for a CTL, liability for that having been conclusively admitted; *ibid*, para.41. The editors agree with that analysis.

inconsistent therewith, and when underwriters decline the notice, their rejection of the assured's offer is not ordinarily, without more, irrevocable.[5]

Acceptance of abandonment

30–06 The analysis in the text and footnotes to this paragraph in the main work was referred to with apparent approval in *The WD Fairway* (above). It was suggested by Tomlinson J. that inconsistent views are put forward in *Arnould*.[6] The criticism appears to be directed at para.30–09, and is addressed in that context below. For the avoidance of doubt, the editors' view of the effect of an acceptance of abandonment is as set out, in summary, at para.30–06 in the main work.

It was common ground in *The WD Fairway* that by accepting notice of abandonment the insurer conclusively admits his liability to pay for a CTL and admits that the offer to cede given by the assured was validly made. However, there was considerable debate as to whether an insurer also irrevocably undertakes, when he accepts the assured's notice, that he will take over the assured's interest in the subject-matter,[7] or whether as was submitted on behalf of underwriters when notice of abandonment has been accepted but payment not yet made, the promise to pay is conditional on the assured being in a position to tender the wreck against payment. This argument was rejected by Tomlinson J.[8] It is not a conditional undertaking. Dealing with the wreck by the assured in a manner inconsistent with the interests of underwriters after acceptance of notice of abandonment will not disentitle the assured from recovering for the CTL, and underwriters do therefore require security in this situation.[9] An equitable lien arises before payment, in circumstances where notice of abandonment had been accepted.[10]

In the circumstances, Tomlinson J. did not need to decide whether acceptance of notice of abandonment constitutes an exercise of the right of election under s.63(1) of the Act, or is to be understood as an irrevocable election to exercise the right which on the promised payment for a CTL will become available to

---

[5] *Ibid*, para.33. There is no reason why declining notice of abandonment should ordinarily amount to an irrevocable election by underwriters not to exercise their rights, to take over the property under s.63(1) or s.79(1). Loss by underwriters of those rights is likely to be achieved only by express agreement or by the assured's reliance on a very clear representation disclaiming future exercise of the right; *ibid*, para.44.

[6] *Ibid*, para.36.

[7] The assured's preferred analysis in *The WD Fairway* was that cession occurs on acceptance of notice of abandonment, rather than on payment following such acceptance, but that argument (which is inconsistent with the analysis in *The Kastor Too*) was not pressed; it was sufficient for the assured to argue that equity would impose an equitable lien in favour of insurers upon their acceptance of the notice of abandonment. The "concession" to that effect was accepted as correct by Tomlinson J., at para.41 in his judgment.

[8] The *WD Fairway (No.2)* [2009] 2 Lloyd's Rep. 191 at para.41.

[9] *Ibid*, para.41. The relevance of this question in the context of *WD Fairway*, where the payment preceded acceptance of the assured's notice, is explained at paras 34 and 40–43.

[10] *Ibid*, para.41. Payment for a total loss, unaccompanied by an acceptance of abandonment or election to take over the property, does not give rise to an equitable lien; see *ibid*, at para.55. As Tomlinson J. stated, there is no reason why equity should intervene to secure insurers' position whilst they take further time to decide whether they wish to assume the burdens of ownership. This analysis is similar to that adopted in relation to the doctrine of subrogation, see *Re Ballast Plc* [2007] Lloyd's Rep. IR 742.

underwriters by virtue of s.79(1).[11] The analysis in *The Kastor Too*[12] might be read in either sense, but the point seems to be of merely academic interest. It is hard to envisage any circumstances where it is likely to matter which view is preferred.

As was recognised in *The WD Fairway (No.2)*, it is unusual for underwriters nowadays to accept notice of abandonment, for the reasons stated in this paragraph of *Arnould*. The usual market practice that is followed when a claim for constructive total loss is settled is described in *The WD Fairway (No.3)*.[13] A cooperative arrangement is commonly made between the assured owners and underwriters whereby the assured facilitates the sale of the vessel, often for scrap, on behalf of underwriters or, if the owners wish to retain the vessel, they account to underwriters for its net residual value, ascertained by agreement or independent valuation. When the assured is to retain the vessel, the agreed residual value will sometimes be deducted from the amount to be paid in respect of the CTL.[14] The process is commonly but inaccurately described as one where the assured buys back the vessel from underwriters.[15] The failure of the parties in *The WD Fairway* to deal with the matter on a consensual basis is believed to have been wholly unprecedented in modern times, in the London market at least.

Abandonment must be absolute and unconditional

Tomlinson J. observed in the course of his judgment in *The WD Fairway (No.2)*[16] **30–09** that the passage in this paragraph of the main work stating that as a general rule no formalities are required to give effect to the transfer of the assured's proprietary interest "which takes place automatically upon acceptance of notice of abandonment" is inconsistent with other passages in Chapter 30 of *Arnould*. We accept that this passage (the words placed here in inverted commas) is in need of correction. Whatever the position may have been prior to the 1906 Act, it is now clear that transfer of the assured's proprietary interest does not take place automatically upon acceptance of notice of abandonment unaccompanied by payment for the total loss, as is indeed stated elsewhere in Chapter 30 of the main work.[17] As *The WD Fairway* shows, acceptance of notice of abandonment gives rise to an equitable lien in respect of the property, prior to payment for a total loss,[18] but it is only where the underwriter has both paid the total loss claim and accepted the notice of abandonment or made a positive election[19] to exercise his right to take over the property under s.63(1) and/or s.79(1) that the assured's proprietary interest is transferred.

---

[11] *Ibid*, para.43.
[12] [2004] 2 Lloyd's Rep. 119 at para.76.
[13] [2009] 2 Lloyd's Rep. 420 at paras 11–12. The process of accounting for the residual value (if any) of an insured cargo is no doubt also dealt with by consensual arrangements of this kind.
[14] *Ibid*, para.12.
[15] *Ibid*, para.11.
[16] [2009] 2 Lloyd's Rep. 191 at para.36.
[17] For example, paras 30–06 and 30–35.
[18] See the discussion at para.30–06 above in this Supplement.
[19] The election may be made by an acceptance of the notice of abandonment. In *The WD Fairway*, the election was made under s.79(1), long after payment of the claim; see para.30–11A below.

The propositions in para.30–09 that as a general rule no formalities are required to give effect to the transfer of the assured's proprietary interest and that where there is a need to comply with formal requirements in order to perfect the transfer this does not preclude a valid abandonment are not affected by *The WD Fairway* where it was accepted on all sides that payment for a CTL, coupled with an express election to take over the interest of the assured in the vessel, will be effective to transfer to insurers the assured's legal or at least equitable title to the vessel.[20]

Where there is a technical obstacle to vesting of the property, such as that recognised by Lord Truro in *Scottish Marine Insurance Co v Turner*,[21] or there are technical requirements to be fulfilled, it is the equitable and not the legal title which vests in the insurer. The trust analysis which derives from the observations of Lord Truro in *Scottish Marine v Turner* was described by Tomlinson J. in *The WD Fairway* as "the conventional analysis".[22] Those underwriters who exercised the right of election under s.79(1) before the vessel's sale (having previously paid their proportions of the total loss), probably acquired a legal title,[23] but for the purpose of the Phase 1 preliminary issues in *The WD Fairway* Tomlinson J. addressed the matter on the basis that the relevant underwriters would have acquired a beneficial interest of less than 100 per cent of the vessel under a trust assumed for the purpose of discussion to be governed by English law. It was not in dispute that where legal ownership of a vessel is divided, under English law the owners with the majority interest are entitled to possession, and would be entitled to call for the judicial sale of the vessel under s.188 of the Law of Property Act, 1925.[24] It was also common ground that insurers who have a subsisting equitable lien could invoke s.188,[25] and that in a case where insurers collectively have a 100 per cent beneficial interest, similarly, the section could be invoked, so as to achieve the vessel's sale.[26] But it was contended that insurers who are co-owners in equity with a beneficial interest of less than 100 per cent are in a less favourable position and cannot procure a judicial sale.[27] The corollary of the rule in *Saunders v Vautier* that where all possible beneficiaries are in agreement they may dispose of trust property as they see fit (it was suggested) is that absence of consent on the part of any person interested under a trust will prevent the termination of the trust and transfer of the legal title.[28] Tomlinson J. did not reach any

---

[20] [2009] 2 Lloyd's Rep. 191 at para.41.

[21] (1853) 1 Macq. H.L. Cas. 334. See *WD Fairway* above, at paras 41 (n.4), 77–78.

[22] [2009] 2 Lloyd's at para.78. Tomlinson J. expressed some doubts about the trust analysis, and suggested that it might be more appropriate, and more efficacious, to classify the equitable proprietary right of insurers as a lien in circumstances where some act of the assured is required in order to effect a transfer of an appropriate share of the legal title to the insurer.

[23] *The WD Fairway* (above) at paras 58, 62, 65; see para.30–11A below in this Supplement.

[24] *Ibid*, paras 66 and 67.

[25] *Ibid*, para.68.

[26] *Ibid*, para.70.

[27] *Ibid*, para.71. As Tomlinson J. observed, it would be surprising if the rights of insurers in this situation were less valuable than if they had the benefit of an equitable lien. It was partly for this reason that he expressed some doubt as to whether the conventional trust analysis is necessarily correct, see n.22 above.

[28] See *ibid* para.71.

conclusions[29] as to the remedies which might be available to insurers in such a situation, where they had less than a 100 per cent beneficial interest, as beneficiaries of a trust created in their favour. This would have entailed consideration of questions with ramifications beyond the realms of marine insurance as to whether relief under s.188(1) of the Law of Property Act 1925 is available to co-owners in equity of a moiety or upwards or only to legal co-owners and of the rule in *Saunders v Vautier*.[30] The editors are content to follow Tomlinson J.'s example and express no view on the point.

Abandonment in cases of partial insurance

The problems discussed at para.30–11 in the main work were considered in *The* **30–11A** *WD Fairway*. This case resembled *Whitworth Bros v Shepherd*,[31] insofar as both cases involved a situation where some but not all of the vessel's insurers accepted notice of abandonment or elected to take over a proprietary interest in the vessel, having paid their proportions of the total loss. The salient facts in *The WD Fairway* were as follows:

(1) *WD Fairway* was a vessel of specialised construction,[32] described as a mega-size trailer hopper dredger, and at the time of her loss was owned by one of the companies in the Boskalis group and registered in the Netherlands.

(2) In March 2007, the vessel became a constructive total loss as a result of a collision off China. Notice of abandonment was given and declined, underwriters agreeing to place the assured in the same position as if a writ/claim form had been issued that day.[33]

(3) In August 2007, the wrecked vessel was towed to Thailand where she remained.

(4) By April 2008, all of the vessel's underwriters had paid their proportions of the CTL claim.[34] Shortly thereafter, payment was also made in respect of the assured's salvage/wreck removal claim which was covered as an additional element under the policy.

(5) A dispute then arose as to the residual open market value of the vessel to which it was common ground that, having paid for the total loss, the

---

[29] The possibility that there may be an implied term requiring the assured to cooperate in enabling the property to be transferred, which is suggested at this point in *Arnould* (para.30–09, fn.51), was recognised but not ruled upon by Tomlinson J. at para.74 in his judgment.

[30] (1841) 41 E.R. 482.

[31] (1884) 12 Ct. of Sess. Cas. (4th). 204. The facts of that case are outlined at para.30–11 in the main work and at para.62 in Tomlinson J.'s judgment in *WD Fairway*.

[32] There were currently only two other vessels in the world of comparable size and capability (*ibid*, para.11).

[33] As Tomlinson J. observed, "This is time—honoured and common if not universal practice;" *ibid*, para.6.

[34] The endorsement recording settlement of the claim did not amount either to an acceptance of notice of abandonment or to an irrevocable election not to take over the vessel; see *The WD Fairway (No.3)* [2009] 2 Lloyd's Rep. 420 para.9 and following, discussed at para.30–24 below in this Supplement.

insurers were entitled. The parties' estimates of value were far apart, and the assured was unwilling to allow the vessel to be put out to tender, which would involve permitting competitors of the Boskalis group access to the vessel and the possibility of her falling into the hands of competitors.

(6) Faced with this impasse, in December 2008 the majority[35] of the underwriters elected to take over the interest of the assured in what remained of the subject-matter insured. The election was made expressly under s.79(1) of the 1906 Act.

(7) The reaction of the Boskalis companies to the insurers' election and the imminent threat of an injunction was swift. On January 9, 2008, the vessel was removed from the Dutch Register of Shipping and sold to another company in the Boskalis group for the nominal sum of 1,000. The purpose of the sale was to frustrate the insurers' contractual entitlement to take over the vessel and any proprietary rights they might have acquired.

(8) The remaining underwriters who had not exercised their election under s.79(1) of the Act sought to do so on January 12 and 15, 2009, i.e. after the sale.

(9) At the time of the vessel's transfer on January 9, 2009 she was not registered under any flag, and she remained unregistered at the time of the proceedings. The vessel was situated in Thailand at the time of transfer.

It was ultimately held by Tomlinson J. that the sale was effective to transfer the title to the vessel under the *lex situs*, Thai law, which was the relevant law for this purpose. None of the underwriters had any proprietary interest in the vessel, under Thai law. However, the claimants were still able to achieve their objective by a wholly different route. Tomlinson J. held that this was an appropriate case in which the jurisdiction under s.423 of the Insolvency Act, 1986, which is not subject to any territorial limitations, should be exercised and proposed (subject to further argument as to precise terms) to order the fourth defendant (the purchasing company) to transfer the vessel to the claimants' nominees with a view to her sale. An order under s.423 was the only way in which effect could be given to the underwriters' contractual entitlement.[36]

---

[35] All but two of the primary layer underwriters, collectively subscribing to 77.75 per cent of that layer, and all but one of the excess layer underwriters, collectively subscribing to 85 per cent, exercised that election in December 2008. The action was brought by the excess underwriters (the primary policy contained an exclusive Dutch jurisdiction clause). The 14th claimant, who had a 15 per cent line on both layers, did not elect to take over the property in December 2008, but only sought to do so after the sale of the vessel in January 2009. An election to take over whatever remains of the subject-matter insured which is exercised after it has already been sold must ordinarily be wholly ineffective, except possibly with regard to the proceeds of sale. In the unusual circumstances of *The WD Fairway*, a successful challenge to the validity of the sale by those insurers who had exercised their election before it took place would no doubt have benefited the 14th claimant as well. In the event, all the claimants obtained relief by a different route, under s.423 of the Insolvency Act, 1986.

[36] *The WD Fairway (No.3)* at para.166. The issues arising with regard to the jurisdiction under the Insolvency Act 1986 are discussed at paras 123–166. Plainly, the possibility that insurers may be able to claim relief under s.423 if all else fails, in those rare cases where their contractual and proprietary rights deriving from abandonment are rendered ineffective, is potentially of some practical importance, but discussion of the subject is beyond the scope of this work. In *Whitworth Bros v Shepherd*

Although the outcome in *The WD Fairway* therefore turned on Thai law and on the Insolvency Act jurisdiction, the position with regard to contractual and proprietary rights of underwriters under English law, in a situation where a majority but not all of the underwriters elect to take over the property, was considered in detail by Tomlinson J. (at the request of the parties) and was on any view relevant to the exercise of the Court's discretion under s.423 of the Insolvency Act.

The principal argument advanced by the assured was that the purported election under s.79(1) in December 2008 was ineffective because it was not an election made by all the subscribing underwriters; only where an insurer who has paid the "whole" of the loss, or insurers who between them have paid the whole of the loss, elect to take over the property will that election be effective. This argument was misconceived. As Tomlinson J. pointed out,[37] it ignored the fact that each insurer has a separate contract with the insured, and that it is with the incidents of each individual contract of insurance that the Act is concerned. It is undoubtedly the position, and is confirmed by *The WD Fairway*, that payment for a total loss coupled with an election by some but not all of the underwriters subscribing to a policy to take over the property under s.63(1) or s.79(1) of the Act, or an acceptance of notice of abandonment by some but not all underwriters, will be effective to confer proprietary rights of some kind under English law, in proportion to the amount of those underwriters' subscriptions. The only question is as to the precise nature of those rights and how, in practice, effect can be given to that election.

As already discussed under paras 30–06 and 30–09 in this Supplement, Tomlinson J. held that underwriters who accept a notice of abandonment are protected by an equitable lien, between the time of such acceptance and payment. Where there is a subsisting equitable lien, which did not arise on the facts in *The WD Fairway*, it would appear to be open to any number of subscribing underwriters who are in that position to apply for an injunction to prevent disposal of the property or for an order for sale.[38]

Where some but not all subscribing insurers have *both* paid their share of a total loss claim *and* elected to take over the property under s.63(1) and/or s.79(1) and/or by express acceptance of the assured's notice of abandonment, those insurers will acquire a legal or at least equitable title to the vessel (on the conventional analysis, at least, the right which is available to insurers in this situation is not classified as an equitable lien).[39]

Since *The WD Fairway* had ceased to be registered under any flag at the time of the sale in January 2009, it is probable that those underwriters who exercised the right of election under s.79(1) became co-owners of the vessel as tenants in common at law as from the time of the vessel's deletion from the Dutch Registry.[40]

(1884) 12 Ct. of Sess. Cas (4th) 204, which was also a case where (albeit for very different reasons) the election to take over the assured's interest in the vessel had become ineffective, the relief sought and recovered by the insurers was an award of the appropriate proportion of her value. That solution would not have been practicable or effective in *The WD Fairway*, but would no doubt be applied in more straightforward cases.

[37] *The WD Fairway (No.2)* at para.66. See also paras 8–13 to 8–15 in the main work, where the principles applying in cases of co-insurance are discussed.

[38] See *ibid*, paras 47, 68.

[39] See *ibid*, paras 77, 78.

[40] *Ibid*, paras 62, 65; G. Bruce et al, *Williams & Bruce's Admiralty Practice*, 3rd ed (1902) at pp 30–31. *The WD Fairway* confirms the analysis suggested in *The Commonwealth* [1907] P. 216, discussed at para.30–11 in the main work.

However, for the purposes of the preliminary issues, the matter was approached on the basis that any interest acquired by those underwriters was an equitable interest (as would seem on any view to have been the position prior to the vessel's deletion from the Dutch registry).

In those cases where an equitable title is acquired by an election exercised by some but not all subscribing insurers, as would be the position where there are formal requirements that have to be met before legal title is transferred, the appropriate analysis under English law is that the relevant underwriters acquire a beneficial interest under a trust.[41] In principle, those underwriters would be entitled to have the appropriate number of whole sixty-fourth shares transferred to them to be registered in their name, and any remaining part one sixty fourth shares would be held on trust by the vessel's owners for themselves and for the insurers in their respective proportions.[42]

As already noted under para.30–09 above in this Supplement, Tomlinson J. held that insurers who between them have acquired a majority interest in the vessel as tenants in common at law together with the assured will be entitled to possession of the vessel and to apply under s.188 of the Law of Property Act 1925 to have the vessel realised by judicial process,[43] but declined at that stage of the proceedings to express any concluded view as to whether co-owners in equity of a moiety or upwards of the shares in a vessel would be entitled to similar relief.[44]

Acceptance of notice of abandonment

30–23   *Note 122*: See also *The WD Fairway (No.2)* [2009] 2 Lloyd's Rep. 191, discussed at para.30–06 above in this Supplement

Acceptance of abandonment must distinctly appear

30–24   In *The WD Fairway*, the endorsement recording the underwriters' agreement to settle the CTL claim contained the words "Net open market residual value of vessel to be accounted to insurers."[45] The endorsement did not amount either to an acceptance of notice of abandonment or election to take over the vessel or to an irrevocable election not to take over the vessel.[46] Another argument, which was raised at one stage, that the insurers impliedly elected to take over the vessel under s.63(1) and/or s.79(1) of the Act by their payment of the assured's salvage/wreck removal claim, was not pursued.[47] That point was conceded having regard to the inclusion of the Waiver Clause[48] in the policy, but Tomlinson J.

---

[41] See para.30–09 in the main work and above in this Supplement.

[42] *The WD Fairway (No.2)* at paras 41 (fn.4) and 61.

[43] *The WD Fairway (No.2)* at paras 67 and 68.

[44] *Ibid*, para.76. The proceedings never reached a stage when this thorny question had to be answered. Tomlinson J.'s inclination, with which the editors are in sympathy, is that the conventional trust analysis may need revisiting and that a Court might feel ready to classify the equitable proprietary right of insurers instead as an equitable lien, should similar problems arise in any future case of divided ownership.

[45] *The WD Fairway (No.3)* [2009] 2 Lloyd's Rep. 420, at para.9.

[46] *Ibid*, paras 9 and following.

[47] *The WD Fairway (No.2)* [2009] 2 Lloyd's Rep. 191 at para.56.

[48] A version of the standard clause discussed at para.30–24 in the main work.

observed that it should not be assumed that this was the only reason why the question had to be answered in that way.[49]

Revocation or withdrawal of notice by assured

Note 139: See also *The WD Fairway (No.2)* [2009] 2 Lloyd's Rep. 191 at para.33 **30–25** per Tomlinson J.: "In the ordinary case, an assured whose notice of abandonment is declined will be treated as continuing to make the offer constituted by the notice unless and until he does some act inconsistent therewith."

Effect of abandonment as entitling the underwriters to salvage

The principles stated in this paragraph of the main work are confirmed by the **30–28** analysis in *The Kastor Too*[50] and *The WD Fairway*.[51]

Other rights incidental to the ownership of the property pass as salvage to underwriters

The proposition in this paragraph of the main work that the underwriters by not **30–32** accepting the abandonment, or by other acts of the like kind, may lose all title to the ultimate benefit of salvage was accepted in *The WD Fairway (No.2)*, above, at para.17, but Tomlinson J. did not regard *Brooks v MacDonnell*[52] as a useful illustration since in that case the abandonment was rejected and it was inherent in the settlement that the underwriters disclaimed any further interest in the insured property. In the opinion of Tomlinson J., the position where underwriters lose all title to the ultimate benefit of salvage cannot ordinarily occur absent an express disclaimer by underwriters of their entitlement.[53]

Effect of abandonment when not accepted

The proposition that underwriters can keep their options open indefinitely was **30–35** referred to with apparent approval in *The WD Fairway (No.2)*.[54]

Note 190: If the underwriter disclaims any interest in whatever remains of the subject-matter insured, he cannot lay claim as abandonee to the proceeds of sale; see *The WD Fairway (No.3)*[55] at paras 14 et seq. The alternative route of laying claim to the proceeds of sale by way of subrogation is also not available in circumstances where the underwriter (who has paid the assured's claim for a CTL) has renounced any interest in the residual value of the vessel, which is afterwards sold

---

[49] Applying the principles set out at para.30–24, it is submitted that the insurers' payment of the salvage claim could not possibly have amounted to an implied acceptance of abandonment, whether or not the policy contained a waiver clause.

[50] [2004] 2 Lloyd's Rep. 199.

[51] [2009] 2 Lloyd's Rep. 191.

[52] (1835) 1 Y. & C. 500.

[53] [2009] 2 Lloyd's Rep. 191 at para.17. The editors agree with that statement.

[54] *Ibid*, para.45.

[55] [2009] 2 Lloyd's Rep. 420. See also *White Star SS Co v North British & Mercantile Ins Co Ltd* (1943) A.M.C. 399 cited with apparent approval as also representing English law in *The WD Fairway (No.2)* above.

by the assured.[56] Except in the widest sense that at the time of the loss the assured has the right to sell his property, he at that stage has no legal or equitable right to which his insurers could be subrogated[57]; if the consequence is that the assured receives more than an indemnity, that is simply the result of underwriters' express choice.

Note 191: See also *The WD Fairway (No.2)*, above.

Underwriters always entitled to salvage

30–36 *Note 198*: See also *The WD Fairway (No.2)*, above, paras 17, 45; *The WD Fairway (No.3)*, above.

Notes 203, 204: The position as regards insurers being subrogated to proceeds of sale was addressed in *The WD Fairway (No.3)*. See the discussion under para.30–35 above in this Supplement. The question raised in note 204, as to why there was no right of subrogation in *Brooks v MacDonnell*,[58] is answered by Tomlinson J. in *The WD Fairway (No.2)*, at para.17; see note 53 above in this Supplement. The reference to *Brooks v MacDonnell* in footnote 204 should be ignored.

---

[56] *The WD Fairway (No.3)* paras 14–16.

[57] *Ibid*, para.16. *Castellain v Preston* (1883) 11 Q.B.D. 380 was distinguished. In that celebrated case, the fire occurred between contract and conveyance and the right to enforce the sale was a right which subsisted at the date of the fire. *Castellain v Preston* does not decide that if an owner sells his property without any discount, after having been indemnified by his insurers, he must account to them in respect of the proceeds.

[58] (1835) 1 Y. & C. 500

Chapter 31

SUBROGATION

Section 79 of the Marine Insurance Act 1906

The law applicable to a subrogation claim is to be determined in accordance with **31–01** the Rome I[1] and Rome II[2] Regulations. The Rome I Regulation distinguishes between contractual subrogation and legal subrogation in respect of a contract claim, and the Rome II Regulation deals with subrogation to non-contractual claims. In the case of contractual subrogation, in accordance with art.14 of Rome I: (1) the relationship between the assured and the insurers is governed by the law applicable to the agreement to transfer subrogation rights (that of the insurance policy if there is no separate agreement); and (2) the law governing the subrogated claim determines whether the claim can be transferred by way of subrogation, the conditions for subrogation and whether the third party's obligations have been discharged. In the case of subrogation which operates by way of law in respect of a contract claim, in accordance with art.15 of Rome II, if the insurers satisfy the claim, the law governing the policy determines whether and to what extent the insurer is entitled to exercise subrogation rights against the third party. In the case of subrogation which operates by way of law in respect of a tort claim, in accordance with art.19, if the insurers satisfy the claim the law which governs the policy determines whether and to what extent the insurer is entitled to exercise subrogation rights against the third party.

Note 3: The relationship between ss.63 and 79 was explained by Tomlinson J. in *Dornoch Ltd v Westminster International BV (The WD Fairway (No.2)* [2009] 2 Lloyd's Rep. 191. Section 63 is concerned with the rights of the insurers in respect of the abandoned subject matter *before* the insurers have made payment, and s.79 is concerned with the rights of the insurers in respect of both the abandoned subject matter and of the assured's rights of suit *after* the insurers have made payment. As far as rights of suit are concerned, the insurers do not acquire any rights by way of subrogation until they have provided an indemnity but once an indemnity has been provided the insurers automatically obtain subrogation rights (s.79(1)). As far as the subject matter is concerned, the insurers acquire an equitable lien over the subject matter when notice of abandonment has been accepted, securing their position between then and the time of payment. Payment for a total loss does not of itself give rise to any lien or interest in the property. It is only when the insurer has both made payment for a total loss and exercised his election to take over the property under s.63(1) or s.79(1) that title to the insured property will pass to the insurer; depending on the circumstances, the insurer will then acquire legal or at least equitable title to the property with retrospective

---

[1] European Parliament and Council Regulation 593/2008/EC.
[2] European Parliament and Council Regulation 864/2007/EC.

effect from the time of loss. If the insurers do not accept the notice of abandonment, they do not obtain an equitable interest in the subject matter under s.63(1), but if they nevertheless choose to make payment then they have an option to take over the insured subject matter under s.79(1).

(d) Liabilities arising from exercise of rights of subrogation

31–40A The assured's right to damages or an indemnity in circumstances where he is prejudiced by the manner in which the insurer has exercised subrogation rights is discussed at para.31–38 in the main work. In some situations, the conduct of litigation in the assured's name may also result in the insurer's incurring a direct liability towards the party against whom a subrogated claim was asserted in a wrongful manner. This point is illustrated by two related cases in which cargo insurers were held liable to the owners of the carrying vessels for damages for inducement of breach of contract.[3] In each of these cases, the insurers were the driving force behind the arrest of the vessel at the suit of the assured and maintenance of that arrest, aimed at forcing the shipowners to give up their right to arbitration of the claim against them by the insured cargo owners and to accept Senegalese jurisdiction, in breach of the arbitration clause incorporated in the bill of lading. The insurers, who were the same in both cases, were acting under express provisions enabling them to conduct litigation without having settled the claim under the policy, but it is submitted that the exercise of a right of subrogation in the same manner would have had identical consequences.

Distinctions between principles of subrogation and abandonment

31–07 *Note 26*: For the distinction between the statutory provisions relating to abandonment (ss.63 and 79) and subrogation (s.79 alone), see *Dornoch Ltd v Westminster International BV, The MD Fairway (No.2)* [2009] 2 Lloyd's Rep. 191, discussed in para.31–01, note 3 of the supplement.

The nature of the rights to which the insurer may be subrogated

31–15 *Note 61*: Section 651 of the Companies Act 1985 has been replaced by ss.1029–1030 of the Companies Act 2006.

(a) The assured's duty not to prejudice the rights of the insurer

31–34 *Note 135*: In *Horwood v Land of Leather* [2010] Lloyd's Rep. IR 453 the court felt that there was an implied term in a contract of insurance that the assured would not prejudice the rights of the insurers by reaching a settlement with the third party wrongdoer in advance of payment of the loss by the insurers. The case in fact turned on breach of an express term which required co-operation.

31–36 *Note 142*: See also *Horwood v Land of Leather* [2010] Lloyd's Rep. IR 453.

---

[3] *Kallang Shipping SA Panama v Axa Assurances Senegal (The Kallang) (No.2)* [2009] 1 Lloyd's Rep. 124; *Sotrade Denizcilik Sanayi ve Ticaret As v Amadou Lo (The Duden)* [2009] 1 Lloyd's Rep. 145.

(c) The incidence of costs

The suggestion in the last sentence of this paragraph that insurers who conducted **31–39** proceedings in their own interests would be likely to be held liable for the costs of the proceedings, has been borne out by the decision in *The Kamal XXVI, The Kamal XXIV and The Arelia.*[4] Although the assured is the nominal claimant, the court in this case exercised its power under s.51 of the Senior Courts Act 1981 to award costs against the insurers even though they were not parties to the proceedings.

Subrogation to an interest in the proceeds of recoveries made by the assured

The right of the insurer to claim from the assured the proceeds of any recovery **31–41A** made by the assured from the third party is illustrated by *Castellain v Preston.*[5] Here, the assured agreed to sell a house to a third party purchaser but, between exchange and completion, the house was destroyed by fire. The assured recovered the costs of making good the fire damage from his insurers, and subsequently obtained the full purchase price from the purchaser, on the basis that the risk had passed to the purchaser on contract. The insurers were held by the Court of Appeal to be entitled to recover from the assured a sum equivalent to that which they had paid, thereby preventing the assured from obtaining two payments in respect of the same loss. The assured's cause of action remained vested in him as a matter of law but subject to the right of the insurers to exercise it in his name, and that was precisely what occurred. The application of that principle is less straightforward in a case where the insurers wish to assert a proprietary claim to the subject matter insured. Where insurers have, following the loss, exercised their right to take over the subject matter under s.63 of the Marine Insurance Act 1906, payment to the assured of the policy moneys automatically confers ownership of the subject matter upon them by virtue of s.79(1) so that no question of subrogation arises. By contrast, if the insurers have not asserted their right to take over the subject matter under s.63, then by reason of s.79(1) payment of the policy moneys confers upon them the option to take over the insured subject matter. If they assert their right to do so, then they obtain title to the subject matter. However, if they do not assert that right, then ownership remains with the assured: it was held in *Dornoch Ltd v Westminster International BV (The WD Fairway) (No.3)* [2009] 2 Lloyd's Rep. 420 that the insurers do not, on payment, obtain any equitable right in the subject matter so that the assured remains free to deal with it as he wishes. In the *WD Fairway (No.3)* certain of the insurers did not, after payment for the loss of the vessel, assert any proprietary claim to the vessel, and the assured proceeded to sell it to a third party. At that point the insurers claimed the proceeds of the sale. Tomlinson J. held that their claim failed: if title to the subject matter remains vested in the assured, and he chooses to sell it, there is no right to which the insurers can be subrogated: the assured is simply exercising his right of ownership. While it is the case that the assured may have profited from receiving both the insurance moneys and the proceeds of sale, that situation arises because the insurers have chosen not to assert their rights

---

[4] [2010] EWHC 2531 (Comm).
[5] (1880) 11 Q.B.D. 380.

under s.79(1). On Tomlinson J.'s analysis, *Castellain v Preston* is not authority for the proposition that an assured, having suffered an insured loss and received indemnification from the insurers, is required to account to the insurers for the proceeds of any sale of the subject matter if they have failed to assert their right to take over that subject matter.

CHAPTER 32

DOUBLE INSURANCE AND CONTRIBUTION

Express terms precluding or modifying the assured's right of recovery in cases of double insurance

Note 34: See also *SHC Capital Ltd v NTUC Income Insurance Co-operative Ltd* **32–14** [2010] S.G.H.C. 224, in which the Singapore High Court held that an insurer who is not, or is only partially, liable to meet a claim, but who pays the claim under protest and only because the other insurer has wrongfully denied liability, is not to be treated as a volunteer. The test is whether payment was made as a matter of "practical necessity".

The relationship between the various types of contract clauses that may be **32–16A** found in policies, restricting the liability of an insurer in the case of double insurance, is complex. If each policy contains a provision which excludes or postpones liability in the event that some other policy is in force, those provisions are self-cancelling and do not operate to prevent the assured from recovering under either policy.[1] If each policy contains a rateable proportion clause, then the clauses are not self-cancelling and each insurer is liable only for its rateable proportion. The most difficult case is that in which one policy excludes or postpones liability in the event of other insurance, and that other policy contains a rateable proportion clause. It was suggested[2] in *National Farmers Union Mutual Insurance Society Ltd v HSBC Insurance (UK) Ltd*[3] that the former provision takes priority, and that—because there is no other insurance—the latter insurer is required to pay 100 per cent of the claim despite its rateable proportion clause, and there is no possibility of contribution being sought by the paying insurer.

Contribution

It has been held in Australia[4] that if an insurer pays a claim and then settles a subro- **32–19** gation action against the wrongdoer or waives subrogation rights, another insurer called upon to contribute to the payment does not of itself have any subrogation rights.

---

[1] *Gale v Motor Union Insurance Co* [1928] 1 K.B. 359; *Weddell v Road Transport and General Insurance Co Ltd* [1932] 2 K.B. 563; *National Employers Mutual General Insurance Association Ltd v Haydon* [1980] 2 Lloyd's Rep. 149.

[2] The point did not arise on the facts, as the position was regulated by express wording.

[3] [2010] EWHC 773 (Comm), doubting dicta to the contrary in *Austin v Zurich General Accident & Liability Insurance Co Ltd* (1944) 77 Ll. L. Rep. 409 and following the New Zealand decision, *State Fire Insurance v Liverpool & London Globe Insurance* [1952] N.Z.L.R. 5. The same view has been adopted in Hong Kong: *Chui Man Kwan v Bank of China Group Insurance Co Ltd* [2008] H.K.E.C. 1190. It is to be noted, however, that in *National Farmers Union Mutual Insurance v HSBC Insurance* the court did not refer to the judgments of the Court of Appeal in *Austin v Zurich* [1945] 2 K.B. 250, which gave unqualified approval of the reasoning at first instance.

[4] *Speno Rail Maintenance Australia Pty Ltd v Metals & Minerals Insurance Pte Ltd* (2009) 253 A.L.R. 364.

CHAPTER 33

REINSURANCE

Definition and forms of reinsurance

The Reinsurance Directive will be repealed and replaced in 2012 by the Solvency **33–02** II Directive, European Parliament and Council Directive 2009/138/EC.

Note 10: *Wasa v Lexington* was further appealed to the House of Lords, [2009] UKHL 40, without significant reference to this point.

Definition and forms of reinsurance

Note 13: For the meaning of "event", see *IRB Brasil Resseguros SA v CX* **33–03** *Reinsurance Company Ltd* [2010] EWHC 974 (Comm).

Note 19: The decision in *Limit No.2 Ltd v Axa Versicherung AG* was reversed on other grounds, [2009] Lloyd's Rep. IR 396.

Regulation of reinsurers

The Reinsurance Directive will be repealed and replaced in 2012 by the Solvency **33–06** II Directive, European Parliament and Council Directive 2009/138/EC.

Insurable interest

The question of insurable interest was addressed by the House of Lords on appeal **33–07** in *Wasa International Insurance v Lexington Insurance*,[1] although no argument was presented to their Lordships on the point and the parties proceeded on the basis that reinsurance is a form of cover on the original subject matter rather than liability insurance. Their Lordships unanimously ruled that reinsurance is not liability insurance. Lord Mance in particular was against the classification of reinsurance in this way: his Lordship rejected the comments of Sedley L.J. in the Court of Appeal and both Lords Mance and Collins emphasised that reinsurers always have the right to rely upon their own coverage terms irrespective of the coverage provided by the direct policy. However, Lord Collins and Lord Phillips, with the concurrence of Lords Walker and Brown, felt that there was much to be said for the proposition that reinsurance is liability insurance, and this would be the case if appropriate language was used in the reinsurance agreement, but that was not the case on the facts. Lord Collins was also wary of a ruling that reinsurance was liability insurance, given the possible consequences for the regulation of reinsurance business if the nature of the policy was redefined as something

---

[1] [2009] UKHL 40.

other than direct cover for which authorisation was required. It may be thought, therefore, that the debate is not over, and that all will depend upon the wording of the reinsurance.

33–08   It follows from the discussion at para.33–07 above that the view of the editors, expressed in the opening sentence of para.33–07 of the main work, that "Sedley LJ's starting point is plainly the correct one", has to be modified in the light of what was said by their Lordships. However, the editors adhere to the following statement in para.33–08 of the main work, that "the identification of the reinsured's interest, and the nature of such interest, depends upon the form and wording of the relevant policy." That proposition is apparent from the views of all of their Lordships, other than perhaps Lord Mance.

Persons who may sue

33–10   The Third Parties (Rights against Insurers) Act 1930 is to be replaced, from a date to be announced, by the Third Parties (Rights against Insurers) Act 2010.

Material facts and reinsurance contracts

33–11   *Note 49*: The decision in *Limit No 2 Ltd v Axa Versicherung AG* was reversed on other grounds, [2009] Lloyd's Rep. IR 396.

   Note 56: See also *Crane v Hannover Ruckversicherungs-Aktiengesellschaft* [2010] Lloyd's Rep. IR 93.

Material facts relating to the reinsurance

33–13   *Note 68*: The Court of Appeal in *Limit No.2 Ltd v Axa Versicherung AG* [2009] Lloyd's Rep. IR 396 partially reversed the first instance decision, although on the separate ground that no relevant misrepresentation had been made.

   Note 85: Claims handling which conforms to usual standards is not a material fact: *Crane v Hannover Ruckversicherungs-Aktiengesellschaft* [2010] Lloyd's Rep. IR 93.

Incorporation of terms

33–23   In *Wasa International Insurance v Lexington Insurance*[2] it was common ground that the words "as original" operated to incorporate the terms of the direct policy into the reinsurance.

   Note 138: See also *Markel Capital Ltd v Gothaer Allgemeine Versicherung AG* [2009] Lloyd's Rep. IR 433.

   Note 143: In *Wasa International Insurance v Lexington Insurance* [2009] Lloyd's Rep. IR 675 Lord Mance, who alone raised this issue, refused to be drawn upon the meaning of the "warranty".

---

[2] [2009] Lloyd's Rep. IR 675.

Conditions for incorporation

The House of Lords, on appeal in *Wasa International Insurance v Lexington* **33–24**
Insurance,[3] did not consider the question whether a term uncertain in its scope can
be incorporated into a reinsurance agreement. Their Lordships did, however, agree
with the Court of Appeal that a judgment interpreting a term which did not have a
dictionary definition at the time of the contract was not, on that ground alone, to
be disregarded. As was pointed out by Lord Collins, it is elementary that an insurer
takes the risk of changes in the law, and a similar risk is run by reinsurers. It is only
where the direct policy does not have an applicable law, so that it is uncertain what
law will be applied to the term, can reinsurers argue that the English law meaning
of the identical words in the reinsurance contract is to prevail.

Note 146: In *Allianz Insurance Co Egypt v Aigaion Insurance Co SA (No.2)*
[2009] Lloyd's Rep. IR 533 (Comm) the direct policy contained a "Deferred
Premium Clause" providing for payment of premium on a quarterly basis. The
reinsurance agreement similarly stated "Deferred Premium Clause" but did not
specify its terms. H.H. Judge Chambers QC held that the reinsurance had
intended to adopt the wording of the insurance provision so that the equivalent
deferred premium clause took effect in the reinsurance. There were no words of
incorporation, and the decision was based not so much on incorporation as on the
presumed intention of the parties to the reinsurance agreement when they chose
to use the words "Deferred Premium Clause".

Note 148: The proposition in this footnote, that a period clause is not of exceptional significance, cannot survive the appeal to the House of Lords in *Wasa
International Insurance v Lexington Insurance* [2009] Lloyd's Rep. IR 675. Their
Lordships there held that if the direct policy did not contain a clear choice of law
provision, so that it was unclear from the outset which law would be applied to
the construction of that policy, the reinsurers were entitled to rely upon the applicable law of the reinsurance agreement (in that case, English law) to provide the
proper construction of significant terms, including the duration clause.

Variations to the underlying risk

Note 169: The House of Lords on appeal in *Wasa International Insurance v* **33–27**
Lexington Insurance [2009] Lloyd's Rep. IR 675 agreed with the Court of Appeal
that a change in the substance of the law governing the direct policy, which led to
a change in the nature of the underlying risk, did not discharge the reinsurers from
liability, as they—like the reinsured—ran the risk of such changes.

Scope of reinsurance

Limit No.2 Ltd v Axa Versicherung AG was reversed on other grounds.[4]   **33–32**

---

[3] [2009] Lloyd's Rep. IR 675.
[4] [2010] Lloyd's Rep. IR 93.

Back to back cover

33–33 The concluding sentences of this paragraph no longer hold good in the light of in *Wasa International Insurance v Lexington Insurance.*[5] They should be substituted as follows.

Thirdly, particular weight is to be given to express reinsurance wordings dealing with the amount[6] of cover, and the presumption of back to back cover is readily rebutted in this context where the words of the two contracts are not expressed in the same terms. It has also been accepted that a duration clause in a reinsurance agreement has special status,[7] so that if there is no chosen applicable law for the direct policy then the reinsurers are entitled to rely upon the meaning of the duration clause as determined by the law applicable to the reinsurance agreement even though the meaning of more or less identical words in the direct policy is given a different meaning by the law which is ultimately found to be applicable to the direct policy. The true principle is whether the parties by their words intended the durations of the two contracts to be consistent or different,[8] and it is unlikely that reinsurers are to be taken to have accepted the meaning of the duration clause in the direct policy where it is uncertain from the outset which law is to be applied to that clause.

The principle of back to back cover is not ousted simply because the words of the direct policy had no clear dictionary meaning at the date of the contract. Further, if those words are subsequently held by the courts of the relevant jurisdiction to have a meaning which could not have been predicted at the time of the contract, so that the liability of the reinsured is significantly greater than had been anticipated at the time, the reinsurers are not relieved from their obligation to provide an indemnity to the reinsured: if reinsurers have agreed to provide cover on the same basis as that offered by the reinsured, and have taken a proportionate share of the premium reflecting that fact, the risk of an unexpected interpretation is borne as much by them as it is borne by the reinsured.[9]

Establishing and quantifying the reinsured's liability under the direct policy

33–35 The proposition in the second sentence, that a judgment of a court is enough to establish and quantify the liability of the reinsured to the assured, was noted by

---

[5] [2009] Lloyd's Rep. IR 675.
[6] *Baker v Black Sea and Baltic General Insurance Co Ltd* [1998] Lloyd's Rep. IR 327. But contrast: *Phillips v Dorintal Insurance* [1987] 1 Lloyd's Rep. 482; *Insurance Co of Pennsylvania v Grand Union Insurance* [1990] 1 Lloyd's Rep. 208; *Goshawk Syndicate Management Ltd and others v XL Speciality Insurance Co* [2004] Lloyd's Rep. IR 683.
[7] *Wasa International Insurance Co Ltd v Lexington Insurance Co* [2009] Lloyd's Rep. IR 675.
[8] *Youell v Bland Welch & Co (No.1)* [1992] 2 Lloyd's Rep. 127; *Municipal Mutual Insurance Ltd v Sea Insurance Ltd* [1998] 2 Lloyd's Rep. 421. Contrast the result in *Commercial Union Assurance Co Plc v Sun Alliance Insurance Group Plc* [1992] 1 Lloyd's Rep. 475. See also Cf *Stronghold Insurance Co Ltd v Bulstrad Insurance and Reinsurance Plc* Unreported March 1, 2008 (noted in *Insurance Law Monthly*), where the words of the insurance and the reinsurance were identical.
[9] For these propositions, see *Wasa International Insurance Co Ltd and AGF Insurance Co Ltd v Lexington Insurance Co* [2008] Lloyd's Rep. IR 510. The House of Lords [2009] Lloyd's Rep. IR 675, overturned the decision of the Court of Appeal, but on the more limited ground that the law to be applied to the direct policy was uncertain.

Lord Mance in *Wasa International Insurance Co Ltd v Lexington Insurance Co*[10] to be based only on dicta and that the point had not been authoritatively determined. Lord Mance chose to leave the point open. None of the other members of the House of Lords chose to comment on this point, which did not arise on the facts of *Wasa*.

Proof of coverage under the terms of the reinsurance agreement

The second limb of the *Scor* test is that "the claim so recognised by [the reinsured] **33–40** falls within the risks covered by the policy of reinsurance as a matter of law." If the reinsurance agreement contains additional terms which limit the reinsurers' liability, e.g., in terms of time, amount or by reference to geographical location, then those terms will take priority over the obligation to follow settlements and the reinsurers will not be liable if any of them are applicable at least insofar as the words make it clear that the liability of the reinsures was not intended to match that of the reinsured.[11]

Where, by contrast, the two contracts are back to back and the reinsurance agreement contains the "full reinsurance" clause which operates to incorporate the terms of the direct policy into the reinsurance, then there is a limited role for the second limb in *Scor*. In most cases it would seem futile for the reinsurers to waive strict proof of liability under the first limb in *Scor*, by recognising a bona fide and businesslike test with respect to the underlying facts and policy terms, and then reserving the right to raise the scope of the policy and its applicability to the loss at the second limb, reinsurance stage. The position established by the authorities is that if the two policies are back to back then the second limb of the *Scor* test is "almost invariably"[12] satisfied if the basis of the assured's claim as recognised by the reinsured arguably falls within the terms of the reinsurance as a matter of law.[13] Accordingly, the reinsured will be entitled to recover under the reinsurance unless the claim as recognised is clearly outside the scope of the reinsurance, or the basis on which the claim is recognised is the subject of an express exclusion, or the reinsured does not put forward any basis for the recognition of the claim but simply pays it.[14] However, there is an important exception where there is no fixed applicable law for the direct policy, as in that situation the

---

[10] [2009] UKHL 40.

[11] *Municipal Mutual Insurance Ltd v Sea Insurance Co Ltd* [1998] Lloyd's Rep. IR 421; *Wasa International Insurance Co v Lexington Insurance Co* [2009] Lloyd's Rep. IR 675. In *Aegis Electrical and Gas International Services Co Ltd v Continental Casualty Co* [2008] Lloyd's Rep. IR 17 it was pointed out that if the insurance and reinsurance are not back to back, the fact that the claim as recognised falls within the terms of the direct policy is not enough to entitle the reinsured to treat that claim as falling within the terms of the reinsurance, because the reinsurers always have the right to rely upon their own wording. See the discussion of back to back cover in para.33–33, above.

[12] The phrase of Lord Collins in *Wasa International Insurance Co v Lexington Insurance Co* [2009] Lloyd's Rep. IR 675.

[13] *Hiscox v Outhwaite (No.3)* [1991] 2 Lloyd's Rep. 524; *Hill v Mercantile and General Reinsurance Co Plc* [1996] 3 All E.R. 865; *Assicuraizioni Generali SpA v CGU General Insurance Plc* [2004] Lloyd's Rep. IR 457; *Aegis Electrical and Gas International Services Co Ltd v Continental Casualty Co* [2008] Lloyd's Rep. IR 17.

[14] *Aegis Electrical and Gas International Services Co Ltd v Continental Casualty Co* [2008] Lloyd's Rep. IR 17.

incorporation of the terms of the direct policy does not prevent the reinsurers from relying upon the meaning of those words in accordance with the law applicable to the reinsurance, at least where the clause in question is a fundamental one. In *Wasa International Insurance Co v Lexington Insurance Co*[15] the direct policy was written against various risks including property damage, for a three year period. The only clause relevant to the governing law was a service of suit clause under which the reinsurers agreed to submit to the jurisdiction of any court of competent jurisdiction in the US. The reinsurance was expressed to be for 36 months and was written "as original", and it was common ground that the terms of the direct policy were incorporated into the reinsurance, A claim was brought against the reinsured in the courts of Washington, and those courts— applying the law of Pennsylvania as dictated by Washington's conflict of laws rules—held that the direct policy provided cover for all property damage whenever occurring, as long as any part of that damage took place in the insured three year period. The outcome was that the reinsured faced liability for about a 50 year period running before, during and after the currency of the policy. The House of Lords ruled that the absence of any choice of law clause in the direct policy meant that the reinsurers were, to avoid uncertainty, entitled to rely upon the English law interpretation of the reinsurance agreement, and under English law there could only be liability for property damage suffered during the period of coverage. It is unclear whether this principle extends to all coverage provisions (the view of Lord Mance) or only to the most significant of the (the view of Lord Collins). Lord Mance was alone in raising the possibility that the same result might have followed even if there had been an express choice of law clause in the direct policy, although the majority view appears to have been that it was the absence of such a choice which gave rise to the right of the reinsurers to rely upon the English law construction of the reinsurance.

Qualified follow the settlements clauses: loss settlements clauses

33–40A The usual form of follow the settlements clause in facultative agreements is unqualified. However, excess of loss treaties written in the London market frequently contain a more limited version, referred to not as "follow the settlements" but as "loss settlements". The clause reads:

> "All loss settlements by the Reassured including compromise settlements . . . shall be binding upon the Reinsurers, providing such settlements are within the terms and conditions of the original policies . . . and within the terms and conditions of this Reinsurance."

In *Hill v Mercantile & General Reinsurance Co Plc*[16] the House of Lords noted that the wording required the reinsured to prove as a matter of law that the loss settlement fell within the terms of the direct policy, so that it was not enough for the reinsured to show that it had acted in a bona fide and businesslike fashion in settling the underlying claims. However, it was subsequently held in *Equitas Ltd v*

---

[15] [2009] Lloyd's Rep. IR 675.
[16] [1996] 3 All E.R. 865.

R&Q Reinsurance Co[17] and *IRB Brasil Resseguros SA v CX Reinsurance Company Ltd*[18] that *Hill* said nothing about how the reinsured could satisfy the burden of proof, and that the burden could be satisfied without proof of actual legal liability. In *Equitas* the reinsured paid claims based on two major losses, the Exxon Valdex grounding and the seizure of aircraft on the invasion of Kuwait. The claims were paid through the LMX Spiral, a complex network of excess of loss reinsurances. It subsequently became clear that a part of each of these losses did not fall within the terms of the underlying cover,[19] and the reinsurers refused to make any payment at all. Gross J. held that the reinsured had, by developing an actuarial model which approximated to (but was unable to recreate precisely) the LMX Spiral, proved its loss. In *IRB Brasil* class actions had been brought against policyholder, and these had been settled by the reinsured. Burton J. upheld the ruling of the arbitrators that the reinsured had satisfied the burden of proof laid down by the loss settlements clause even though it was certain that not all of the claims contained in the class action settlements were valid or properly valued: on the balance of probabilities, the total sum for which the claims had been settled represented the reinsured's actual liability. It will be seen, therefore, that even under a restricted follow the settlements clause of this type, although the reinsured is required to prove its loss as a matter of law, it can do so in the case of a treaty where there are multiple underlying claims on a "swings and roundabouts" basis.

Allocation of losses

An important aspect of determining the coverage of an insurance and reinsurance **33–40B** contract is allocation of losses occurring over a lengthy period to the appropriate year of coverage. Although there is no presumption that losses have occurred in regular and consistent fashion, in practice, where this can legitimately be inferred, that approach is sometimes adopted so that in effect losses are allocated on a time on risk basis. Thus in *Municipal Mutual Insurance Ltd v Sea Insurance Co Ltd*[20] the assured faced pilferage claims over a three year period, and these were allocated by the reinsured on the assumption that the losses had occurred equally across the period of coverage, so that they could be allocated on that basis to insurance and reinsurance years of cover. That approach was upheld by the Court of Appeal. Similarly in *IRB Brasil Resseguros SA v CX Reinsurance Company Ltd*[21] the court upheld the view of the arbitrators that losses which arose from product liability claims were to be allocated to insurance and reinsurance policy years on the basis that the losses followed a regular pattern.

Defence costs

Note 260: The English and Scottish Law Commissions have proposed the reversal **33–42** of the *Sprung* rule: see Issues Paper 6, March 2010.

---

[17] [2009] EWHC 2787 (Comm).
[18] [2010] EWHC 974 (Comm).
[19] *King v Brandywine Reinsurance Co* [2005] 1 Lloyd's Rep. 655; *Scott v Copenhagen Re Co* [2003] Lloyd's Rep. IR 696.
[20] [1998] Lloyd's Rep. IR 421.
[21] [2010] EWHC 974 (Comm).

THE INSTITUTE CARGO CLAUSES 1/1/09

These clauses are purely illustrative. Different policy conditions may be agreed. The specimen clauses are available to any interested person upon request. In particular:

(a)   in relation to any clause which excludes losses from the cover, insurers may agree a separate insurance policy covering such losses or may extend the clause to cover such events;
(b)   in relation to clauses making cover of certain risks subject to specific conditions each insurer may alter the said conditions.

1/1/09

INSTITUTE CARGO CLAUSES (A)

RISKS COVERED

Risks

1.   This insurance covers all risks of loss of or damage to the subject-matter insured except as excluded by the provisions of Clauses 4, 5, 6 and 7 below.

General Average

2.   This insurance covers general average and salvage charges, adjusted or determined according to the contract of carriage and/or the governing law and practice, incurred to avoid or in connection with the avoidance of loss from any cause except those excluded in Clauses 4, 5, 6 and 7 below.

"Both to Blame Collision Clause"

3.   This insurance indemnifies the Assured, in respect of any risk insured herein, against liability incurred under any Both to Blame Collision Clause in the contract of carriage. In the event of any claim by carriers under the said Clause, the Assured agree to notify the Insurers who shall have the right, at their own cost and expense, to defend the Assured against such claim.

EXCLUSIONS

4.   In no case shall this insurance cover
   4.1   loss damage or expense attributable to wilful misconduct of the Assured
   4.2   ordinary leakage, ordinary loss in weight or volume, or ordinary wear and tear of the subject-matter insured
   4.3   loss damage or expense caused by insufficiency or unsuitability of packing or preparation of the subject-matter insured to withstand the ordinary incidents of the insured transit where such packing or preparation is carried out by the Assured or their employees or prior to the attachment of this insurance (for the

purpose of these Clauses "packing" shall be deemed to include stowage in a container and "employees" shall not include independent contractors)

4.4 loss damage or expense caused by inherent vice or nature of the subject-matter insured

4.5 loss damage or expense caused by delay, even though the delay be caused by a risk insured against (except expenses payable under Clause 2 above)

4.6 loss damage or expense caused by insolvency or financial default of the owners managers charterers or operators of the vessel where, at the time of loading of the subject-matter insured on board the vessel, the Assured are aware, or in the ordinary course of business should be aware, that such insolvency or financial default could prevent the normal prosecution of the voyage This exclusion shall not apply where the contract of insurance has been assigned to the party claiming hereunder who has bought or agreed to buy the subject-matter insured in good faith under a binding contract

4.7 loss damage or expense directly or indirectly caused by or arising from the use of any weapon or device employing atomic or nuclear fission and/or fusion or other like reaction or radioactive force or matter.

5. 5.1 In no case shall this insurance cover loss damage or expense arising from

    5.1.1 unseaworthiness of vessel or craft or unfitness of vessel or craft for the safe carriage of the subject-matter insured, where the Assured are privy to such unseaworthiness or unfitness, at the time the subject-matter insured is loaded therein

    5.1.2 unfitness of container or conveyance for the safe carriage of the subject-matter insured, where loading therein or thereon is carried out

        prior to attachment of this insurance or

        by the Assured or their employees and they are privy to such unfitness at the time of loading.

  5.2 Exclusion 5.1.1 above shall not apply where the contract of insurance has been assigned to the party claiming hereunder who has bought or agreed to buy the subject-matter insured in good faith under a binding contract.

  5.3 The Insurers waive any breach of the implied warranties of seaworthiness of the ship and fitness of the ship to carry the subject-matter insured to destination.

6. In no case shall this insurance cover loss damage or expense caused by

  6.1 war civil war revolution rebellion insurrection, or civil strife arising therefrom, or any hostile act by or against a belligerent power

  6.2 capture seizure arrest restraint or detainment (piracy excepted), and the consequences thereof or any attempt thereat

  6.3 derelict mines torpedoes bombs or other derelict weapons of war.

7. In no case shall this insurance cover loss damage or expense

  7.1 caused by strikers, locked-out workmen, or persons taking part in labour disturbances, riots or civil commotions

  7.2 resulting from strikes, lock-outs, labour disturbances, riots or civil commotions

  7.3 caused by any act of terrorism being an act of any person acting on behalf of, or in connection with, any organisation which carries out activities directed towards the overthrowing or influencing, by force or violence, of any government whether or not legally constituted

  7.4 caused by any person acting from a political, ideological or religious motive.

DURATION

Transit Clause
8. 8.1 Subject to Clause 11 below, this insurance attaches from the time the subject-matter insured is first moved_in the warehouse or at the place of storage (at the place named in the contract of insurance) for the purpose of the_immediate loading into or onto the carrying vehicle or other conveyance for the commencement of transit,

continues during the ordinary course of transit

and terminates either

  8.1.1 on completion of unloading from the carrying vehicle or other conveyance in or at the final warehouse or place of storage at the destination named in the contract of insurance,

  8.1.2 on completion of unloading from the carrying vehicle or other conveyance in or at any other warehouse or place of storage, whether prior to or at the destination named in the contract of insurance, which the Assured or their employees elect to use either for storage other than in the ordinary course of transit or for allocation or distribution, or

  8.1.3 when the Assured or their employees elect to use any carrying vehicle or other conveyance or any container for storage other than in the ordinary course of transit or

  8.1.4 on the expiry of 60 days after completion of discharge overside of the subject-matter insured from the oversea vessel at the final port of discharge, whichever shall first occur.

  8.2 If, after discharge overside from the oversea vessel at the final port of discharge, but prior to termination of this insurance, the subject-matter insured is to be forwarded to a destination other than that to which it is insured, this insurance, whilst remaining subject to termination as provided in Clauses 8.1.1 to 8.1.4, shall not extend beyond the time the subject-matter insured is first moved for the purpose of the commencement of transit to such other destination.

  8.3 This insurance shall remain in force (subject to termination as provided for in Clauses 8.1.1 to 8.1.4 above and to the provisions of Clause 9 below) during delay beyond the control of the Assured, any deviation, forced discharge, reshipment or transhipment and during any variation of the adventure arising from the exercise of a liberty granted to carriers under the contract of carriage.

Termination of Contract of Carriage
9. If owing to circumstances beyond the control of the Assured either the contract of carriage is terminated at a port or place other than the destination named therein or the transit is otherwise terminated before unloading of the subject-matter insured as provided for in Clause 8 above, then this insurance shall also terminate *unless prompt notice is given to the Insurers and continuation of cover is requested when this insurance shall remain in force, subject to an additional premium if required by the Insurers,* either

  9.1 until the subject-matter insured is sold and delivered at such port or place, or, unless otherwise specially agreed, until the expiry of 60 days after arrival of the subject-matter insured at such port or place, whichever shall first occur, or

  9.2 if the subject-matter insured is forwarded within the said period of 60 days (or any agreed extension thereof) to the destination named in the contract of insurance or to any other destination, until terminated in accordance with the provisions of Clause 8 above.

Change of Voyage
10. 10.1 Where, after attachment of this insurance, the destination is changed by the Assured, *this must be notified promptly to Insurers for rates and terms to be agreed. Should a loss occur prior to such agreement being obtained cover may be provided but only if cover would have been available at a reasonable commercial market rate on reasonable market terms.*

10.2 Where the subject-matter insured commences the transit contemplated by this insurance (in accordance with Clause 8.1), but, without the knowledge of the Assured or their employees the ship sails for another destination, this insurance will nevertheless be deemed to have attached at commencement of such transit.

CLAIMS

Insurable Interest
11. 11.1 In order to recover under this insurance the Assured must have an insurable interest in the subject-matter insured at the time of the loss.

11.2 Subject to Clause 11.1 above, the Assured shall be entitled to recover for insured loss occurring during the period covered by this insurance, notwithstanding that the loss occurred before the contract of insurance was concluded, unless the Assured were aware of the loss and the Insurers were not.

Forwarding Charges
12. Where, as a result of the operation of a risk covered by this insurance, the insured transit is terminated at a port or place other than that to which the subject-matter insured is covered under this insurance, the Insurers will reimburse the Assured for any extra charges properly and reasonably incurred in unloading storing and forwarding the subject-matter insured to the destination to which it is insured.

This Clause 12, which does not apply to general average or salvage charges, shall be subject to the exclusions contained in Clauses 4, 5 6 and 7 above, and shall not include charges arising from the fault negligence insolvency or financial default of the Assured or their employees.

Constructive Total Loss
13. No claim for Constructive Total Loss shall be recoverable hereunder unless the subject-matter insured is reasonably abandoned either on account of its actual total loss appearing to be unavoidable or because the cost of recovering, reconditioning and forwarding the subject-matter insured to the destination to which it is insured would exceed its value on arrival.

Increased Value
14. 14.1 If any Increased Value insurance is effected by the Assured on the subject-matter insured under this insurance the agreed value of the subject-matter insured shall be deemed to be increased to the total amount insured under this insurance and all Increased Value insurances covering the loss, and liability under this insurance shall be in such proportion as the sum insured under this insurance bears to such total amount insured.

In the event of claim the Assured shall provide the Insurers with evidence of the amounts insured under all other insurances.

14.2 **Where this insurance is on Increased Value the following clause shall apply:**
The agreed value of the subject-matter insured shall be deemed to be equal to the total amount insured under the primary insurance and all Increased Value

insurances covering the loss and effected on the subject-matter insured by the Assured, and liability under this insurance shall be in such proportion as the sum insured under this insurance bears to such total amount insured.

In the event of claim the Assured shall provide the Insurers with evidence of the amounts insured under all other insurances.

BENEFIT OF INSURANCE

15. This insurance

    15.1 covers the Assured which includes the person claiming indemnity either as the person by or on whose behalf the contract of insurance was effected or as an assignee,

    15.2 shall not extend to or otherwise benefit the carrier or other bailee.

MINIMISING LOSSES

<u>Duty of Assured</u>

16. It is the duty of the Assured and their employees and agents in respect of loss recoverable hereunder

    16.1 to take such measures as may be reasonable for the purpose of averting or minimising such loss, and

    16.2 to ensure that all rights against carriers, bailees or other third parties are properly preserved and exercised

and the Insurers will, in addition to any loss recoverable hereunder, reimburse the Assured for any charges properly and reasonably incurred in pursuance of these duties.

<u>Waiver</u>

17. Measures taken by the Assured or the Insurers with the object of saving, protecting or recovering the subject-matter insured shall not be considered as a waiver or acceptance of abandonment or otherwise prejudice the rights of either party.

AVOIDANCE OF DELAY

18. It is a condition of this insurance that the Assured shall act with reasonable despatch in all circumstances within their control.

LAW AND PRACTICE

19. This insurance is subject to English law and practice.

NOTE:- Where a continuation of cover is requested under Clause 9, or a change of destination is notified under Clause 10, there is an obligation to give prompt notice to the Insurers and the right to such cover is dependent upon compliance with this obligation.

© Copyright: 11/08 – Lloyd's Market Association (LMA) and International Underwriting Association of London (IUA).

CL382
01/01/2009

These clauses are purely illstrative. Different policy conditions may be agreed. The specimen clauses are available to any interested person upon request. In particular:

(a)   in relation to any clause which excludes losses from the cover, insurers may agree a separate insurance policy covering such losses or may extend the clause to cover such events;

(b)   in relation to clauses making cover of certain risks subject to specific conditions each insurer may alter the said conditions.

1/1/09

INSTITUTE CARGO CLAUSES (B)

RISKS COVERED

Risks

1.   This insurance covers, except as excluded by the provisions of Clauses 4, 5, 6 and 7 below,

   1.1   loss of or damage to the subject-matter insured reasonably attributable to

      1.1.1   fire or explosion

      1.1.2   vessel or craft being stranded grounded sunk or capsized

      1.1.3   overturning or derailment of land conveyance

      1.1.4   collision or contact of vessel craft or conveyance with any external object other than water

      1.1.5   discharge of cargo at a port of distress

      1.1.6   earthquake volcanic eruption or lightning,

   1.2   loss of or damage to the subject-matter insured caused by

      1.2.1   general average sacrifice

      1.2.2   jettison or washing overboard

      1.2.3   entry of sea lake or river water into vessel craft hold conveyance container or place of storage,

   1.3   total loss of any package lost overboard or dropped whilst loading on to, or unloading from, vessel or craft.

General Average

2.   This insurance covers general average and salvage charges, adjusted or determined according to the contract of carriage and/or the governing law and practice, incurred to avoid or in connection with the avoidance of loss from any cause except those excluded in Clauses 4, 5, 6 and 7 below.

"Both to Blame Collision Clause"

3.   This insurance indemnifies the Assured, in respect of any risk insured herein, against liability incurred under any Both to Blame Collision Clause in the contract of carriage. In the event of any claim by carriers under the said Clause, the Assured agree to notify the Insurers who shall have the right, at their own cost and expense, to defend the Assured against such claim.

EXCLUSIONS

4.   In no case shall this insurance cover

   4.1   loss damage or expense attributable to wilful misconduct of the Assured

   4.2   ordinary leakage, ordinary loss in weight or volume, or ordinary wear and tear of the subject-matter insured

   4.3   loss damage or expense caused by insufficiency or unsuitability of packing or preparation of the subject-matter insured to withstand the ordinary incidents of the insured transit where such packing or preparation is carried out by the Assured or their employees or prior to the attachment of this insurance (for the purpose of these Clauses "packing" shall be deemed to include stowage in a container and "employees" shall not include independent contractors)

4.4 loss damage or expense caused by inherent vice or nature of the subject-matter insured

4.5 loss damage or expense caused by delay, even though the delay be caused by a risk insured against (except expenses payable under Clause 2 above)

4.6 loss damage or expense caused by insolvency or financial default of the owners managers charterers or operators of the vessel where, at the time of loading of the subject-matter insured on board the vessel, the Assured are aware, or in the ordinary course of business should be aware, that such insolvency or financial default could prevent the normal prosecution of the voyage

This exclusion shall not apply where the contract of insurance has been assigned to the party claiming hereunder who has bought or agreed to buy the subject-matter insured in good faith under a binding contract

4.7 deliberate damage to or deliberate destruction of the subject-matter insured or any part thereof by the wrongful act of any person or persons

4.8 loss damage or expense directly or indirectly caused by or arising from the use of any weapon or device employing atomic or nuclear fission and/or fusion or other like reaction or radioactive force or matter.

5. 5.1 In no case shall this insurance cover loss damage or expense arising from

  5.1.1 unseaworthiness of vessel or craft or unfitness of vessel or craft for the safe carriage of the subject-matter insured, where the Assured are privy to such unseaworthiness or unfitness, at the time the subject-matter insured is loaded therein

  5.1.2 unfitness of container or conveyance for the safe carriage of the subject-matter insured, where loading therein or thereon is carried out

    prior to attachment of this insurance or

    by the Assured or their employees and they are privy to such unfitness at the time of loading.

  5.2 Exclusion 5.1.1 above shall not apply where the contract of insurance has been assigned to the party claiming hereunder who has bought or agreed to buy the subject-matter insured in good faith under a binding contract.

  5.3 The Insurers waive any breach of the implied warranties of seaworthiness of the ship and fitness of the ship to carry the subject-matter insured to destination.

6. In no case shall this insurance cover loss damage or expense caused by

  6.1 war civil war revolution rebellion insurrection, or civil strife arising therefrom, or any hostile act by or against a belligerent power

  6.2 capture seizure arrest restraint or detainment, and the consequences thereof or any attempt thereat

  6.3 derelict mines torpedoes bombs or other derelict weapons of war.

7. In no case shall this insurance cover loss damage or expense

  7.1 caused by strikers, locked-out workmen, or persons taking part in labour disturbances, riots or civil commotions

  7.2 resulting from strikes, lock-outs, labour disturbances, riots or civil commotions

  7.3 caused by any act of terrorism being an act of any person acting on behalf of, or in connection with, any organisation which carries out activities directed towards the overthrowing or influencing, by force or violence, of any government whether or not legally constituted

  7.4 caused by any person acting from a political, ideological or religious motive.

DURATION

Transit Clause

8.   8.1   Subject to Clause 11 below, this insurance attaches from the time the subject-matter insured is first moved_in the warehouse or at the place of storage (at the place named in the contract of insurance) for the purpose of the_immediate loading into or onto the carrying vehicle or other conveyance for the commencement of transit,

continues during the ordinary course of transit

and terminates either

8.1.1   on completion of unloading from the carrying vehicle or other conveyance in or at the final warehouse or place of storage at the destination named in the contract of insurance,

8.1.2   on completion of unloading from the carrying vehicle or other conveyance in or at any other warehouse or place of storage, whether prior to or at the destination named in the contract of insurance, which the Assured or their employees elect to use either for storage other than in the ordinary course of transit or for allocation or distribution, or

8.1.3   when the Assured or their employees elect to use any carrying vehicle or other conveyance or any_container for storage other than in the ordinary course of transit or

8.1.4   on the expiry of 60 days after completion of discharge overside of the subject-matter insured from the oversea vessel at the final port of discharge,

whichever shall first occur.

8.2   If, after discharge overside from the oversea vessel at the final port of discharge, but prior to termination of this insurance, the subject-matter insured is to be forwarded to a destination other than that to which it is insured, this insurance, whilst remaining subject to termination as provided in Clauses 8.1.1 to 8.1.4, shall not extend beyond the time the subject-matter insured is first moved for the purpose of the_commencement of transit to such other destination.

8.3   This insurance shall remain in force (subject to termination as provided for in Clauses 8.1.1 to 8.1.4 above and to the provisions of Clause 9 below) during delay beyond the control of the Assured, any deviation, forced discharge, reshipment or transhipment and during any variation of the adventure arising from the exercise of a liberty granted to carriers under the contract of carriage.

Termination of Contract of Carriage

9.   If owing to circumstances beyond the control of the Assured either the contract of carriage is terminated at a port or place other than the destination named therein or the transit is otherwise terminated before unloading of_the subject-matter insured as provided for in Clause 8 above, then this insurance shall also terminate *unless prompt notice is given to the Insurers and continuation of cover is requested when this insurance shall remain in force, subject to an additional premium if required by the Insurers*, either

9.1   until the subject-matter insured is sold and delivered at such port or place, or, unless otherwise specially agreed, until the expiry of 60 days after arrival of the subject-matter insured at such port or place, whichever shall first occur,

or

9.2   if the subject-matter insured is forwarded within the said period of 60 days (or any agreed extension thereof) to the destination named in the contract of insurance or to any other destination, until terminated in accordance with the provisions of Clause 8 above.

208

Change of Voyage
10. 10.1 Where, after attachment of this insurance, the destination is changed by the Assured, *this must be notified_promptly to Insurers for rates and terms to be agreed. Should a loss occur prior to such agreement being obtained cover may be provided but only if cover would have been available at a reasonable commercial market rate on reasonable market terms.*

10.2 Where the subject-matter insured commences the transit contemplated by this insurance (in accordance with Clause 8.1), but, without the knowledge of the Assured or their employees the ship sails for another destination, this insurance will nevertheless be deemed to have attached at commencement of such transit.

CLAIMS

Insurable Interest
11. 11.1 In order to recover under this insurance the Assured must have an insurable interest in the subject-matter insured at the time of the loss.

11.2 Subject to Clause 11.1 above, the Assured shall be entitled to recover for insured loss occurring during the period covered by this insurance, notwithstanding that the loss occurred before the contract of insurance was concluded, unless the Assured were aware of the loss and the Insurers were not.

Forwarding Charges
12. Where, as a result of the operation of a risk covered by this insurance, the insured transit is terminated at a port or place other than that to which the subject-matter insured is covered under this insurance, the Insurers will reimburse the Assured for any extra charges properly and reasonably incurred in unloading storing and forwarding the subject-matter insured to the destination to which it is insured.

This Clause 12, which does not apply to general average or salvage charges, shall be subject to the exclusions contained in Clauses 4, 5, 6 and 7 above, and shall not include charges arising from the fault negligence insolvency or financial default of the Assured or their employees.

Constructive Total Loss
13. No claim for Constructive Total Loss shall be recoverable hereunder unless the subject-matter insured is reasonably abandoned either on account of its actual total loss appearing to be unavoidable or because the cost of recovering, reconditioning and forwarding the subject-matter insured to the destination to which it is insured would exceed its value on arrival.

Increased Value
14. 14.1 If any Increased Value insurance is effected by the Assured on the subject-matter insured under this insurance the agreed value of the subject-matter insured shall be deemed to be increased to the total amount insured under this insurance and all Increased Value insurances covering the loss, and liability under this insurance shall be in such proportion as the sum insured under this insurance bears to such total amount insured.

In the event of claim the Assured shall provide the Insurers with evidence of the amounts insured under all other insurances.

14.2 **Where this insurnace is on Increased Value the following clause shall apply:**
The agreed value of the subject-matter insured shall be deemed to be equal to the total amount insured under the primary insurance and all Increased

Value insurances covering the loss and effected on the subject-matter insured by the Assured, and liability under this insurance shall be in such proportion as the sum insured under this insurance bears to such total amount insured.

In the event of claim the Assured shall provide the Insurers with evidence of the amounts insured under all other insurances.

BENEFIT OF INSURANCE
15. This insurance
    15.1 covers the Assured which includes the person claiming indemnity either as the person by or on whose behalf the contract of insurance was effected or as an assignee,
    15.2 shall not extend to or otherwise benefit the carrier or other bailee.

MINIMISING LOSSES

Duty of Assured
16. It is the duty of the Assured and their employees and agents in respect of loss recoverable hereunder
    16.1 to take such measures as may be reasonable for the purpose of averting or minimising such loss, and
    16.2 to ensure that all rights against carriers, bailees or other third parties are properly preserved and exercised

and the Insurers will, in addition to any loss recoverable hereunder, reimburse the Assured for any charges properly and reasonably incurred in pursuance of these duties.

Waiver
17. Measures taken by the Assured or the Insurers with the object of saving, protecting or recovering the subject-matter insured shall not be considered as a waiver or acceptance of abandonment or otherwise prejudice the rights of either party.

AVOIDANCE OF DELAY
18. It is a condition of this insurance that the Assured shall act with reasonable despatch in all circumstances within their control.

LAW AND PRACTICE
19. This insurance is subject to English law and practice.

NOTE:- Where a continuation of cover is requested under Clause 9, or a change of destination is notified under Clause 10, there is an obligation to give prompt notice to the Insurers and the right to such cover is dependent upon compliance with this obligation.
© Copyright: 11/08 – Lloyd's Market Association (LMA) and International Underwriting Association of London (IUA).

CL383
01/01/2009

These clauses are purely illustrative. Different policy conditions may be agreed. The specimen clauses are available to any interested person upon request. In particular:

(a) in relation to any clause which excludes losses from the cover, insurers may agree a separate insurance policy covering such losses or may extend the clause to cover such events;

(b) in relation to clauses making cover of certain risks subject to specific conditions each insurer may alter the said conditions.

1/1/09

INSTITUTE CARGO CLAUSES (C)

RISKS COVERED

Risks
1. This insurance covers, except as excluded by the provisions of Clauses 4, 5, 6 and 7 below,
    1.1 loss of or damage to the subject-matter insured reasonably attributable to
        1.1.1 fire or explosion
        1.1.2 vessel or craft being stranded grounded sunk or capsized
        1.1.3 overturning or derailment of land conveyance
        1.1.4 collision or contact of vessel craft or conveyance with any external object other than water
        1.1.5 discharge of cargo at a port of distress,
    1.2 loss of or damage to the subject-matter insured caused by
        1.2.1 general average sacrifice
        1.2.2 jettison.

General Average
2. This insurance covers general average and salvage charges, adjusted or determined according to the contract of carriage and/or the governing law and practice, incurred to avoid or in connection with the avoidance of loss from any cause except those excluded in Clauses 4, 5, 6 and 7 below.

"Both to Blame Collision Clause"
3. This insurance indemnifies the Assured, in respect of any risk insured herein, against liability incurred under any Both to Blame Collision Clause in the contract of carriage. In the event of any claim by carriers under the said Clause, the Assured agree to notify the Insurers who shall have the right, at their own cost and expense, to defend the Assured against such claim.

EXCLUSIONS
4. In no case shall this insurance cover
    4.1 loss damage or expense attributable to wilful misconduct of the Assured
    4.2 ordinary leakage, ordinary loss in weight or volume, or ordinary wear and tear of the subject-matter insured
    4.3 loss damage or expense caused by insufficiency or unsuitability of packing or preparation of the subject-matter insured to withstand the ordinary incidents of the insured transit where such packing or preparation is carried out by the Assured or their employees or prior to the attachment of this insurance (for the purpose of these Clauses "packing" shall be deemed to include stowage in a container and "employees" shall not include independent contractors)
    4.4 loss damage or expense caused by inherent vice or nature of the subject-matter insured

4.5 loss damage or expense caused by delay, even though the delay be caused by a risk insured against (except expenses payable under Clause 2 above)

4.6 loss damage or expense caused by insolvency or financial default of the owners managers charterers or operators of the vessel where, at the time of loading of the subject-matter insured on board the vessel, the Assured are aware, or in the ordinary course of business should be aware, that such insolvency or financial default could prevent the normal prosecution of the voyage This exclusion shall not apply where the contract of insurance has been assigned to the party claiming hereunder who has bought or agreed to buy the subject-matter insured in good faith under a binding contract

4.7 deliberate damage to or deliberate destruction of the subject-matter insured or any part thereof by the wrongful act of any person or persons

4.8 loss damage or expense directly or indirectly caused by or arising from the use of any weapon or device employing atomic or nuclear fission and/or fusion or other like reaction or radioactive force or matter.

5. 5.1 In no case shall this insurance cover loss damage or expense arising from

    5.1.1 unseaworthiness of vessel or craft or unfitness of vessel or craft for the safe carriage of the subject-matter insured, where the Assured are privy to such unseaworthiness or unfitness, at the time the subject-matter insured is loaded therein

    5.1.2 unfitness of container or conveyance for the safe carriage of the subject-matter insured, where loading therein or thereon is carried out
       prior to attachment of this insurance or
       by the Assured or their employees and they are privy to such unfitness at the time of loading.

5.2 Exclusion 5.1.1 above shall not apply where the contract of insurance has been assigned to the party claiming hereunder who has bought or agreed to buy the subject-matter insured in good faith under a binding contract.

5.3 The Insurers waive any breach of the implied warranties of seaworthiness of the ship and fitness of the ship to carry the subject-matter insured to destination.

6. In no case shall this insurance cover loss damage or expense caused by

6.1 war civil war revolution rebellion insurrection, or civil strife arising therefrom, or any hostile act by or against a belligerent power

6.2 capture seizure arrest restraint or detainment, and the consequences thereof or any attempt thereat

6.3 derelict mines torpedoes bombs or other derelict weapons of war.

7. In no case shall this insurance cover loss damage or expense

7.1 caused by strikers, locked-out workmen, or persons taking part in labour disturbances, riots or civil commotions

7.2 resulting from strikes, lock-outs, labour disturbances, riots or civil commotions

7.3 caused by any act of terrorism being an act of any person acting on behalf of, or in connection with, any organisation which carries out activities directed towards the overthrowing or influencing, by force or violence, of any government whether or not legally constituted

7.4 caused by any person acting from a political, ideological or religious motive.

DURATION

Transit Clause

8. 8.1 Subject to Clause 11 below, this insurance attaches from the time the subject-matter insured is first moved_in the warehouse or at the place of storage (at the place named in the contract of insurance) for the purpose of the_immediate

loading into or onto the carrying vehicle or other conveyance for the commencement of transit,

continues during the ordinary course of transit

and terminates either

8.1.1 on completion of unloading from the carrying vehicle or other conveyance in or at the final warehouse or place of storage at the destination named in the contract of insurance,

8.1.2 on completion of unloading from the carrying vehicle or other conveyance in or at any other warehouse or place of storage, whether prior to or at the destination named in the contract of insurance, which the Assured or their employees elect to use either for storage other than in the ordinary course of transit or for allocation or distribution, or

8.1.3 when the Assured or their employees elect to use any carrying vehicle or other conveyance or any container for storage other than in the ordinary course of transit or

8.1.4 on the expiry of 60 days after completion of discharge overside of the subject-matter insured from the oversea vessel at the final port of discharge,

whichever shall first occur.

8.2 If, after discharge overside from the oversea vessel at the final port of discharge, but prior to termination of this insurance, the subject-matter insured is to be forwarded to a destination other than that to which it is insured, this insurance, whilst remaining subject to termination as provided in Clauses 8.1.1 to 8.1.4, shall not extend beyond the time the subject-matter insured is first moved for the purpose of the commencement of transit to such other destination.

8.3 This insurance shall remain in force (subject to termination as provided for in Clauses 8.1.1 to 8.1.4 above and to the provisions of Clause 9 below) during delay beyond the control of the Assured, any deviation, forced discharge, reshipment or transhipment and during any variation of the adventure arising from the exercise of a liberty granted to carriers under the contract of carriage.

Termination of Contract of Carriage

9. If owing to circumstances beyond the control of the Assured either the contract of carriage is terminated at a port or place other than the destination named therein or the transit is otherwise terminated before unloading of the subject-matter insured as provided for in Clause 8 above, then this insurance shall also terminate *unless prompt notice is given to the Insurers and continuation of cover is requested when this insurance shall remain in force, subject to an additional premium if required by the Insurers*, either

9.1 until the subject-matter insured is sold and delivered at such port or place, or, unless otherwise specially agreed, until the expiry of 60 days after arrival of the subject-matter insured at such port or place, whichever shall first occur,

or

9.2 if the subject-matter insured is forwarded within the said period of 60 days (or any agreed extension thereof) to the destination named in the contract of insurance or to any other destination, until terminated in accordance with the provisions of Clause 8 above.

Change of Voyage

10. 10.1 Where, after attachment of this insurance, the destination is changed by the Assured, *this must be notified promptly to Insurers for rates and terms to be*

agreed. Should a loss occur prior to such agreement being obtained cover may be provided but only if cover would have been available at a reasonable commercial market rate on reasonable market terms.

10.2 Where the subject-matter insured commences the transit contemplated by this insurance (in accordance with Clause 8.1), but, without the knowledge of the Assured or their employees the ship sails for another destination, this insurance will nevertheless be deemed to have attached at commencement of such transit.

CLAIMS

Insurable Interest

11. 11.1 In order to recover under this insurance the Assured must have an insurable interest in the subject-matter insured at the time of the loss.

11.2 Subject to Clause 11.1 above, the Assured shall be entitled to recover for insured loss occurring during the period covered by this insurance, notwithstanding that the loss occurred before the contract of insurance was concluded, unless the Assured were aware of the loss and the Insurers were not.

Forwarding Charges

12. Where, as a result of the operation of a risk covered by this insurance, the insured transit is terminated at a port or place other than that to which the subject-matter insured is covered under this insurance, the Insurers will reimburse the Assured for any extra charges properly and reasonably incurred in unloading storing and forwarding the subject-matter insured to the destination to which it is insured.

This Clause 12, which does not apply to general average or salvage charges, shall be subject to the exclusions contained in Clauses 4, 5, 6 and 7 above, and shall not include charges arising from the fault negligence insolvency or financial default of the Assured or their employees.

Constructive Total Loss

13. No claim for Constructive Total Loss shall be recoverable hereunder unless the subject-matter insured is reasonably abandoned either on account of its actual total loss appearing to be unavoidable or because the cost of recovering, reconditioning and forwarding the subject-matter insured to the destination to which it is insured would exceed its value on arrival.

Increased Value

14. 14.1 If any Increased Value insurance is effected by the Assured on the subject-matter insured under this insurance the agreed value of the subject-matter insured shall be deemed to be increased to the total amount insured under this insurance and all Increased Value insurances covering the loss, and liability under this insurance shall be in such proportion as the sum insured under this insurance bears to such total amount insured.

In the event of claim the Assured shall provide the Insurers with evidence of the amounts insured under all other insurances.

14.2 **Where this insurance is on Increased Value the following clause shall apply:**
The agreed value of the subject-matter insured shall be deemed to be equal to the total amount insured under the primary insurance and all Increased Value insurances covering the loss and effected on the subject-matter insured by the Assured, and liability under this insurance shall be in such proportion as the sum insured under this insurance bears to such total amount insured.

In the event of claim the Assured shall provide the Insurers with evidence of the amounts insured under all other insurances.

BENEFIT OF INSURANCE

15. This insurance

    15.1 covers the Assured which includes the person claiming indemnity either as the person by or on whose behalf the contract of insurance was effected or as an assignee,

    15.2 shall not extend to or otherwise benefit the carrier or other bailee.

MINIMISING LOSSES

Duty of Assured

16. It is the duty of the Assured and their employees and agents in respect of loss recoverable hereunder

    16.1 to take such measures as may be reasonable for the purpose of averting or minimising such loss, and

    16.2 to ensure that all rights against carriers, bailees or other third parties are properly preserved and exercised

and the Insurers will, in addition to any loss recoverable hereunder, reimburse the Assured for any charges properly and reasonably incurred in pursuance of these duties.

Waiver

17. Measures taken by the Assured or the Insurers with the object of saving, protecting or recovering the subject-matter insured shall not be considered as a waiver or acceptance of abandonment or otherwise prejudice the rights of either party.

AVOIDANCE OF DELAY

18. It is a condition of this insurance that the Assured shall act with reasonable despatch in all circumstances within their control.

LAW AND PRACTICE

19. This insurance is subject to English law and practice.

NOTE:- Where a continuation of cover is requested under Clause 9, or a change of destination is notified under Clause 10, there is an obligation to give prompt notice to the Insurers and the right to such cover is dependent upon compliance with this obligation.
© Copyright: 11/08 – Lloyd's Market Association (LMA) and International Underwriting Association of London (IUA).
CL384
01/01/2009

These clauses are purely illustrative. Different policy conditions may be agreed. The specimen clauses are available to any interested person upon request. In particular:

(a)   in relation to any clause which excludes losses from the cover, insurers may agree a separate insurance policy covering such losses or may extend the clause to cover such events;
(b)   in relation to clauses making cover of certain risks subject to specific conditions each insurer may alter the said conditions.

1/1/09

INSTITUTE STRIKES CLAUSES (CARGO)

RISKS COVERED

Risks
1.   This insurance covers, except as excluded by the provisions of Clauses 3 and 4 below, loss of or damage to the subject-matter insured caused by
  1.1   strikers, locked-out workmen, or persons taking part in labour disturbances, riots or civil commotions
  1.2   any act of terrorism being an act of any person acting on behalf of, or in connection with, any organisation which carries out activities directed towards the overthrowing or influencing, by force or violence, of any government whether or not legally constituted
  1.3   any person acting from a political, ideological or religious motive.

General Average
2.   This insurance covers general average and salvage charges, adjusted or determined according to the contract of carriage and/or the governing law and practice, incurred to avoid or in connection with the avoidance of loss from a risk covered under these Clauses.

EXCLUSIONS

3.   In no case shall this insurance cover
  3.1   loss damage or expense attributable to wilful misconduct of the Assured
  3.2   ordinary leakage, ordinary loss in weight or volume, or ordinary wear and tear of the subject-matter insured
  3.3   loss damage or expense caused by insufficiency or unsuitability of packing or preparation of the subject-matter insured to withstand the ordinary incidents of the insured transit where such packing or preparation is carried out by the Assured or their employees or prior to the attachment of this insurance (for the purpose of this Clause 3.3 "packing" shall be deemed to include stowage in a container and "employees" shall not include independent contractors)
  3.4   loss damage or expense caused by inherent vice or nature of the subject-matter insured
  3.5   loss damage or expense caused by delay, even though the delay be caused by a risk insured against (except expenses payable under Clause 2 above)
  3.6   loss damage or expense caused by insolvency or financial default of the owners managers charterers or operators of the vessel where, at the time of loading of the subject-matter insured on board the vessel, the Assured are aware, or in the ordinary course of business should be aware, that such insolvency or financial default could prevent the normal prosecution of the voyage
      This exclusion shall not apply where the contract of insurance has been assigned to the party claiming hereunder who has bought or agreed to buy the subject-matter insured in good faith under a binding contract

216

3.7 loss damage or expense arising from the absence shortage or withholding of labour of any description whatsoever resulting from any strike, lockout, labour disturbance, riot or civil commotion

3.8 any claim based upon loss of or frustration of the voyage or adventure

3.9 loss damage or expense directly or indirectly caused by or arising from the use of any weapon or device employing atomic or nuclear fission and/or fusion or other like reaction or radioactive force or matter

3.10 loss damage or expense caused by war civil war revolution rebellion insurrection, or civil strife arising therefrom, or any hostile act by or against a belligerent power.

4. 4.1 In no case shall this insurance cover loss damage or expense arising from

    4.1.1 unseaworthiness of vessel or craft or unfitness of vessel or craft for the safe carriage of the subject-matter insured, where the Assured are privy to such unseaworthiness or unfitness, at the time the subject-matter insured is loaded therein

    4.1.2 unfitness of container or conveyance for the safe carriage of the subject-matter insured, where loading therein or thereon is carried out

        prior to attachment of this insurance or

        by the Assured or their employees and they are privy to such unfitness at the time of loading.

4.2 Exclusion 4.1.1 above shall not apply where the contract of insurance has been assigned to the party claiming hereunder who has bought or agreed to buy the subject-matter insured in good faith under a binding contract.

4.3 The Insurers waive any breach of the implied warranties of seaworthiness of the ship and fitness of the ship to carry the subject-matter insured to destination.

DURATION

Transit Clause

5. 5.1 Subject to Clause 8 below, this insurance attaches from the time the subject-matter insured is first moved in the warehouse or at the place of storage (at the place named in the contract of insurance) for the purpose of the immediate loading into or onto the carrying vehicle or other conveyance for the commencement of transit,

continues during the ordinary course of transit

and terminates either

    5.1.1 on completion of unloading from the carrying vehicle or other conveyance in or at the final warehouse or place of storage at the destination named in the contract of insurance,

    5.1.2 on completion of unloading from the carrying vehicle or other conveyance in or at any other warehouse or place of storage, whether prior to or at the destination named in the contract of insurance, which the Assured or their employees elect to use either for storage other than in the ordinary course of transit or for allocation or distribution, or

    5.1.3 when the Assured or their employees elect to use any carrying vehicle or other conveyance or any container for storage other than in the ordinary course of transit or

    5.1.4 on the expiry of 60 days after completion of discharge overside of the subject-matter insured from the oversea vessel at the final port of discharge,

    whichever shall first occur.

5.2 If, after discharge overside from the oversea vessel at the final port of discharge, but prior to termination of this insurance, the subject-matter insured is to be forwarded to a destination other than that to which it is insured, this insurance, whilst remaining subject to termination as provided in Clauses 5.1.1 to 5.1.4, shall not extend beyond the time the subject-matter insured is first moved for the purpose of the commencement of transit to such other destination.

5.3 This insurance shall remain in force (subject to termination as provided for in Clauses 5.1.1 to 5.1.4 above and to the provisions of Clause 6 below) during delay beyond the control of the Assured, any deviation, forced discharge, reshipment or transhipment and during any variation of the adventure arising from the exercise of a liberty granted to carriers under the contract of carriage.

Termination of Contract of Carriage

6. If owing to circumstances beyond the control of the Assured either the contract of carriage is terminated at a port or place other than the destination named therein or the transit is otherwise terminated before unloading of the subject-matter insured as provided for in Clause 5 above, then this insurance shall also terminate *unless prompt notice is given to the Insurers and continuation of cover is requested when this insurance shall remain in force, subject to an additional premium if required by the Insurers*, either

6.1 until the subject-matter insured is sold and delivered at such port or place, or, unless otherwise specially agreed, until the expiry of 60 days after arrival of the subject-matter insured at such port or place, whichever shall first occur,

or

6.2 if the subject-matter insured is forwarded within the said period of 60 days (or any agreed extension thereof) to the destination named in the contract of insurance or to any other destination, until terminated in accordance with the provisions of Clause 5 above.

Change of Voyage

7. 7.1 Where, after attachment of this insurance, the destination is changed by the Assured, *this must be notified promptly to Insurers for rates and terms to be agreed. Should a loss occur prior to such agreement being obtained cover may be provided but only if cover would have been available at a reasonable commercial market rate on reasonable market terms.*

7.2 Where the subject-matter insured commences the transit contemplated by this insurance (in accordance with Clause 5.1), but, without the knowledge of the Assured or their employees the ship sails for another destination, this insurance will nevertheless be deemed to have attached at commencement of such transit.

CLAIMS

Insurable Interest

8. 8.1 In order to recover under this insurance the Assured must have an insurable interest in the subject-matter insured at the time of the loss.

8.2 Subject to Clause 8.1 above, the Assured shall be entitled to recover for insured loss occurring during the period covered by this insurance, notwithstanding that the loss occurred before the contract of insurance was concluded, unless the Assured were aware of the loss and the Insurers were not.

Increased Value

9. 9.1 If any Increased Value insurance is effected by the Assured on the subject-matter insured under this insurance the agreed value of the subject-matter insured shall

be deemed to be increased to the total amount insured under this insurance and all Increased Value insurances covering the loss, and liability under this insurance shall be in such proportion as the sum insured under this insurance bears to such total amount insured.

In the event of claim the Assured shall provide the Insurers with evidence of the amounts insured under all other insurances.

9.2 **Where this insurance is on Increased Value the following clause shall apply:**
The agreed value of the subject-matter insured shall be deemed to be equal to the total amount insured under the primary insurance and all Increased Value insurances covering the loss and effected on the subject-matter insured by the Assured, and liability under this insurance shall be in such proportion as the sum insured under this insurance bears to such total amount insured.

In the event of claim the Assured shall provide the Insurers with evidence of the amounts insured under all other insurances.

BENEFIT OF INSURANCE

10. This insurance
  10.1 covers the Assured which includes the person claiming indemnity either as the person by or on whose behalf the contract of insurance was effected or as an assignee,
  10.2 shall not extend to or otherwise benefit the carrier or other bailee.

MINIMISING LOSSES

Duty of Assured

11. It is the duty of the Assured and their employees and agents in respect of loss recoverable hereunder
  11.1 to take such measures as may be reasonable for the purpose of averting or minimising such loss, and
  11.2 to ensure that all rights against carriers, bailees or other third parties are properly preserved and exercised

and the Insurers will, in addition to any loss recoverable hereunder, reimburse the Assured for any charges properly and reasonably incurred in pursuance of these duties.

Waiver

12. Measures taken by the Assured or the Insurers with the object of saving, protecting or recovering the subject-matter insured shall not be considered as a waiver or acceptance of abandonment or otherwise prejudice the rights of either party.

AVOIDANCE OF DELAY

13. It is a condition of this insurance that the Assured shall act with reasonable despatch in all circumstances within their control.

LAW AND PRACTICE

14. This insurance is subject to English law and practice.

NOTE:- Where a continuation of cover is requested under Clause 6, or a change of destination is notified under Clause 7, there is an obligation to give prompt notice to the Insurers and the right to such cover is dependent upon compliance with this obligation.

© Copyright: 11/08 – Lloyd's Market Association (LMA) and International Underwriting Association of London (IUA).

CL386
01/01/2009

These clauses are purely illustrative. Different policy conditions may be agreed. The specimen clauses are available to any interested person upon request. In particular:

(a) in relation to any clause which excludes losses from the cover, insurers may agree a separate insurance policy covering such losses or may extend the clause to cover such events;

(b) in relation to clauses making cover of certain risks subject to specific conditions each insurer may alter the said conditions.

1/1/09

INSTITUTE WAR CLAUSES (CARGO)

RISKS COVERED

Risks
1. This insurance covers, except as excluded by the provisions of Clauses 3 and 4 below, loss of or damage to the subject-matter insured caused by
   1.1 war civil war revolution rebellion insurrection, or civil strife arising therefrom, or any hostile act by or against a belligerent power
   1.2 capture seizure arrest restraint or detainment, arising from risks covered under 1.1 above, and the consequences thereof or any attempt thereat
   1.3 derelict mines torpedoes bombs or other derelict weapons of war.

General Average
2. This insurance covers general average and salvage charges, adjusted or determined according to the contract of carriage and/or the governing law and practice, incurred to avoid or in connection with the avoidance of loss from a risk covered under these Clauses.

EXCLUSIONS
3. In no case shall this insurance cover
   3.1 loss damage or expense attributable to wilful misconduct of the Assured
   3.2 ordinary leakage, ordinary loss in weight or volume, or ordinary wear and tear of the subject-matter insured
   3.3 loss damage or expense caused by insufficiency or unsuitability of packing or preparation of the subject-matter insured to withstand the ordinary incidents of the insured transit where such packing or preparation is carried out by the Assured or their employees or prior to the attachment of this insurance (for the purpose of these Clauses "packing" shall be deemed to include stowage in a container and "employees" shall not include independent contractors)
   3.4 loss damage or expense caused by inherent vice or nature of the subject-matter insured
   3.5 loss damage or expense caused by delay, even though the delay be caused by a risk insured against (except expenses payable under Clause 2 above)
   3.6 loss damage or expense caused by insolvency or financial default of the owners managers charterers or operators of the vessel where, at the time of loading of the subject-matter insured on board the vessel, the Assured are aware, or in the ordinary course of business should be aware, that such insolvency or financial default could prevent the normal prosecution of the voyage
   This exclusion shall not apply where the contract of insurance has been assigned to the party claiming hereunder who has bought or agreed to buy the subject-matter insured in good faith under a binding contract
   3.7 any claim based upon loss of or frustration of the voyage or adventure

3.8 loss damage or expense directly or indirectly caused by or arising from any hostile use of any weapon or device employing atomic or nuclear fission and/or fusion or other like reaction or radioactive force or matter.

4. 4.1 In no case shall this insurance cover loss damage or expense arising from
   4.1.1 unseaworthiness of vessel or craft or unfitness of vessel or craft for the safe carriage of the subject-matter insured, where the Assured are privy to such unseaworthiness or unfitness, at the time the subject-matter insured is loaded therein
   4.1.2 unfitness of container or conveyance for the safe carriage of the subject-matter insured, where loading therein or thereon is carried out

   prior to attachment of this insurance or

   by the Assured or their employees and they are privy to such unfitness at the time of loading.
   4.2 Exclusion 4.1.1 above shall not apply where the contract of insurance has been assigned to the party claiming hereunder who has bought or agreed to buy the subject-matter insured in good faith under a binding contract.
   4.3 The Insurers waive any breach of the implied warranties of seaworthiness of the ship and fitness of the ship to carry the subject-matter insured to destination.

DURATION

Transit Clause

5. 5.1 This insurance
   5.1.1 attaches only as the subject-matter insured and as to any part as that part is loaded on an oversea vessel

   and
   5.1.2 terminates, subject to 5.2 and 5.3 below, either as the subject-matter insured and as to any part as that part is discharged from an oversea vessel at the final port or place of discharge,

   or

   on expiry of 15 days counting from midnight of the day of arrival of the vessel at the final port or place of discharge,
   whichever shall first occur;
   nevertheless,
   subject to prompt notice to the Insurers and to an additional premium, such insurance
   5.1.3 reattaches when, without having discharged the subject-matter insured at the final port or place of discharge, the vessel sails therefrom,

   and
   5.1.4 terminates, subject to 5.2 and 5.3 below, either as the subject-matter insured and as to any part as that part is thereafter discharged from the vessel at the final (or substituted) port or place of discharge,

   or

   on expiry of 15 days counting from midnight of the day of re-arrival of the vessel at the final port or place of discharge or arrival of the vessel at a substituted port or place of discharge, whichever shall first occur.
   5.2 If during the insured voyage the oversea vessel arrives at an intermediate port or place to discharge the subject-matter insured for on-carriage by oversea vessel or by aircraft, or the subject-matter insured is discharged from the vessel at a port or place of refuge, then, subject to 5.3 below and to an additional premium if required, this insurance continues until the expiry of 15 days counting from midnight of the day of arrival of the vessel at such port or place, but thereafter reattaches as the subject-matter insured and as to any part as that part is loaded

on an on-carrying oversea vessel or aircraft. During the period of 15 days the insurance remains in force after discharge only whilst the subject-matter insured and as to any part as that part is at such port or place. If the subject-matter insured is on-carried within the said period of 15 days or if the insurance reattaches as provided in this Clause 5.2

5.2.1   where the on-carriage is by oversea vessel this insurance continues subject to the terms of these Clauses,

or

5.2.2   where the on-carriage is by aircraft, the current Institute War Clauses (Air Cargo) (excluding sendings by Post) shall be deemed to form part of the contract of insurance and shall apply to the on-carriage by air.

5.3   If the voyage in the contract of carriage is terminated at a port or place other than the destination agreed therein, such port or place shall be deemed the final port of discharge and this insurance terminates in accordance with 5.1.2. If the subject-matter insured is subsequently reshipped to the original or any other destination, then *provided notice is given to the Insurers before the commencement of such further transit and subject to an additional premium*, this insurance reattaches

5.3.1   in the case of the subject-matter insured having been discharged, as the subject-matter insured and as to any part as that part is loaded on the on-carrying vessel for the voyage;

5.3.2   in the case of the subject-matter not having been discharged, when the vessel sails from such deemed final port of discharge;

thereafter this insurance terminates in accordance with 5.1.4.

5.4   The insurance against the risks of mines and derelict torpedoes, floating or submerged, is extended whilst the subject-matter insured or any part thereof is on craft whilst in transit to or from the oversea vessel, but in no case beyond the expiry of 60 days after discharge from the oversea vessel unless otherwise specially agreed by the Insurers.

5.5   *Subject to prompt notice to Insurers, and to an additional premium if required*, this insurance shall remain in force within the provisions of these Clauses during any deviation, or any variation of the adventure arising from the exercise of a liberty granted to carriers under the contract of carriage.

(For the purpose of Clause 5

"arrival" shall be deemed to mean that the vessel is anchored, moored or otherwise secured at a berth or place within the Harbour Authority area. If such a berth or place is not available, arrival is deemed to have occurred when the vessel first anchors, moors or otherwise secures either at or off the intended port or place of discharge

"oversea vessel" shall be deemed to mean a vessel carrying the subject-matter from one port or place to another where such voyage involves a sea passage by that vessel)

Change of Voyage

6.   6.1   Where, after attachment of this insurance, the destination is changed by the Assured, *this must be notified promptly to Insurers for rates and terms to be agreed. Should a loss occur prior to such agreement being obtained cover may be provided but only if cover would have been available at a reasonable commercial market rate on reasonable market terms.*

6.2   Where the subject-matter insured commences the transit contemplated by this insurance (in accordance with Clause 5.1), but, without the knowledge of the Assured or their employees the ship sails for another destination, this insurance will nevertheless be deemed to have attached at commencement **of** such transit.

7. **Anything contained in this contract which is inconsistent with Clauses 3.7, 3.8 or 5 shall, to the extent of such inconsistency, be null and void.**

CLAIMS

<u>Insurable Interest</u>
8. 8.1 In order to recover under this insurance the Assured must have an insurable interest in the subject-matter insured at the time of the loss.

8.2 Subject to Clause 8.1 above, the Assured shall be entitled to recover for insured loss occurring during the period covered by this insurance, notwithstanding that the loss occurred before the contract of insurance was concluded, unless the Assured were aware of the loss and the Insurers were not.

<u>Increased Value</u>
9. 9.1 If any Increased Value insurance is effected by the Assured on the subject-matter insured under this insurance the agreed value of the subject-matter insured shall be deemed to be increased to the total amount insured under this insurance and all Increased Value insurances covering the loss, and liability under this insurance shall be in such proportion as the sum insured under this insurance bears to such total amount insured.

In the event of claim the Assured shall provide the Insurers with evidence of the amounts insured under all other insurances.

9.2 **Where this insurance is on Increased Value the following clause shall apply:**
The agreed value of the subject-matter insured shall be deemed to be equal to the total amount insured under the primary insurance and all Increased Value insurances covering the loss and effected on the subject-matter insured by the Assured, and liability under this insurance shall be in such proportion as the sum insured under this insurance bears to such total amount insured.
In the event of claim the Assured shall provide the Insurers with evidence of the amounts insured under all other insurances.

BENEFIT OF INSURANCE
10. This insurance
10.1 covers the Assured which includes the person claiming indemnity either as the person by or on whose behalf the contract of insurance was effected or as an assignee,
10.2 shall not extend to or otherwise benefit the carrier or other bailee.

MINIMISING LOSSES

<u>Duty of Assured</u>
11. It is the duty of the Assured and their employees and agents in respect of loss recoverable hereunder
11.1 to take such measures as may be reasonable for the purpose of averting or minimising such loss, and
11.2 to ensure that all rights against carriers, bailees or other third parties are properly preserved and exercised

and the Insurers will, in addition to any loss recoverable hereunder, reimburse the Assured for any charges properly and reasonably incurred in pursuance of these duties.

Waiver

12. Measures taken by the Assured or the Insurers with the object of saving, protecting or recovering the subject-matter insured shall not be considered as a waiver or acceptance of abandonment or otherwise prejudice the rights of either party.

AVOIDANCE OF DELAY

13. It is a condition of this insurance that the Assured shall act with reasonable despatch in all circumstances within their control.

LAW AND PRACTICE

14. This insurance is subject to English law and practice.

NOTE:– Where a reattachment of cover is requested under Clause 5, or a change of destination is notified under Clause 6, there is an obligation to give prompt notice to the Insurers and the right to such cover is dependent upon compliance with this obligation.

© Copyright: 11/08 – Lloyd's Market Association (LMA) and International Underwriting Association of London (IUA).

CL385
01/01/2009

Index